Pocket Fruit Knives

A SYNOPSIS OF THEIR HISTORY FROM THE UNITED KINGDOM, FRANCE, NORTHERN EUROPE & USA

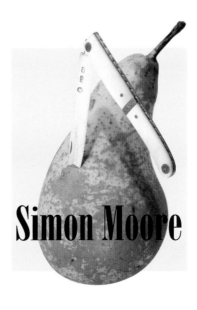

Simon Moore

Copyright © Simon Moore, 2008
First published: July 2008

Published by Antique Knives Ltd.
PO BOX 3892, Farnham Common, Slough, SL1 0JS, England.
Design, photography, layout and production:
David Watson, Graphic Solutions, Farnham Common, England.

www.antique-knives.co.uk

British Library Cataloguing in Publication Data
A catalogue record for this book is available from the British Library

ISBN 978-0-9559507-0-4

(*Cover illustration*): the author, Harriet St Leger & Florence King enjoying a fruit course *à la mode* c.1780, complete with nutmeg and some Constantia wine.
(*below*): a Georgian pocket fruit knife c.1790 with nacre scales inlaid with engraved gilt rosettes and an engraved gilt band midway, showing French influence.
Photo credit: Patricia Cain.
(*End-papers*): from JJ Perret's *L' Art du Coutelier*, 1771

Pocket Fruit Knives: Price Guide

The following price guide information is provided to help dealers and collectors appreciate the relative values of Pocket Fruit Knives.

All prices are estimates of value at the time of publication, and are a matter of opinion - backed up with 40 years of collecting in this field. The "true value" of a knife is the amount a buyer is prepared to pay at a particular time but this depends on many factors including fashion, rarity, condition, supply and demand.

Key:

A £1-49,
B £50-99,
C £100-199,
D £200-499,
E £500-999,
F £1,000-2,000
G £2,000-5,000
H £5,000-10,000
J £10,000+

Abbreviations:
upper: (u).
lower: (l),
clockwise: (c/w)
left to right: (l-r)
top to bottom: (t-b).

In cases where the value spans two price bands this is indicated as e.g. E/F = £800-1500
All prices reflect condition.

page	plate	price	page	plate	price
2	1.2 (c/w)	F, E, D, D, C	52	3.2, 3.3	E, E
3	1.3	E	53	3.4	D
5	1.7 (u), 1.7 (l)	B, C	54	3.6	E/F
6	1.8, 1.9	F, E	55	3.8, 3.9	F, E
7	1.10 (u), 1.10 (l)	C, D	56	3.10.	E, E
8	1.11, 1.12 (u, l l-r)	C; D; B, B, A	57	3.14, 3.15	E/F, E/F
10	1.13, 1.14	J, E	58	3.16	D
11	1.15, 1.16	E, B	59	3.17	F/G
12	1.17	D	60	3.18	F
13	2.1 (u), 2.1 (l)	E, E	61	3.22, 3.33	D/E, E
14	2.2, 2.3, 2.4	E, D, E	62	3.24	E/F
15	2.5	F/G	63	3.26-3.27, 3.28	E/F, D
17	2.11	E	64	3.29, 3.30	C, C
18	2.13	E	65	3.32 (l-r), 3.33, 3.34	E, C, F; D, C
20	2.17	J	66	3.35, 3.36, 3.37	D, D, D
21	2.20.	F/G	67	3.38 (u), 3.38 (l)	D/E, D/E
22	2.23 (c/w at top)	F, E, D, E, D, E, C	67	3.39 (u), 3.39 (l)	D/E, D/E
23	2.24	F/G	68	3.40.	C
24	2.25 (each)	F, F	69	3.42	E/F
26	2.29	H/J	70	3.44, 3.45	D, D
28	2.32	E/F	71	4.1 (l-r)	D, D, C, C, D, B
29	2.33, 2.34	H, E/F	72	4.2	E
30	2.35, 2.36	E, F/G	73	4.3, 4.4	E, D, D
31	2.37, 2.38	F/G, F/G, E/F	74	4.5, 4.6, 4.7	D, E, C
32	2.39, 2.40	E, E/F	75	4.8 (l-r)	D, D, C, C, D, B
33	2.41, 2.42	F, E/F	75	4.9	D
34	2.43	C	76	4.10 (t-b)	D, D, C, C, C, C
35	2.46, 2.47	E, D	76	4.11	D
36	2.48, 2.49	H, D/E	77	4.12 (t-b)	C/D, C, C, C/D
37	2.50.	H/J	78	4.13	E/F
38	2.51 (c/w top left)	D, E, C, D, C	79	4.14 (l-r)	C/D, D, D, C/D
39	2.53, 2.54	D, D	80	4.15	E
40	2.55	D/E	81	4.17 (l-r)	D/E, C, C, C, C, C, E, C
41	2.57	E	82	4.18, 4.19	C, C, C/D
43	2.59	F	83	4.20, 4.21, 4.22	C/D; C/D, C, B/C
44	2.60.	G	84	4.23	F/G
45	2.61	F	85	4.26	B
46	2.62, 2.63	same piece above	91	4.44	F/G
47	2.64	E/F	94	4.51	B/C
48	2.65	F	96	4.58	D
49	2.67	E	98	4.62	C, C
50	2.68	D	99	4.63	E
51	3.1 (u l-r)	E/F, E/F, B, C	100	4.64	D/E
51	3.1 (l l-r)	E, F, C, F			

page	plate	price
101	5.1	F
102	5.2 (each)	Too complex - each is mentioned later
103	5.3, 5.4	C, E
104	5.5 (l-r); 5.6, 5.7 (l-r)	D, F, D/E; E, C, B
105	5.8, 5.9	C/D, E/F
106	5.10, 5.12	D/E, D/E
107	5.14, 5.15	E, B
108	5.17, 5.18	E/F, D, D
109	5.19, 5.20 (l-r)	D/E; C, [D], B, C
110	5.21 ,5.22 ,5.23	J, J, J
113	5.25	J
114	5.26	D
115	5.28	C/D
116	5.31/2, 5.33	D, D, E
117	5.34	C, C
118	5.36, 5.37, 5.38	D/E, C, C, C, C/D
119	5.39-5.42	C, C, C/D
120	5.43, 5.44	B, B/C
121	5.45 (l&r),[t-b]; 5.46	D, D [D/E, D/E, D/E]; C, C
122	5.47	G
123	5.49	D/E
124	5.50.	G
125	5.52, 5.53, 5.54	F/G, B, D/E
126	5.55, 5.56	F, D/E
127	5.57	C
128	5.58, 5.59	F, C
129	5.60, 5.61 (l-r)	A/B; B/C, B/C, C
130	5.62, 5.63	D, C, D; D
131	6.1	E
132	6.2, 6.3	C, C
133	6.4	D/E, C
134	6.6	D/E
135	6.7, 6.8	C, C; B/C
136	6.9, 6.10	B, A
138	6.14, 6.15	D, D; D
139	6.16	C
140	6.19	D/E
141	6.22	C/D
143	6.23, 6.24, 6.25	C, B/C, E
144	6.27 (l-r); 6.28, 6.29	A/B, B, B; C, B/C
145	6.30.	G
149	6.35, 6.36	C, D
150	6.37, 6.38	D, A/B
152	7.2	C
153	7.4, 7.5	B, B/C; B/C
154	7.7, 7.8	C, B
155	7.9, 7.10 (l-r)	B/C; B, C/D, C/D
156	7.11, 7.12, 7.13	D/E; B/C, C; B, B/C
157	7.14 (top)	C/D
157	7.14 (fan)	C, C, C; B/C, B, B, B/C
158	7.16, 7.17	C, B
159	7.18, 7.19	C/D, C/D; D/E
160	7.20. (l-r)	B, B/C, B
161	7.22, 7.23	D, D
162	7.24 (l-r)	B/C, B/C, B, C
163	7.25	B/C
164	7.26, 7.27	C, C/D
165	7.31	D
167	7.35	C/D
168	7.36, 7.37	C, C
169	7.38, 7.39	C/D, C
170	7.40.	D
171	7.41. 7.42	C, C/D
172	7.43, 7.45	C, C/D; C
173	7.46, 7.47	C; C, B/C
174	7.48, 7.50	B/C, E
175	7.51 (l-r)	B, B, A/B, A/B, A
175	7.53 (l-r)	A, A, A, A/B, A
176	7.58	A
177	7.59	B/C
178	7.60, 7.61 (per pair)	C/D, C/D
179	7.62	C
180	7.63 (l-r), 7.64	C/D, C, C/D; D
181	7.65, 7.67	D, C/D
182	7.68, 7.69	C/D, C
183	7.70, 7.71	C, C
184	7.72, 7.73	D, B/C
185	7.74, 7.75	B/C, B/C; C/D
186	7.76, 7.77 (c/w)	C/D; B, B, B/C, B, A/B
187	7.78, 7.80	C, B/C, C
189	7.81	C/D
189	7.82	C
190	7.83	C/D
191	7.84, (t-b); 7.85	C, C, B/C; C, C
192	7.86, 7.87	D, C/D
193	7.88	E/F
194	7.89	F/G
195	8.1	A, A, A, A
196	8.2, 8.3	C, B/C
197	8.4	C/D
198	8.5, 8.6	B/C, B
199	8.7, 8.8 (c/w)	B/C; B/C, B/C, B, C, B/C
200	8.10.	C/D
201	8.11	A/B, A/B
202	8.14, 8.15, 8.16	C/D, B, B
203	8.17, 8.18	A, A
204	8.19, 8.20	B, B, B; B
205	8.22	B
207	8.25	C
208	8.27	D
209	8.28, 8.29	A, A, A
210	8.31 (= 8.32)	B
211	8.33, 8.34	C/D; B/C, B/C
212	8.35, 8.36, 8.37	A/B; A, A; A
213	8.38, 8.39	A, A; A, A, A
214	8.40, 8.41	B/C; C
215	8.42, 8.43	B; B/C
216	8.46	B
221	8.54, 8.55	B/C, B/C
222	8.56, 8.57	B/C, B
223	8.58, 8.59	B/C, B
224	8.61	B
225	9.1 (c/w)	B/C, B/C, B/C
226	9.2, 9.3	B, A/B
227	9.5	B
229	9.10.	B/C, B/C
230	9.11, 9.12	B, B/C, B; B
231	9.13, 9.14	B/C; B
232	9.15, 9.16	B; B/C
233	9.17, 9.18	C, B
234	9.20, 9.21	B, C
235	9.22	C/D
236	9.23, 9.24	E, C
237	9.25, 9.26	D, B
238	9.27	B
239	9.28, 9.29	F, F
240	9.30.	F
257	10.18, 10.19	B/C, B
259	10.21	C/D
260	10.23, 10.24	B/C, A
262	10.28	A
263	10.33, 10.34	A, A
264	10.37	A/B
265	10.38, 10.39, 10.40	A, B, A
267	10.48	E/F
268	10.51	B

Contents

French or English?
This knife was made
c.1760-1770, it has a
soft spring and a smooth
opening/closing action and
belongs to 'The period of
Confusion' (Chapter 3).

Three items from the 18th century (*above*) and three sets from the 19th century (*below*).

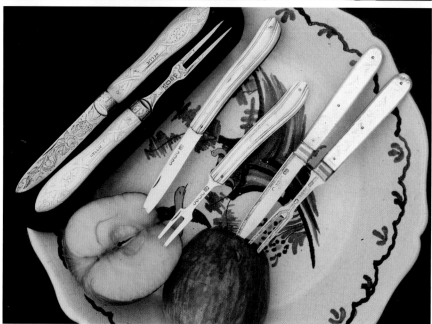

Dedication

This book is dedicated to many people, primarily to Harriet and Jenny but also to those collectors who have passed on and who were known and dear to me: John Carss, Bill Karsten, Ted Kleinman and Norman Cox. They were never rivals, but always friends and valued sources of information.

Watercolour greeting from Mary Kleinman to the author following a house move in 1991

Beautifully inscribed pistol grip pocket fruit knife given from LB to EH in 1780.

Preface

In 1988 I was asked by Ted Donohoe, a well-known London dealer, why I had written a Shire booklet about pen and other folding knives when there were no longer any interesting examples of folding fruit knives in The Antiques Trade. Folding (or pocket) fruit knives and forks were certainly readily available as charming and inexpensive collectables in 1968, when I first started to collect them. Indeed there were many really fine examples circulating in The Trade until about 1987 when there started a gradual decline in the number of finer examples. Since 1999, the number has fallen dramatically. This naturally has stimulated a rapid and deserved price rise for the more desirable items. As prices have risen, so the more unusual and finer quality items have re-emerged but are snapped up by discerning collectors. Many are sold on e-bay, and auction houses are becoming less fussy about selling finer items as single lots. There are those who have deep pockets who have thousands of such items in their collections and who will pay any price to acquire a different piece. As with all collectables this can be frustrating for researchers since certain items, which could yield much information, are hidden away from public view until the collector either dies or moves onto another topic.

I have always had a boyish enthusiasm for pocket-knives. As I reached maturity I found that pocket fruit knives and forks were more aesthetically pleasing, and no-one else appeared to be collecting them or had written anything about them! Such fresh pasture naturally prompted a crusade for research and providing information, perhaps even being the first to write about them. My first article appeared in 1975 and began to pave the way, I hoped, for adding to my own collection as interest was stimulated and more pieces came on the market. I naively assumed that others would not be that much interested and I hoped that rival collectors would only regard this as a passing fad. I was largely wrong of course, as the items are much too charming to give up after a short period of collecting, but some collectors, who had started slightly before me, did come out of the woodwork and were delighted to show me their finds. I have since discovered that there is at least one really interesting and informative pocket fruit knife in each collection and that a 'complete' collection can never exist. I have similarly found that in 40 years of collecting, selling and observing, I still do not know the subject completely – there is still that one knife or fork lurking somewhere with a different story to tell.

The manufacture of pocket fruit knives has been restricted to England and to France, where they originated. Other countries seem not to have had much use for such leisure items, with the exception of the USA during the later 19th century, for a 50-60 year period. Occasional, commissioned

Invoice and earlier receipt of JJ & H Thornhill of New Bond Street, London 1824 & 1820

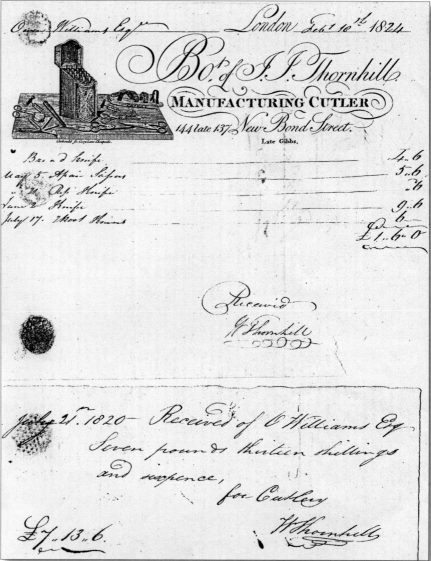

Reverse scale of multi-bladed pocket fruit knife by Joseph Rodgers 1904, with later scrimshaw decoration for the author.

items, have been made throughout the rest of Europe and in Russia where knives attributed to some of Fabergé's workmasters have come to light.

French pocket fruit knives have been around for over 300 years and French makers have frequently excelled in the manufacture and decoration of such an otherwise-modest item. Even the basic mechanism was technologically more advanced but often ignored in Britain, probably for political reasons at the beginning of the 18th century.

I must apologise in advance to those who read through this book and find some areas of slight repetition, but this is to help those who need to have information for specific periods without reading the entire text.

Finally, I am deeply indebted to those who were so generous in showing me their collections as, without them, I would not have been able to amass the information for this book.

Simon Moore 2003-7

Acknowledgements

I would like to offer my heartfelt thanks to the many collectors who were generous in letting me photograph items from their collections. Based on my collection alone, there would have been large areas of empty space.

Foremost among these is James Rowbotham whose keenness has always helped me to be *au courant* with unusual styles appearing on e-bay and at auctions and to Kyle Grauman who has an excellent eye and knack of finding the unusual.

I also acknowledge help from the following people, some of whom, alas are no longer with us: John and Sally Carss, Ted, Mary and Daniel Kleinman, Norman Cox, Dennis Lough, Cynthia and Jeremy Secker, Cindy and Jim Taylor, Ken Goldman, Bill Brown and, last but not least, all those dealers who helped me amass some interesting pieces in my early days of collecting, especially Peter and Janet Cameron.

Also, to Jackie Richardson of the Sheffield Assay Office, 137 Portobello Street, S1 4DS, Drs David Hibberd and Alan Harrington for much help with editing the text.

Oliver Crimmen of the Fish Section at the Natural History Museum, London for helping to identify the various fish skins that are generically termed as shagreen or *galuchat*.

Finally, many thanks are due to Alan Harrington for financial assistance with this project.

Victoria & Albert Museum, South Kensington, London. SW7 2RL.

Musée de la coutellerie, 63300 Thiers, France.

Musée de Breuil St Germain, 52200 Langres, France.

Musée de Strasbourg, 67076, Strasbourg, Alsace, France.

Koninklijk Museum voor Schone Kunsten, Antwerp.

Scarborough & Filey Amenities Council, YO11 2HG.

The Army & Navy Club, Pall Mall, London SW1Y 5JN.

Messrs S J Phillips, Ltd., New Bond Street, London, W1A 3DL

Christie's South Kensington, 85 Old Brompton Road, London SW7 3LD.

Messrs Woolley & Wallis Auctioneers, Castle Street, Salisbury, SP1 3SU.

Hampshire County Council Wardrobe, Chilcomb Lane, Winchester, SO23 8RD.

Daniel Bexfield Antiques, 26 Burlington Arcade, London W1J 0PU.

Alex Szolin: www.antiquities.co.uk

St Cross Chapel, Winchester, SO23 9SD.

I have always maintained a boyish interest in pocket knives and purchased my first pocket fruit knife at Portobello Road in 1968. It was Georgian, 1818 and cost £1; two more purchases were made during the same day and that started my interest. There were not many other collectors in those days nor was there anything written about them. I have always found them fascinating and am still learning about them, their apparently infinite diversity and the sheer number of them show how popular they were in their time, mainly between 1780 and 1930.

Simon Moore 2007

1 A brief history of pocket & fruit knives in Europe up to 1650

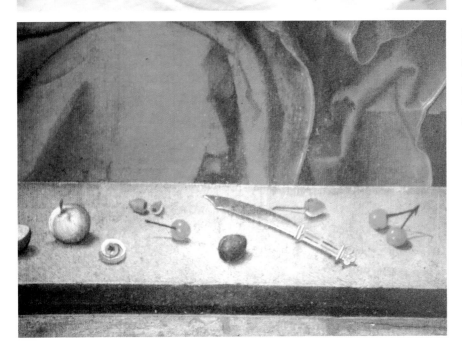

Detail from triptych by
Jean de Mabuse,
showing typical Flemish
fruit knife, c.1530.
*Courtesy of St Cross Chapel,
Winchester.*
Plate 1.1

Selection of Roman folding cutlery: (*clockwise*) Silver spoon c.6th Century A.D. Bronze-handled folding spoon with leonine handle, knife blade & spike. Three folding knife hafts: ivory cat in the form of a table leg, two bronze lovers and a hare coursing haft, 2nd-3rd century A.D.
Plate 1.2

Introduction

Folding knives have a long history dating back to the time of Christ when they were made and used by the Roman and Ancient Greek cultures. The science of making hard-edged knives from precious metals had presumably been perfected by the Ancient Egyptians, probably well before the reign of Tutankhamen (c.1370 BC) - a gold-bladed dagger was found among his funerary regalia.

Roman folding knives were made from a simple iron or steel-edged blade that pivoted on a haft of bone, ivory, wood or cast bronze. Each haft could be formed to tempt a wide range of customers or as an intending owner desired but many have been found that conform to a standard design depicting hare coursing (*above*).

The Roman love of the chase is reflected in many such hafts and Roman legionaries and army officers may have owned such pieces since these have turned up in archaeological digs all over their former empire. Some folding knives were also made as part of folding spoons, another Roman invention apparently, and they also produced finer silver examples. Post Roman Empire folding knives are scarce. A few have been found throughout Europe (*p.3*) but there appears to have been little use for them at this time.

Merovingian pocket knife with ivory haft and silver band mounts. *(Courtesy of Thiers Cutlery Museum).* *Plate 1.3*

Master of Frankfurt, self-portrait with wife, enjoying a dish of cherries, c.1480: the knife is typical of the mid-15th century. *(Courtesy of Koninklijk Museum voor schone kunsten, Antwerp).* *Plate 1.4*

The beginnings of knives made specifically for cutting fruit or assisting in the serving and consumption of dessert courses can be traced back, rather vaguely, to the Middle Ages. Later mediaeval paintings occasionally depict diners eating a dessert or fruit course at a time when the consumption of such luxuries was reserved for the noble and well-to-do merchant classes. Fruit knives, and forks especially, have been mentioned in literature and in period inventories. They have been traditionally made slightly smaller and more decorative in order to appeal to their wealthy users *(plate 1.4)*. In England, forks were reserved almost solely for sweetmeat eating until the later 17th century, when table forks became accepted as the norm. Carbon steel blades are vulnerable to fruit acids and quickly darken when used to slice and cut up fruit; stainless steel was not discovered until the early 1900s. Silver and gold, however, are not attacked or stained by fruit acids, nor do these metals add any taint to the fruit, but have the disadvantage of being costlier as well as softer and more vulnerable.

Two painting details depicting 16th century dessert courses showing period table cutlery.
Plates 1.5 &1.6

During the 14th to 16th centuries folding knives were largely supplanted by the universal knife-in-a-sheath which was easier (cheaper) to make and less easy to lose (*above*).

The mid-17th century finally saw the arrival of folding knives with a spring-back to hold the blade open or closed, and this feature revolutionised the pocket knife industry. Cutlers in both London and the expanding town of Sheffield produced many folding, steel-bladed pocket knives with differently shaped blades and hafts as they experimented to find the most practical designs.

French cutlers also produced many such pieces at this time and a few added a silver blade to their pocket knives, which fruit acid would not discolour nor taint; in effect they produced the first-known folding fruit knives.

Knives for fruit, cheese or dessert continued to be made as smaller versions of their table or pocket knife (steel-bladed) cousins. This partial size diminution of table and pocket cutlery didn't arrive in England until about the reign of Queen Anne and seems to have evolved throughout the rest of Europe at about the same time.

16th century commoners' knives: leather, wood and pewter sheaths.
Plate 1.7

(*above*) Mediaeval clasp
knife c.1380. Bone
zoomorphic haft.
Plate: 1.8
(*below*) Elizabethan pocket
knife with rotating haft
opening mechanism,
dated 1585.
Inscription reads:
A TRUSTY FRENDE IS
HARDE TO FIND / IN
GOD IS AL MI TRUSTE.
1585
Plate: 1.9

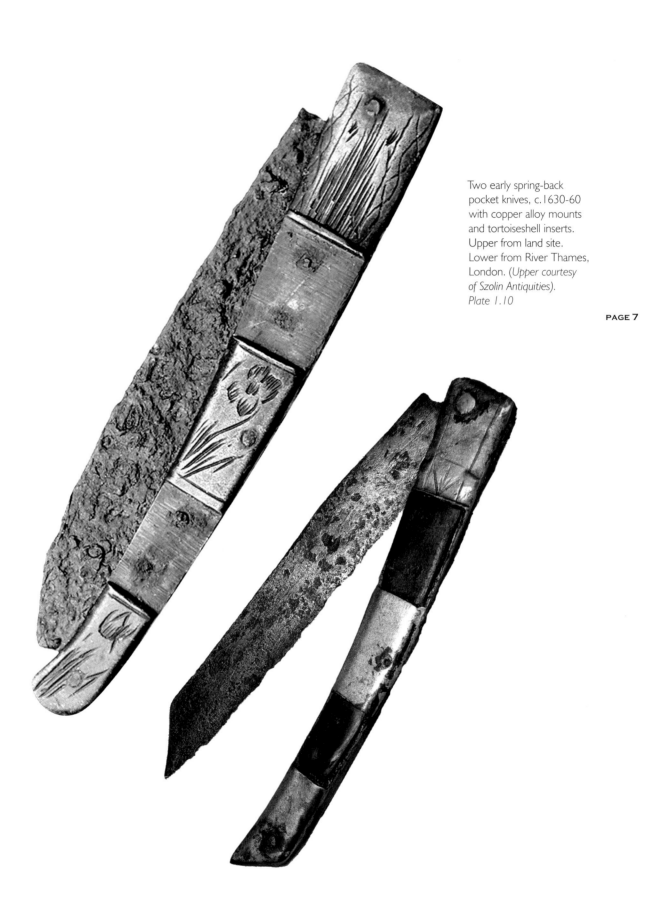

Two early spring-back pocket knives, c.1630-60 with copper alloy mounts and tortoiseshell inserts. Upper from land site. Lower from River Thames, London. (*Upper courtesy of Szolin Antiquities*). Plate 1.10

Small-sized English pocket knives were multi-purpose and traditional implements and would have included fruit cutting before the arrival of the silver blade. *(above)* An excavated item cased in pewter, c.1760. *(below)* An array of brass-hafted knives in various sizes, including a political motto. These tended to be heavily French-influenced in style. *Plates 1.11 & 1.12*

Folding cutlery (including spoons) had been a standard item for travellers in Europe since Roman times but although these were artistically designed, they show little use of richer materials until the mediaeval period. The appearance of precious-metal folding or collapsible spoons generally began in Europe during the middle to later mediaeval period, although a few, such as one found in a Bishop's grave at Scarborough, may predate this period by several centuries *(plate 1.13)* indicating a cultural awareness and influence that may have come from the Norse countries.

The first known pocket fruit knives

Folding knives incorporating silver or precious metal blades appeared first in France around 1670/80, although René d'Allemagne (1938) suggests the beginning of the 18th century. At first, the silver (or gilt or gold) blade doubled with one of steel and a few examples have been discovered from this period with additional tools such as saws and hooks. The style of these knives is magnificent: French cutlers showed themselves as superior in the manufacture of table and folding cutlery at this time. D'Allemagne also adds that these knives were very expensive and only a few people would have been wealthy enough to own one. Their appearance almost coincided with the evolution of folding knives (and forks) with spring-backs. This altered the trend and trade in pocket cutlery which had hitherto been rather quiet due to the knife-in-a-sheath that everyone carried. The demand for folding cutlery is shown to have increased at this time since sheathed (portable) cutlery started to wane in popularity as hosts began to supply their guests with table cutlery. In 1663 Samuel Pepys noted that only the top two tables at a City of London banquet had been set with cutlery and the other guests had been obliged to bring their personal cutlery.

During the mid 17th century, designs for pocket-knives in England were rather basic with steel blades and thick tortoiseshell, horn or wood used as scaling materials. In France, they were better esteemed and many were made more decorative, the tortoiseshell being cross-banded with silver that incorporated human figures and animals (*ref. chapter 2*).

The trend for French wares in England was exemplified by the apparent gift of Charles II to his mistress Nell Gwyn, in about 1680, of a silver-hafted twin-bladed folding knife. The silver casing was decorated with feasting figures *à la mode* (*plate 2.17*). This knife was made with two blades, one of silver-backed steel and one of silver. While it was evolving and being tested for popularity on the market, this particular knife design (known as a *Couteau-sans-clou*) didn't change much for about 70 years. Once the trend for folding fruit knives reached England in about 1750 and, to a much lesser extent, other European countries, decorative styles evolved more quickly. Trend setting with such new and fashionable accoutrements may also have exacerbated rivalries between England and France, already at political odds, and stimulated an amazing array of new mechanical and decorative designs.

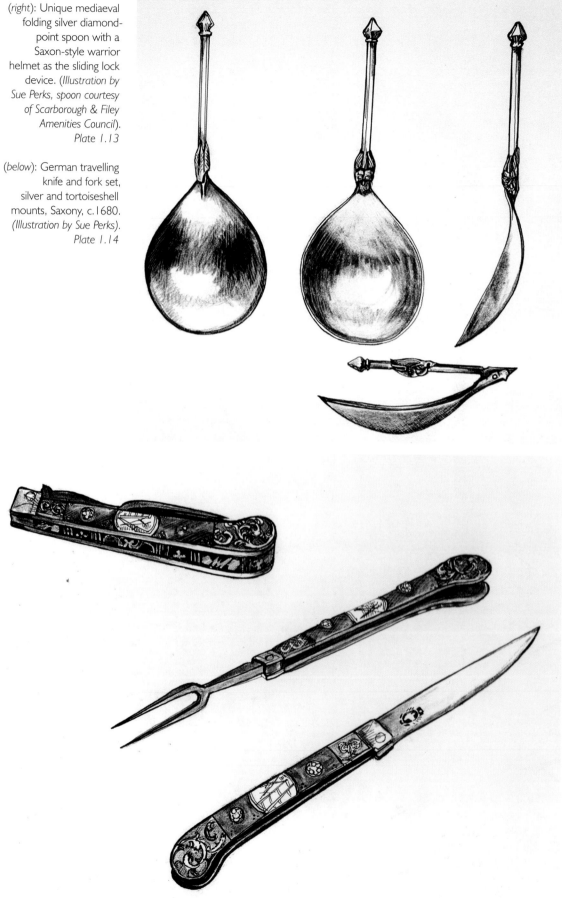

(*right*): Unique mediaeval folding silver diamond-point spoon with a Saxon-style warrior helmet as the sliding lock device. (*Illustration by Sue Perks, spoon courtesy of Scarborough & Filey Amenities Council*). Plate 1.13

(*below*): German travelling knife and fork set, silver and tortoiseshell mounts, Saxony, c.1680. (*Illustration by Sue Perks*). Plate 1.14

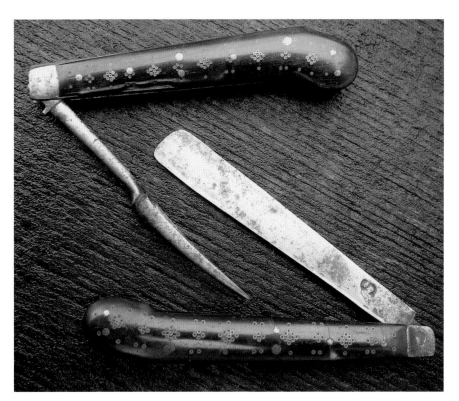

English silver travelling knife and fork set with tortoiseshell scales inlaid with *piqué* silver circles, c.1700.
Plate 1.15

German travelling fork c.1730, with scales of horn inlaid with Islamic-style *piqué*.
Plate 1.16

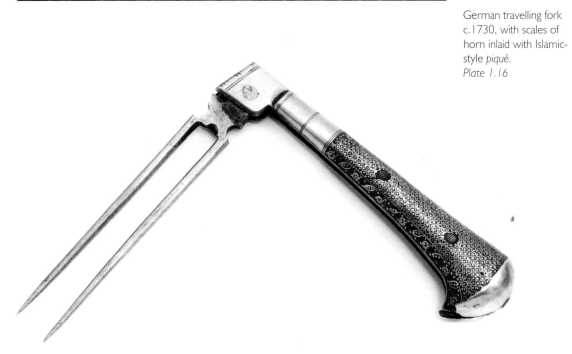

Dutch pocket knife,
c.1400 with crude haft
of wooden slats rivetted
together. Note the thumb
rest protruding from the
back of the blade, enabling
it to be held open.
Plate 1.17

2 A brief history of early French pocket fruit knives

Plate 2.1

A typical early 18th century *couteau-sans-clou* with cutler's mark only of a cross over an ermine. Above, a typical French-style pocket fruit knife from Thomas Gray of Eastcheap, London, c.1770, complete with a sleeper shark shagreen and silver *étui*.

Detail of Still Life by
Conrad Mannlich,
(1701-1758) showing
fruits and a *Couteau-sans-
clou* c.1730 *(courtesy of
Musée de Strasbourg)*.
Plate 2.2

*Couteau-sans-clou, c.1720,
scaled with nacre, with
similar scalloped borders
to the knife above.
Plate 2.3*

Collecting Note

Collecting French pocket fruit knives may seem rather specialised but they are most important since the trend for precious-metal-bladed pocket-knives appears to have started in France, coupled with a superiority of both design and mechanism.

I have always been amazed at the diversity, beauty and cunning construction of pocket fruit knives generally but particularly those from France.

Evolution of pocket and other portable fruit knives in France

The invention of the spring-back pocket-knife sometime during the early to mid 17th century caused a rapid increase in eating fashion. The portability of knives was essential

given that guests or patrons had to supply their own 'eating irons' or else use their fingers. Most carried a small eating knife in a sheath, preferring this to the old-fashioned and folding clasp knife which was only prevented from accidentally opening by the blade being gripped by the haft sides of organic material - normally bone or wood (*plate 1.8*). Across Europe the spring-back pocket knife, guaranteed by its own design not to open in its owner's pocket or purse, became swiftly *de rigueur*. Examples were bladed with steel, some with matching fork blades, for travellers. Some were made with two blades, one at each end, and maximised the use of the spring. At the same time, some pocket knives were made with

Pair of steel-bladed
eating knives with silver
openwork tracery-
decorated hafts, known
as *Bérain* style. c.1680
Jean Bérain was a designer
(1637-1711). (ex Sotheby,
Ridpath collection
catalogue, 1942).
Plate 2.4

additional springs, blades and tools. Apart from the master blade of steel, there may also have been a stone pick (for horses' hooves), a saw, pruning blades, a bodkin, or even scissors. Silver blades appear not to have been added to these extra tools until the later 17th century, as a fashionable accompaniment for those who could regularly afford the luxury of eating fruit. The haft naturally became the cutler's or silversmith's canvas, reflecting this touch of luxury, being scaled with tortoiseshell and overlaid with silver or even gold tracery, or scaled with plain or engraved nacre (mother-of-pearl). For those who still considered folding knives, however grand, were too 'gentleman farmerish' for their tastes, elegantly sheathed pairs of knives, one bladed in like manner with steel and the other with precious metal, were also made.

An elegant pocket knife that could encompass a multitude of functions was required, including a precious metal blade for fruit eating: the 'rivetless' *Couteau-sans-clou* arrived and quickly found its niche in gentlemen's pockets.

Hallmarking

At this time the testing and hallmarking of silver was considerably less refined than it later became; such small items as knife blades did not warrant the added expense of assay and hallmarking. Silver blades were not marked with any quality control mark until the mid-18th or even early 19th century when hallmarking laws were tightened up. Hallmarking laws were slackened at the time of the French Revolution (1789) and particularly during the ensuing Terror of 1792-3.

Small silver (less than 1.5 ounces troy) required a maker's mark only; the same applied to gold of less than 1 ounce troy. Earlier pieces were often left totally unmarked, especially if made outside of Paris. A few were stamped with a provincial crowned date-letter mark, often imitating those of the Capital. From 1819 to 1838, the laws were tightened up further to the extent that pieces lacking hallmarks or those with obscured or obliterated marks would have to be re-assayed and marked at full cost or be destroyed. This has inevitably led to confusion and the misdating of earlier pieces, particularly those from the late 17th and early 18th centuries, and which were subsequently marked with an eagle's head (c.1780) or the tiny crab-in-cinquefoil mark introduced in 1838. Even the tiny Swan mark (1893-1970) could be applied to an unmarked silver blade 200 or more years after it had been made if it was

Mullet (star) hallmark on *couteau-sans-clou*, c.1720 - struck later to conform with hallmarking regulations, Montpellier, c.1780.
Plate 2.6

Some 'hallmarks' are no more than engraved signatures *(A Caen)* since these blades were not submitted for assay..
Plate 2.7

Crab hallmark (c.1850) on *couteau-sans-clou*, and eagle's head mark on the top corner of the upper blade for Bourg, c.1780.
Plate 2.8

exported or even sold at auction if of unknown, or sometimes even known, origin. Many antique French-hallmarked and foreign pieces were subsequently marked with the Swan (*above*). This was due to a piece being sold during a later period, (*Directoire, Régence, Empire &c*).

The author has noted in museum collections and displays how many of these early knives have been erroneously dated to the mid-19th century, by which time the overall decorative styles had completely changed.

A boar's head mark denoted that a provincial assay had been checked in Paris using a touch needle – an old fashioned but convenient way of checking metal quality by comparing a line-scrape from the blade on a slate (or touchstone) against that of a needle of known quality (*plate 2.16*).

Multi-marked *couteau-sans-clou* blade with four later but legally-required marks, two of which have been struck upside down, and one later control mark. The open hand is a Parisian counter-mark for 1762-1768. The inverted vine leaf may be the town mark for Péronne 1768-1774. The inverted hunting horn is a second Paris counter-mark for 1768-1774. The smaller mark in the oval cartouche is the swan used as a quality control mark when precious metal objects came back into France between 1893 and 1970. Note how the hand mark, in particular, has distorted the engraved lines surrounding it and how all the other marks, except for the maker's *(au verso)* have been struck onto the engraving so that the deepest cuts still score through the marks suggesting that the knife was made and engraved some years before these marks were struck, probably c.1720.
Plate 2.9

PAGE 17

Rare maker's mark, for this period, of CG with a flambeau between; maybe for C. Guyot of Langres c.1720. Makers for these knives would have been deemed unimportant as goldsmiths at the time and their marks are virtually impossible to identify. Stylistically the mark belongs to the period between 1680 and 1750.
Plate 2.10

The *couteau* with all of these marks on the silver blade. The crowned Croix de Lorraine cutler's mark is for Guyot of Langres, c.1720.
Plates 2.11 & (inset) 2.12

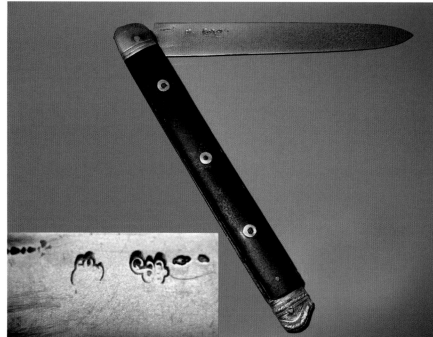

(*above*): A gold spring-backed fruit knife, c.1785: note the animal's head counter-mark (*right*) which has a *Bigorne* back-stamp (*enlarged just below*). (*below*): an English fruit knife, 1783, may have appeared at a French auction being struck with the tiny swan mark and back-stamped on a *bigorne* to prevent fraudulent copying of hallmarking dies.
Plate 2.13

The gold blade of this knife has been inserted into a harder-wearing steel tang.
Plate 2.14

Full set of hallmarks on a silver Berge knife blade c.1773-83. Left and right of centre are the dog's head and monogram for Orléans 1774-80, the crowned letter T or I is a possible date letter, the LM with the key (*below right*) is the mark of an anonymous/unknown maker of many such blades. The handshake mark (*upper right*) is the Paris control mark for 1783.
Plate 2.15

From about 1780, a full set of hallmarks (*poinçons*) is normally found on precious metal blades. Paris hallmarks were changed annually and were struck on the reverse side of the blade so as not to deface the obverse surface. One or two quality control marks were also struck and from May 1838 these were struck onto the blade against an anvil engraved with a series of running insects and a dividing line down the middle and known as a *bigorne*, leaving an imprint on the obverse side of the blade. The reason for this was to prevent control marks from being copied or fraudulently struck. Information about French hallmarking is fairly plentiful since the publication of Carré's *Les Poinçons de l'Orfèvrerie Française* (1928) but the subject is still quite complicated when relating to precious metal knife blades due to the low importance of mere blades in silver circles; little has been explained about them apart from brief mentions in Pagé's *La coutellerie depuis l'origine jusqu'à nos jours* (1896) and an entry in a 1900 exhibition catalogue (Picard).

In a presumed economy-driven society, many of the Paris retailers appear to have purchased or even contracted the making of precious metal blades from provincial rather than Parisian goldsmiths, from nearby towns such as Rouen and particularly from Orléans. The main reason, however, stems from blade-smiths working in these towns. Each of these towns, where blades were submitted for assay and hallmarking, had their own assay office and a set of local hallmarking dies. One prolific workshop, whose sponsor mark of LM with an upright key between the letters, produced many such blades and is listed anonymously as a master goldsmith from Orléans in 1775, (Beuque &

Frapsauce 1982); there is nothing else currently known about this producer.

Some Paris retailers would have requested that their company mark should be stamped onto the steel blade and also onto the precious metal blade if there were not too many quality control marks already upon it. This, in view of the check on the quality of provincial-made blades by the Paris office, often including the thin precious metal layers coating the bolsters and caps, and the addition of tiny quality control marks of their own, meant that there was often no room for an additional retailer's mark until the 19th century!

Magnificent *couteau-sans-clou* by an unidentified French cutler whose trademark was three pellets, or a crown above letter I or A. An eagle's head silver mark was added c.1785 when hallmarking laws were tightened up. Reputed to have been given to Nell Gwyn by King Charles II, c.1670-80. The knife was donated by Captain Philip (late of Scots Greys) to the Army & Navy Club, London in 1888.
(Drawing by Sue Perks).
Plate 2.17

(inset): The same cutler's mark on another pocket knife, c.1680
(ref. Plate 2.26)

(below): Haft figures from tracery-decorated knives from the same period as above and depicting *(l to r)* a countryman, a cup-bearer and a dog, a giraffe, and two wild men (woodwoses). Note the concealed rivet heads blended into the decoration, such as the enlarged curl below the cup bearer's hind leg.
Plate 2.18

Silver spines ornamenting all four springs on a multi-bladed *couteau-sans-clou*.
Plate 2.19

Knife made at Langres by Diderot (c.1700) (*Courtesy of Musée du Breuil de St Germain, Langres*).
Plate 2.20

Couteaux-sans-Clous

These are twin-bladed spring-back knives with steel and silver blades. The name *sans clous* (rivetless) is derived from the rivets being either hidden under the scales or disguised into the haft design.

The earliest of these knives appears to date from the third quarter of the 17th century when spring-backed knives, as opposed to gravity or clasp knives, were still in their comparative infancy. Despite their rather unrefined mechanism, known as 'hard spring' - a square tang and thick-section spring that exerted considerable force on the blade's tang so that the blade had to be closed cautiously, they belong to a group of folding knives with the most amazing decoration.

Many knives of this type were single and steel-bladed with hafts sumptuously decorated in the manner of period table knives. Their silver ornament (described below) could even extend to an additional engraved silver tongue that flicked into position, covering the blade slot when the blade was opened or a blade slot that gradually opened as the blade was closed (*plates 2.25 & 2.29*).

Two examples of scallop ricassi, designed to 'lubricate' steel blade hinges on *couteaux*. That below is false, being engraved onto an early *Berge* knife blade but copying the style of that above.

(below): A more stylised scallop shell on an early 18th century pocket knife blade stamped with a clear cutler's mark.
Plates 2.21 & 2.22

POCKET FRUIT KNIVES: 2 A BRIEF HISTORY OF EARLY FRENCH POCKET FRUIT KNIVES

The form of these early precious-metal-bladed knives followed the dictates of the 'blade-at-either-end' knife although a few were multi-bladed. Each knife was assembled and the parts riveted together, the rivet heads either being filed flush with the web (liner) of sheet steel and concealed beneath the scales (usual for more brittle nacre scales) or capped with silver rosettes and blended by engraving into the silver tracery decoration (plates 2.15 & 2.18). Either way, the rivets were cunningly concealed, giving rise to the title Couteau-sans-clou or 'knife without rivet'. Some of these had considerable skill lavished upon them; exposed metal could be nothing but silver so that the springs and all other exposed base metal surfaces, apart from the actual faces of the steel blades themselves, were coated with pre-decorated strips of silver sheet soldered onto the steel (plate 2.19). Steel master blades were also frequently decorated with a short silver panel, usually depicting an engraved scallop shell, which prevented the thicker end of the steel blade from rusting and seizing up if the knife should become damp or remain unused for a while. The slippery physical property of silver acts as a natural lubricant to prevent such blade seizure.

Silver traceries or appliqué openwork were heat-pressed into organic scales, usually tortoiseshell since its darkness contrasts well

Another triumph of French fruit knife making: a twin silver-bladed couteau-sans-clou featuring an unusual double-edged blade (left) for cutting grapefruit and other tougher-skinned fruit. The inscription plaques are both engraved COVTOFIN. (detail): part of the openwork silver tracery featuring a woman and a bird, c.1700.
Plate 2.24
(facing page): Couteaux-sans-clous c.1670-1730, and a similar-styled pocket knife (centre) by the same cutler as the Nell Gwyn knife marked I or A with three pellets or crown above. Note how some steel blades have silver scalloped bases.
Plate 2.23

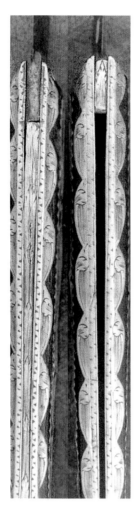

PAGE 24

The final touch of French elegance! The left-hand haft fitted with a springy tongue of engraved silver to conceal the open blade slot.
Plate 2.25

Two similar pocket knives with Bérain-style hafts, c.1700. The left knife with an English replacement blade stamped SPARLING (John Smith of Sheffield, or Robert Sparling of London c.1770).
Plate 2.26

Invoice from Robert Sparling to His Grace the Duke of Norfolk, dated 26th of July 1776.
Plate 2.27

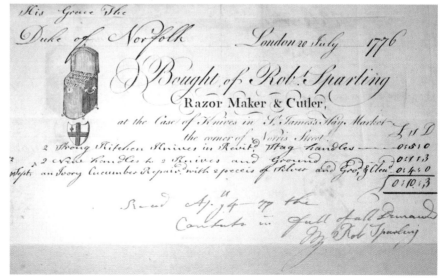

with silver and forms a flexible organic layer between the iron web and the silver decoration. The edges of many silver haft traceries were scalloped so that the silver could be folded down along the bevelled edges of the organic scaling material to hold it in place. The silver edges were engraved with panels of punctated cross-hatching, scrollwork, and panels of tightly engraved lines. The openwork that covered the scales themselves was also cut and engraved with figures of wild men, harlequins, angels, birds, plants and scrollwork (*plate 2.18*). This openwork style is much derived from Jean Bérain (1637-1711), whose fantastic designs, incorporating metal-inlaid figures, were much favoured by King Louis XIV and later influenced the work of André-Charles Boulle with his unique style of furniture. The purpose of these knives can only be guessed. Silver blades were meant for fruit cutting although the hunting scene shown on the silver blade of the knife in *plate 2.31* is somewhat misleading. The steel

blades could be used for anything from cutting a sausage to slitting a throat! Sometimes a motto was added to the haft *COVTO FIN / COVPE BIEN* (a finely-made knife cuts well).

The family firm of Beligné started in 1610 and still exists in name, at Nogent in Burgundy. At this time, Didier Beligné was the King's cutler and worked in nearby Langres. He decorated silver blades with a characteristic engraved border (*above*), presumably imitated by others, as similarly-made but equally fine knives have appeared, but are unmarked or unsigned.

Couteaux-sans-clous were evidently popular due to the numbers that still turn up in the Antique Trade while many are in museum collections. Most show wear and tear in the form of nacre cracks and missing silver ornaments so their condition should not be judged too severely.

(top left): Beligné's trademark and *(right)* typical decoration on silver knife blades. (*Courtesy of Musée du Breuil de St Germain, Langres*).
Plate 2.28
(top): Note the later 'Crab' hallmark, c.1850 which appears as a black circle.

Amazing pocket knife by *Aubin* of Caen, c.1700, with overlays of engraved gold. As the blade is opened, these close together (*below*) and as the blade is closed (*below*), these open to reveal the blade slot. The tortoiseshell haft has been inlaid in the usual Bérain style, but with gold and shaped slivers of ormer shell. (*Courtesy of Galerie Reboul, Paris*). *Plate 2.29*

The style and decoration was used on both folding and rigid-bladed knives throughout the first half of the 18th century but cutlers also produced a springless style of folding

knife, possibly invented around the turn of the 17th century, although decorated in the same style as before, known as the *Couteau de* or *à la Berge*.

Dilemmas

1. Pagé (1896) states that the style of 'rivetless decoration' was typical for folding knives made at the end of Louis XV's reign (1715-1774) or maybe during the *Régence* (1715-1723) [the earlier period is possible judging by the decorative style attributed to Jean Bérain]. Pagé's indecision is significant since the Ridpath collection catalogue (Sotheby 1942) shows a pair of knives with identically decorated hafts listed as being made during the late 17th century (*plate 2.4*). The style may have lasted for almost 100 years.

2. No one is quite sure why a Parisian cutler, named *Berge*, should be credited with having his name connected with a

Decorative panels and inscription plaques spelling out: COVTO FIN COVPE BIEN *(a fine knife cuts well)* from knife upper left. p.22 *Plate 2.30*

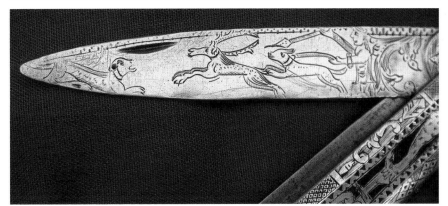

A stag hunting scene stylishly engraved on the same knife's fruit blade. *Plate 2.31*

knife that appears to predate his birth by up to 40 years. He presumably made and marketed a great number and perhaps the type of knife was named by association rather than after an unknown or earlier inventor. The earliest-presumed knife of this type can be seen at the Victoria and Albert Museum in London. The steel blade is inlaid with rosettes of copper alloy arranged in cinquefoils, while the silver blade and the haft have been sawn with areas of Bérain-style openwork cunningly inlaid with slivers of tortoiseshell in the manner of *plique à jour* enamel

(plate 2.33). If this is Berge's (unsigned) masterpiece it could suggest that he might have been born as early as c.1670. Although this dating is debatable, on stylistic grounds, he could have made the knife c.1730 in retro style.

Another fine *couteau-sans-clou*, but with interlacing ornaments of cut steel. The steel blade has been stamped with a cutler's mark of a boot crowned: c.1730.
Plate 2.32

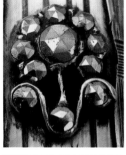

Berge Knives (leading to Empire knives)

The *Couteau à tête de compas*, as it was originally known according to Pagé (1896), swiftly assumed the name of *Couteau de* or *à la Berge* sometime during the mid to later 18th century. Although hardly any personal details seem to exist about Berge, not even his first name, he is frequently mentioned, first in Jean-Jacques Perret's *L'Art du coutelier* (1771), then in Pagés *La coutellerie depuis l'origine jusqu'à nos jours* (1896) who (latterly) quotes him as being the creator of this style of twin-bladed knife. More recently, Dominique Pascal (*Couteaux de poche*, 2004) mentions Berge and his knives and has been trying to glean more material from sources other than Perret and Pagé, yet none seem to exist. Despite the knife mentioned in dilemma 2 (*page 26*) Berge appears to have been born in the early to mid-18th century, worked in Paris and maybe inherited his father's cutlery business, producing many twin-bladed pocket fruit knives whose blades were situated at the same end of the haft – but this history is all supposition. The blade material followed the tradition of one blade of steel and the other of precious metal. These knives lacked a spring but

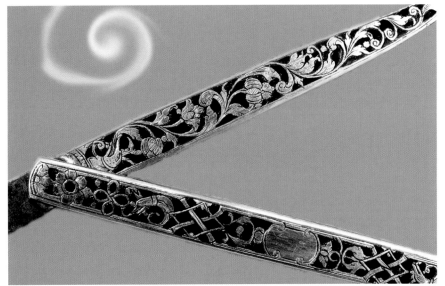

Early Berge knife in the style of a *couteau-sans-clou*. The fruit blade (shown) comprises excised silver inlaid with shaped slivers of tortoiseshell, c.1700. *(Courtesy of Victoria & Albert Museum, London).*
Plate 2.33

Early *Berge* knife, c.1720. Note the decorative and concealed-rivet style of the *couteau-sans-clou*. *(Courtesy of D Kleinman).*
Plate 2.34

the two blades backed onto each other. Both blades could not, therefore, be more than half-opened simultaneously giving the appearance of a geometrician's compass. Full-scale production of knives with the Berge mechanism seems to have begun during the first quarter of the 18th century. The style was evidently popular and continued well into the 19th century when it was largely superseded by single-bladed fruit knives not unlike those produced in England and was even copied by English cutlers who produced smaller replicas (*ref. plate 4.2*). Earlier *Berge* knives were decorated in similar manner to the *Couteaux-sans-clous* and some were engraved on the silver blade

A more typical and later *Berge* knife with gold-striped haft ornaments but a silver blade, by LM of Orléans with the Warden's crowned italic P for 1784; the boar's head is a later Parisian mark showing that the blade was checked with a touch needle assay.
Plate 2.35

Superb nacre-hafted *Berge* knife: silver and steel blades, the nacre haft inlaid with gold rather than silver *piqué posé* twigs and ormer shell, c.1770.
(Courtesy of SJ Phillips, London)
Plate 2.36

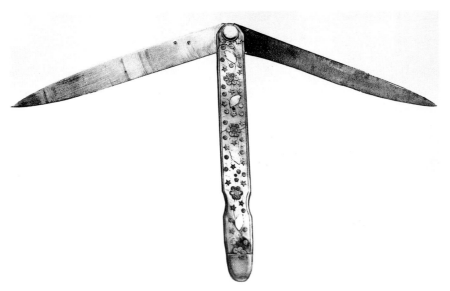

Two similar types of *Berge* knives with inlaid nacre hafts and one English style knife c.1790.
(From d'Allemagne's *Accessoires*, 1928).
Plates 2.37 & 2.38

with Tenniel-styled faces in profile or flying birds (*plates 2.34 & 2.52*). The steel blade backs were normally lined with spines of precious metal matching those of the fruit blade, so that an unbroken line of gold or silver was always visible along the back, whichever blade was open. In 1740 French cutlers were forbidden to ornament their work with gold or silver, but this ruling was repealed in 1765 after many complaints and infractions. By about 1770, a fashion for further decoration had superseded the 'rivetless' look, and the rivet heads were often adorned with tiny rosettes of gold or silver in the form of stars, tiny cinquefoils or flower heads. The handles of these knives were fashioned from two plates of decorative material, usually nacre

Berge knife with a fruit blade of gold, Péronne town mark, c.1768-74, cross-hatched nacre scales with gold sunflower rosettes and a typical green-stained sting-ray *galuchat* hinge-lidded box.
Plate 2.39

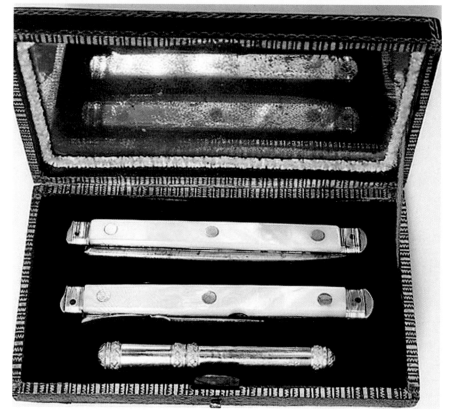

Fine Empire set, complete with needle case, gilt and steel-bladed knife and gilt fork set in a plush case, complete with mirror, c.1800.
Plate 2.40

or tortoiseshell, without any form of supporting web (liner) since this would have interfered with the knife's action or marred its delicate lines. The haft was decorated in a variety of ways: nacre was usually crosshatched or diagonally striped. Both nacre and tortoiseshell were often inlaid with diagonal or longitudinal strips of gold or silver alternating with rosettes (*plates 2.35 & 2.46*) and this style is very occasionally found on silver hafts, banded with gilt oblique stripes.

Another beautiful *Berge* knife with a gold blade assayed for Paris 1761-2. The nacre haft has been overlaid with 'encrustations' of carved ormer shell and gold formed into be-ribboned groups of Arcadian pipes, tambourines, hats and swords. The cutler's mark of the ermine is often noted on steel blades for knives of such high quality. *(Courtesy of Galerie Reboul, Paris)*
Plate 2.41

Superb *Berge* knife with gold fruit blade, the haft decorated and part-overlaid with rich blue enamel on a *guilloché* background, unmarked but c.1770.
Plate 2.42

Some hafts were even more extravagantly decorated with twigs of gold supporting flowers and leaves of pink and green abalone or ormer shell or combined with Arcadian pipes and shepherd hats of gold and shell (*above*). More extravagant still were enamelled handles beautifully fashioned within a framework of four colour gold, perhaps with an in-built timepiece or portrait miniature and studded with tiny diamonds or split pearls (*plate 2.50*).

The ends of each handle were finished with caps of precious metal, often minutely control-hallmarked, either square-ended, wavy or scallop-shaped at the bolster where the blade was attached, and usually scallop-shaped at the other end. If the haft was fashioned from nacre then the capped ends were underlaid with wood, sometimes combined with sealing wax, so that the fissile mother-of-pearl was protected against cracking or chipping if the knife was accidentally dropped.

Gilt-bladed *Berge* knife c.1780-91, again by LM of *Orléans* with a key between. Note the shoe and goose head marks on the gold sheet plating the wood-covered bolster, which are Parisian control marks 1775-81, making the knife c.1780-81 in date. (Sponsors' marks were outlined with a lozenge cartouche from 1794 in Paris and the rest of France from 1797 onwards). *Plate 2.43*

(detail): Plate 2.44

Close-up of two bolsters showing the thin gold caps (hallmarked) which have become damaged, exposing the protective wooden underlay. Compare the crude iron rivets of these two knives with that shown in *plate 2.39*. *Plate 2.45*

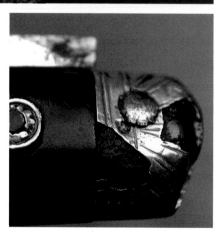

Each knife was sold in a velvet-lined wooden case veneered with either green-stained shagreen (*galuchat* - refer to Knife Boxes page 42) or morocco leather. For those who preferred spring-backed knives, similar cases were made to contain two matching knives, one with a steel blade, the other bladed with precious metal, although these were largely made during the late 18th and early 19th centuries. Many were made with lock-back mechanisms and the haft scales were often inlaid with longitudinal strips of precious metal as before. They are known as *Empire* knives (*couteaux de l'Empire*) due to their being made mainly during the Napoleonic Empire period. However, cutlers appear to have abandoned the Berge design in about 1820 in favour of other styles as tastes moved on, and twin-bladed spring-back knives reigned supreme throughout much of the 19th century. Softer precious metal blades were often mounted into a steel tang if in contact with a steel spring, to prevent or reduce

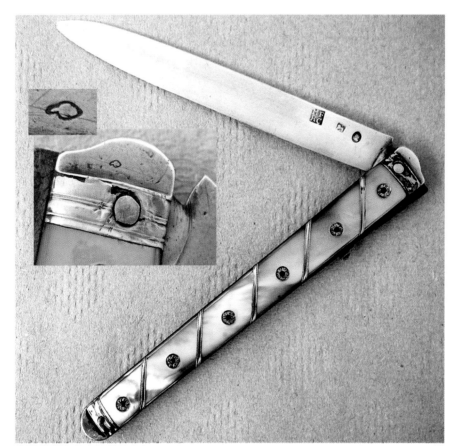

Couteau de l'Empire with the usual fine nacre scales diagonally-striped with gold wire. The Eagle's head mark signifies Paris, 1781-1789 but the blade assayed in Sheffield at around the same time, bearing the sponsor mark of Mathew Fenton, Richard Creswick and William Watson. The crudeness of the rivet suggests that the blade may have been added later and yet the knife's smooth and perfect action suggests originality! This may be a typical knife of 'mixed race'.
Plate 2.46

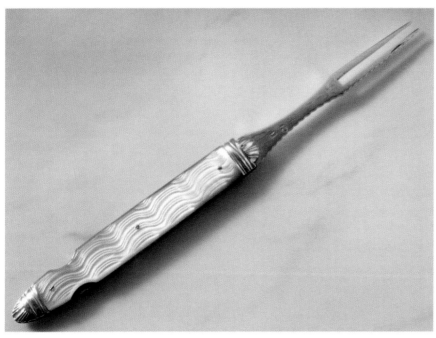

An English fork c.1790 mounted on a Berge knife haft. Despite appearances this does seem to be an original 'mixed race' piece.
Plate 2.47

wear – a feature overlooked by English manufacturers.

'Mixed Race' knives and forks are not so uncommon from this time, although the reasons for their existence can only be guessed. Beautiful French hafts, often hallmarked as such but bladed with Sheffield silver, have turned up in The Trade occasionally. One is shown (plate 2.46), comprising a typical Empire knife with a beautiful gold-striped and nacre-scaled haft with Paris 'bird beak' control marks struck onto the bolsters, but bearing

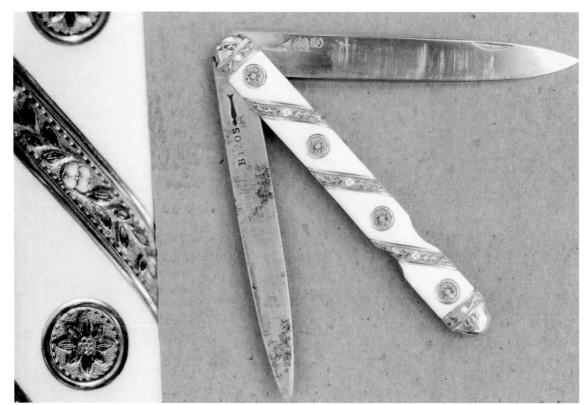

Two typical *Berge* knives of the 1780-1820 period and with full sets of contemporary hallmarks. The upper knife with fine enamelling by Bizos of Paris who may have been the retailer. Below, a more modest knife with fine stamped rosettes laid into nacre scales (marks explained on page 18).
Plates 2.48 & 2.49

a Sheffield blade, all c.1790. If the blade replaced an original then it must have been broken or damaged shortly after purchase. The owner must have had it repaired in England and this might explain the rather crudely hammered hinge rivet which slightly protrudes rather than being covered by the gold bolster bands. Despite this, the action of the knife is

certainly up to French standards. There were also some French-style English knives made at this and slightly later times (*ref. page 72*).

During the late 18th and early 19th centuries, a few even more luxurious knives, in *Berge* and other styles, were bladed with Damascus steel, which has a fine *moiré* finish,

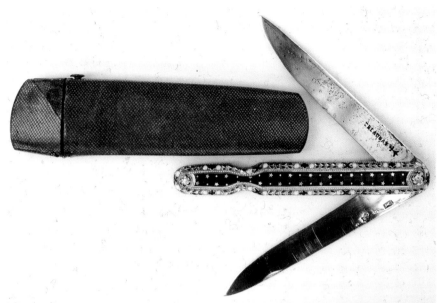

Another rich man's knife: the haft superbly enamelled and set with split pearls. Mark of Montpellier c.1770, but retailed by Delaunay of Paris.
Plate 2.50

(detail): Plate 2.52

matched with a blade of silver or gold. A certain Monsieur Treppoz (still working in 1819) in the St Honoré region of Paris is said to have "Worked in Damascus steel (*acier damassé*) and was one of the first artists to have introduced Damascus steel into cutlery making" (D'Allemagne, 1928). Such fine blades of superior steel, partnered with gold, continued to be made with hafts decorated with enamels and split pearls and were produced to match the splendours of Louis XVI's reign (1774-1793) and the Napoleonic period (1793-1815) and echoing those of the *Régence* (1715-1723) and the reign of Louis XV (1723-1774). Many of these were produced at places outside of Paris, such as Orléans, and precious metal blades often bear the assay marks of even smaller provincial French towns such as Péronne (*plate 2.39*) where there was a resident goldsmith. Retailers' marks are often additionally found on either or both the blades, typically Touron, Cardeilhac, Delaunay and Christofle, particularly on those of superior quality (*above*).

A selection of typical *Berge* knives c.1740-1790, including one with a typical 'bird-on-thistle' motif rather crudely engraved on the silver blade (*below*). The tortoiseshell-scaled knife comprises a single (steel) blade, known as an *Empire* knife, since its form became more popular after the Revolution - it would have been paired with a precious metal-bladed knife.
Plate 2.51

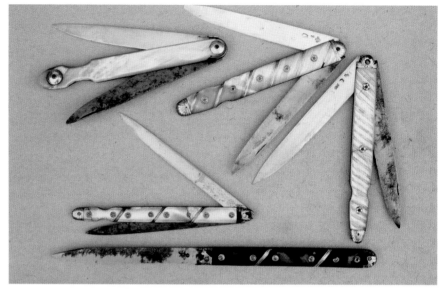

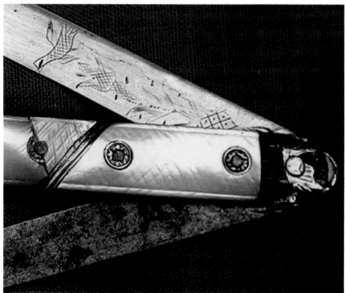

Note the engraved wooden underlay supporting the thin gold plating of the bolster and the later-replaced triangular chip of nacre.
Plate 2.52

Berge and Empire knives seem to have suffered slightly less wear and tear than *couteaux-sans-clous*. This can be attributed to their greater fragility, being discarded or recycled when damaged or that the more discerning kept them as objects to impress. Despite the age disparity all of these would have been through a tough period of French history.

Upper: *Berge* knife with gold blade, the haft unusually of silver, diagonally striped with gold bands and engraved with bright-cut work, unmarked, c.1770. *Plate 2.53*

Lower: spring-backed pocket fruit knife c.1760-75, later marked with the 19th century swan. Note the wriggle-engraved bird motif again. *Plate 2.54*

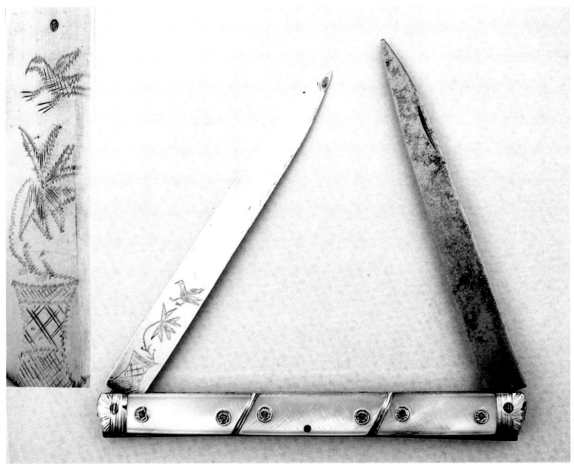

Plate 2.56

Unusual nacre-scaled pocket fruit knife, single bladed but the haft has *Berge* influence. Engraved with Arcadian figures, c.1770.
Plate 2.55

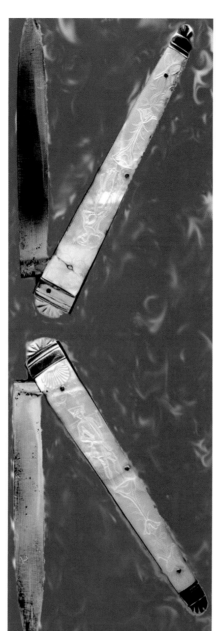

Backs of *Berge* knives showing how the spine decoration is often (but not always) continued along the blade back. If the blade has been replaced it will probably not co-ordinate as well as these.
Plate 2.56

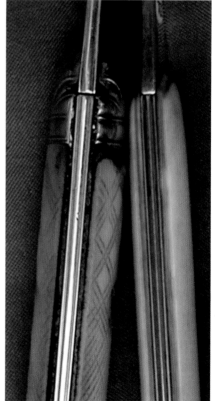

Gold and steel-bladed pocket fruit knife, c.1780-1820 with scales of serpentine, and bolsters and caps of two-coloured gold. The marks are for ?Rouen, counter-marked in Paris c.1788. This form of haft became more usual for dessert and fruit knives of the Napoleonic and even later periods. Note that the gold blade has been mounted on a steel tang (ref. also p.18).
Plate 2.57

Green-stained sting-ray/dogfish skin (galuchat) boxes with brass or gilt-brass hinges. The left with birds'-eye studs, is c.1730, the mid three are mid to later 18th century, the right-hand iron hinge is early 19th century.
Plate 2.58

Knife boxes

French cutlers never seemed to tire of inventing types of knife that could be carried in the pocket, all of them housed in beautiful hinge-lidded wooden containers veneered with either leather or, more usually, rubbed-down and polished green-stained shagreen (shark or ray skin) which they generically termed *galuchat*. D'Allemagne (1938) describes *galuchat* as lizard or snake skin which was glued onto a green-stained *transparent* (layer) so that the green colour showed through the skin. More recent research has identified sting-ray skin, with its micro-rhomboidal scales, as the top quality shagreen used to adorn many such boxes although (Perfettini,1988) states that many of these knife cases were veneered with a fine-grained dog-fish skin, rather than D'Allemagne's suggestion of lizard. He also says that the skins were initially used as abrasive pads until they became smooth. Today the term *galuchat* is used generically to describe any such fish skin used as a decorative veneer.

Most of these boxes were hinge-lidded and the hinge can give an idea of date. If the hinge comprised a trio (or more) of 'birds eye' rivets (domed and with concentric circles) then it dates from the late 17th to mid 18th century. If the hinge was of gilt brass in two parts externally, normally with 4 pins attaching it to the box, then it was likely made during the later 18th century. If the hinge was in the form of a tube, usually of iron, it was an early 19th century development. Some boxes were simply made with pull-off lids (*page 52*).

Berge knives were invariably sold in these fine boxes, which were internally lined with velvet and for those who preferred spring-backed *Empire* knives, similar cases were made with two slots to contain two matching knives following the normal blade material conventions.

Reference: Jean Perfettini: *Le galuchat*. Vial, 1988.

Other French pocket fruit knives

Smaller-size pocket fruit knives began to appear during the 1720s. These were between 7 and 10 centimetres long when closed, much like later English examples. Due to their similarity in size and shape, they are often difficult to differentiate from English examples of the same period and which evolved from these *mi-siècle* French styles. Few were ever hallmarked, their small size excusing them from the otherwise stringent French hallmarking laws, until the post Revolution era. For easier comparison they are placed in the next chapter due to their similarity to evolving English knives.

Couteaux aux lames de réchanges

These are exchangeable-bladed knives comprising a single haft and two blades (steel and precious metal) that could be attached to the haft by using a notched tang that clipped into a spring-loaded mechanism inside the haft (*plates 2.59 (above) & 2.60*). Pressing on the top rosette on the reverse side of the haft, or a similar release button, released the blade, sometimes quite violently, so that it could either be exchanged for the other blade or simply put away. They were made largely between 1770 and 1830 and the style was also copied in England shortly after (*page 109*).

Couteau à lames de réchange of gold and steel, the steel blade with an unidentified cutler's mark, c.1800.
Plate 2.59

A *couteau à lames de réchange* in a more Empire style with Romanesque haft ornamentations in two-colour gold, on scales of top-quality nacre. A complex double group of hallmarks c.1775-1785, on the gold blade denotes its Parisian origin. The steel blade has been marked with the well-known cutler/retailer's name of A. Peter.
Plate 2.60

Couteaux gigognes
This translates as 'nesting knives' (like a Russian Doll) and these are even more remarkable. Comprising a non-collapsible knife in a shagreen *étui*, the blade was made from thin sheets of steel cunningly forged together to form a hollow blade. A smaller precious metal-bladed fruit knife was made to fit exactly inside this knife and a toothpick was made to fit inside the fruit knife. The thinness of the steel blade has meant that few of these amazing but rather impractical knives have survived intact, let alone in perfect condition; many of the steel blades have been ruptured or otherwise damaged.

Couteaux d'Estaings

Estaing knives were invented by a French admiral during the late 18th century and somewhat followed the design of the *Couteau gigogne*. However, the steel blade was fitted inside an enveloping blade of silver that acted as the fruit knife, and which clipped into the haft on one side. The haft rosettes were substituted by metal buttons, two of which were sprung and connected to a lever system inside the haft. One button released the silver envelope blade while the other unlocked the steel blade so that it could be extended to twice its length for use as a carving knife or even a weapon. When retracted the knife blade fitted inside an open-ended *étui* of shagreen. On a historical note, Admiral d'Estaing was born in 1729 and was involved in fighting in America (c.1778) and the West Indies. Despite his honourable standing, he fell foul of the Revolution and was executed in 1794.

Couteau d'Estaing as a fruit knife, c.1800, with its *galuchat* (shagreen) sheath and scales of ivory. The silver buttons release the blade-extending lock mechanism.
Plate 2.61

The same knife with the
blade extended and with
the mechanism exposed.
Plates 2.62 & 2.63

PAGE 46

Like the *Couteaux gigognes*, few
of these knives have survived in
perfect condition: the fragile silver
enveloping blade has frequently
been ruptured, broken or lost and
unsuspecting buyers can be offered
the extending steel-bladed knife as

complete. The mechanism too
is vulnerable to abuse or rough
handling and often becomes
jammed. Some knowledge of the
mechanism is useful so that this, at
least, can be corrected.

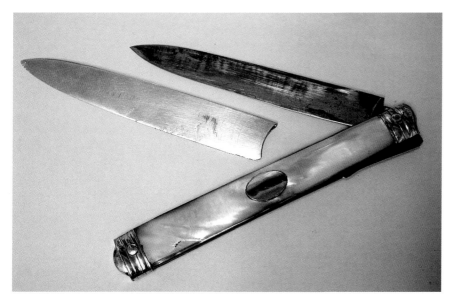

Highly unusual folding lock-back version of a *d'Estaing* knife showing how it had become adapted into a more conventional style by the first to second quarter of the 19th century. *Plate 2.64*

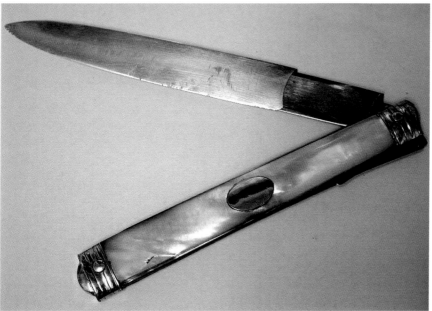

Conclusion

There is no doubt that French pocket cutlery and fruit knives especially, were much esteemed throughout Europe and yet they have been quoted as being cheap to buy – a well-made knife of humbler materials could cost a mere two *liards* (small copper coins) and a fork would cost one *sou* (centime)! Despite this apparent cheapness there was nothing cheap about their manufacture and even some of the humblest antique French pocket and knives have survived and found their way into highly reputable collections.

Silver gilt-bladed French
pocket fruit knife with a
solid haft of tortoiseshell,
steam-treated to compress
the sheets of shell
together. This amazing
example of gold *piqué*
combines both *posé* and
clouté work, c.1760.
Plate 2.65

Worked back of blade of
previous knife, inlaid with
an undulating silver wire
along the back.
Plate 2.66

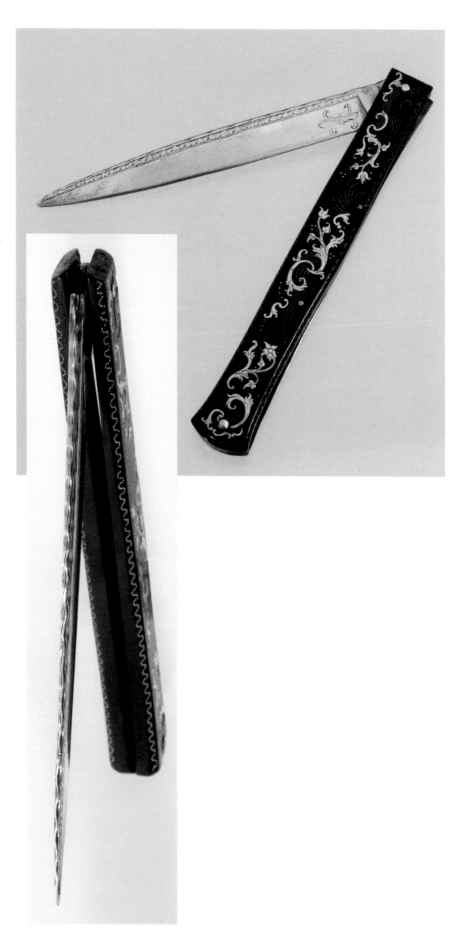

Large *Couteau-sans-clou* with rather cut-down steel blade c.1720. The silver blade bears a single, tiny (worn) Paris silver guarantee mark struck between 1809 and 1819 in a circular cartouche. The cross on the shield resembles that of the Swiss Canton Helvetica. *Plate: 2.67*

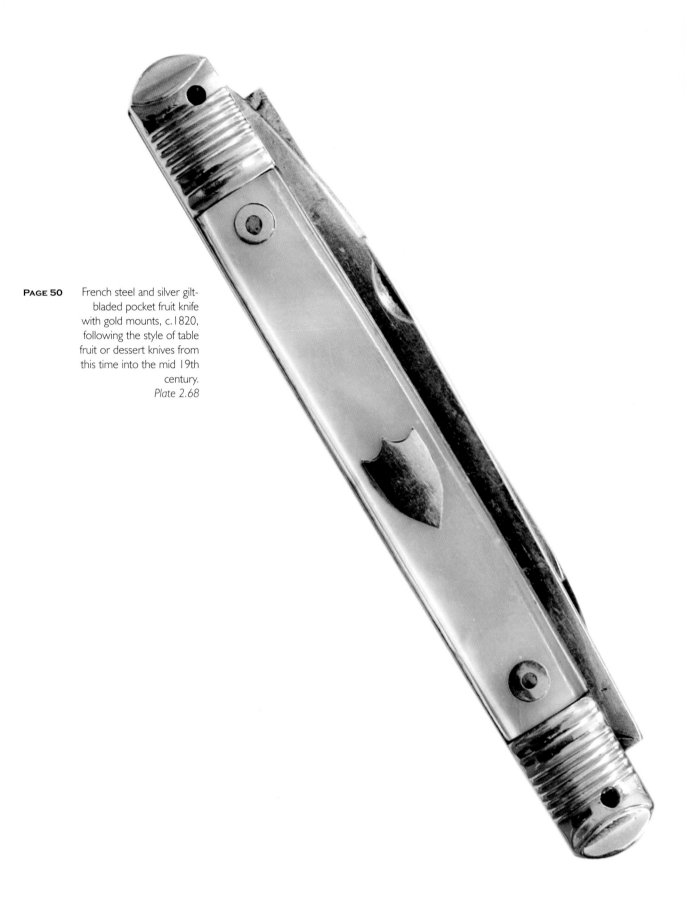

PAGE 50 French steel and silver gilt-
bladed pocket fruit knife
with gold mounts, c.1820,
following the style of table
fruit or dessert knives from
this time into the mid 19th
century.
Plate 2.68

3 Evolution of English fruit knives to c.1770, the period of 'confusion'

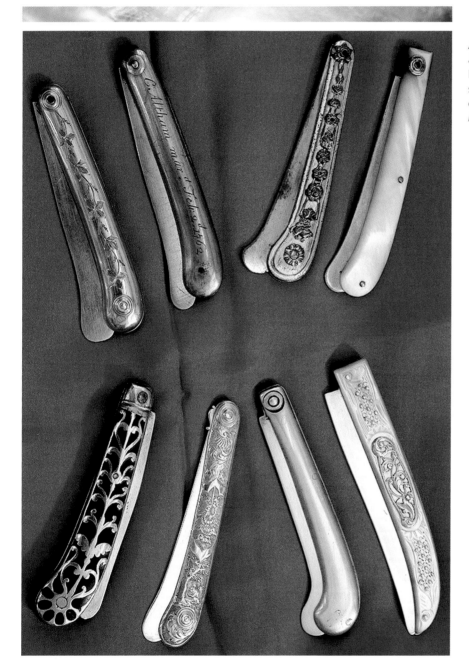

A selection of French & English pocket fruit knives, c.1730-1770, so similar that it is difficult to distinguish between them. *Plate 3.1*

Whether Charles II's gift to mistress Gwyn of a French pocket fruit knife prompted the introduction of a new trend to the English, we shall never know. It would evidently appear doubtful since folding, or other forms of pocket fruit knife, were apparently not made by English cutler/goldsmiths until the early to mid-18th century. This may have been due to regulations forbidding cutlers to work with precious metals.

Two fruit knives marked GRAY only, with green-stained ivory hafts. The upper knife in the *Berge* style and the lower in French Empire. Both in green-stained fish-skin (*galuchat*) boxes with pull-off lids c.1780-1800. The upper box is made from sting-ray skin, the lower from sleeper shark. *Plates 3.2 & 3.3*

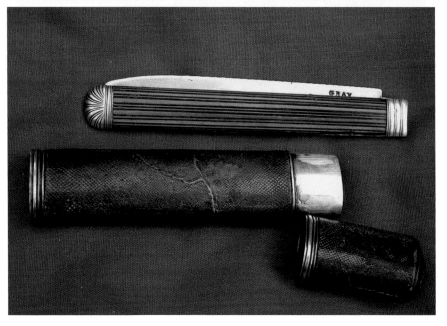

The earliest English pocket fruit knives appear to have been made around the mid-18th century and they so exactly imitated the French knives that it is frequently difficult to assign a country of origin during this period (*plate 3.1*). At the time, English regulations on hallmarking small precious metal objects (weighing less than 10 pennyweights) were waived, and the same applied to small French precious metal items which would normally have borne some regulatory hallmarks, thus augmenting the confusion. However, a few knife blades were submitted for assay and one was recently discovered bearing the Paris mark of a script capital A with a crown, (*plates 3.4 & 3.5*) which was used between 1727 and 1732, suggesting that these small fruit knives may have been initiated sometime about 1720 or slightly earlier and also suggesting a Baroque leading into Rococo decoration. Another small hallmarked knife with plain nacre scales, a gold blade, struck with the hound's head (Paris, 1762-68) and a slightly pointed and curved terminal has also recently come to light. These knives may have come from Rococo *étuis*, their shape, size and decoration being suggestive of this, with nacre scales scroll-engraved and gold wire *piqué* or panels, the ends often engraved with a fish head.

These smaller folding fruit knives were often part of an *étui* - a period hold-all for small implements or tools for manicure, sewing and drawing, each of which also held a small knife, measuring about 6 - 8 centimetres when closed (*plate 3.17*). Differentiation is tenuous at least since French examples of these knives tended to have a circular tang, (*plates 3.18 & 3.19*) sometimes with

a small upper lug to the back of the blade, while English knives tended to be plainer and made with a square ricasso that abutted onto a circular or squared tang (*plate 3.28*). Some of these knives were multi-purpose, made with steel blades, but many were reserved for fruit with the usual precious-metal blade and would have been more unique in purpose and

A rather worn gilt French example and, unusually, marked for a small item (8cm closed) with the crowned script A for Paris c.1727-1732.
This single mark is most useful for assigning some periodicity for this type of knife whether French or English-derivative.
The silver screw is a later addition.
Plates 3.4 & 3.5

Two similar-sized knives, bladed with gold and bearing the Paris discharge marks for 1762-8 *(upper)* and 1738-44 *(lower)*. The style for both is similar to the unmarked item, bottom right of the chapter heading illustration and opposite page *(plate 3.8)*, suggesting that it might also belong to the Louis XV period. *Plates 3.6 & 3.7*

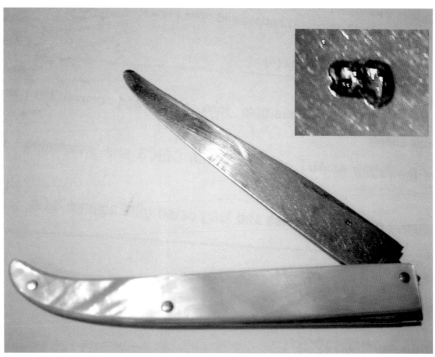

so were sold in solo *étuis (plates 3.22 & 3.23)*. Small fruit knives, whose blades weighed less than 10 penny-weight, were exempted from hallmarking from 28th May 1739 (12 Geo. II c.26) and remained unmarked, making it hard to differentiate French from English, or French imported into England and subsequently inscribed!

During the later 18th century this confusing period of 'Who made

what?' continued, exacerbated further during the 1770s and 80s by an English sword cutler named Thomas Gray. Apart from weaponry, Gray also sold 'fancy goods', presumably to boost his business in Eastcheap (London). Many French style folding fruit knives bear the stamped name of GRAY on their blades but have no other identifying marks *(page 52)* so that one cannot say whether these knives were made by Gray himself, or

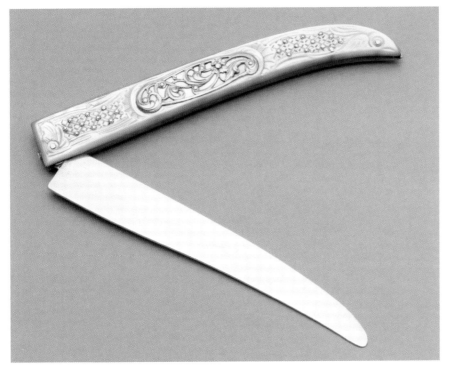

Superbly decorated Louis XV gold-bladed fruit knife, c.1740-50 with a central panel of gold *chinoiserie*, and of gold *piqué clouté*. Note that the curved terminal has been engraved and riveted to resemble a fish's head.
Plate: 3.8

This knife is most likely to be French despite being unmarked and typifies the 'confusion' of this period. The decorative Bérain-style overlay lacks the detail of the earlier knives and the blade shape suggests c.1720-50.
Plate 3.9

by his journeymen, or more likely commissioned from France using his name as sole retailer.

The Birmingham-based plating firm of S. Colmore also used the French style in the manufacture of knives with some of the earliest-known close-plated blades (*plate 3.10*), that is, made by soldering a thin envelope of silver sheet around a steel blade. These silver envelopes were of much thicker silver than those produced using the early 19th century process and little wear has been detected on Colmore's blades. He evidently patented this technique since the blades of earlier knives (c.1770) have been very lightly stamped with the mark COLMORE PATENT within a pointed oval (navette) cartouche. In 1790, the

Two Colmore patent knives c.1770, showing remarkable Anglo-French influence with the wavy-ended hafts (nearest to blade) and lock-back mechanisms. The haft decoration and navette-shaped shield are more typically English.
Plate 3.10

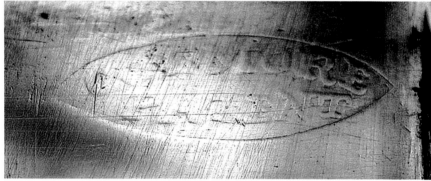

The navette-shaped trademark on the smaller knife has been stamped in very shallow relief.
Plate 3.11

Shallow relief stellar decoration along the upper edge of the larger knife's blade.
Plate 3.12

Maker marks on the larger knife blade for S Colmore and *Colmore Patent* registered in 1790; the IH may be for John Harrison.
Plate 3.13

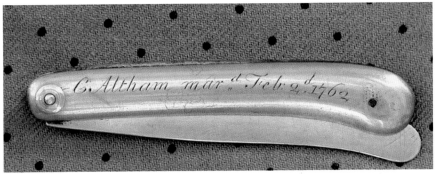

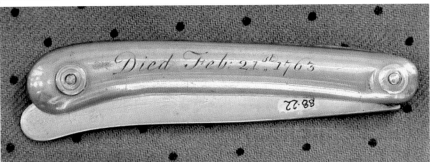

Remembrance knife to C. Altham married in 1762, died just over a year later. These knives are not hallmarked so this inscription, recording a microcosm of history, has been instrumental in recording the knife style for the period, yet there are those who would have had it removed!
Plate 3.14

A similar knife in gold, but showing that in later Victorian times, a little extra decoration in the form of scrolling leaves, was often considered to be quite the norm. Note how these two knives are quite plain, compared to French, and how the blade tips of these two knives protruded from the end of the haft for easier opening until c.1770.
Plate 3.15

mark was registered in Sheffield and altered to S.C I.H and Colmore (over) Patent within a rectangular cartouche (see *plate 3.13*). The earlier mark seems not to have been registered at either the Birmingham or Sheffield Assay Office.

also used the idea of reverse chasing and some of his blades are decorated with many tiny devices in the form of stars and crosses, shallowly chased from the reverse of the silver sheet before it was made into an envelope for soldering onto the steel blade. The relief of these devices is so minute (up to 5 microns) that they are barely visible as decoration *(plate 3.12)* and can only be just seen by tilting the blade.

The style of the knives by Gray and Colmore is unmistakably French at

a time when France was becoming increasingly less influential in English pocket fruit knife designs. As the Revolution and the ascendancy of Bonaparte fuelled anti-French feelings in England, English cutler/goldsmiths may have felt the further need to sever design influences with France and Catholicism.

The first folding fruit knives to have been made in England in about 1750, were usually quite plain and made entirely from gold or silver. They copied the period fashion dictates of pocket and table knives, so their blades were curved into round-tipped scimitars and the hafts were curved downward like the butt of a contemporary pistol. When open, the knife resembled an elongated letter S and when closed,

A fine French lady's pocket fruit knife c.1770. The form is more *couteau* than *Berge* with a blade at each end of the gold haft. The steel blade marked Bernat would likely have been used as a sewing aid. The delicate silver blade is much too frail and small for actual use and was probably just an *á la mode* accessory. *Plate 3.16*

the rounded blade tip protruded about 5-10 mm from the end of the haft to facilitate opening (*plates 3.14 & 3.15*). Whether made as cheaper versions, contemporary fakes or not, examples of this delicate style of knife were also made of copper (or copper alloy such as brass) and then gilt. Today the copper often shows through the worn areas of gilt, but in their time these may have been sold as gold; whatever the intent, they were finely made (*plate 3.34*). Many a pocket fruit knife (or a steel-bladed pocket knife) was sold as a standard item for an *étui*, sometimes with delicate scissors, mounted needle, dance card of ivory and a bodkin-*cum*-ear scoop. This entourage might be sold in a fine porcelain *étui*, perhaps from the Chelsea factory, but pocket fruit knife-and-fork sets in such *étuis* are scarce from this time. A young society lady would have gratefully received such a fashionable gift from her parents, even an admirer.

Cutlers who also worked with precious metals appeared to have made pocket fruit knives, although at this time, London cutlers were not allowed to use precious metals in their work unless it was closely vetted by the Goldsmiths' Company. Although the London Goldsmiths' Company would have frowned upon Sheffield cutlers who also worked with gold and silver, their regulations and powers could not easily be enforced at such a distance.

Construction

There is little documentation on the method of constructing these knives and even Jean-Jacques Perret (1771) records little about the actual basic construction other than describing the half-finished product. The precious metal hafts were made with great skill since the metal is quite thin. In those days, goldsmiths would likely have rolled out just enough gold to make a sheet of the correct size and then wrought the desired shape of the haft by careful hammering

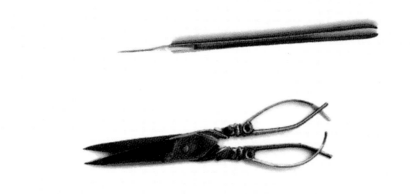

Typical fine porcelain *étui* attributed to Gouyn of W London c.1755, in the Chelsea style. Note the typical gold-hafted fruit knife of the period - French or English? There is also a bodkin topped with a small golden spoon - probably an ear scoop, scissors and forceps. *Plate 3.17*

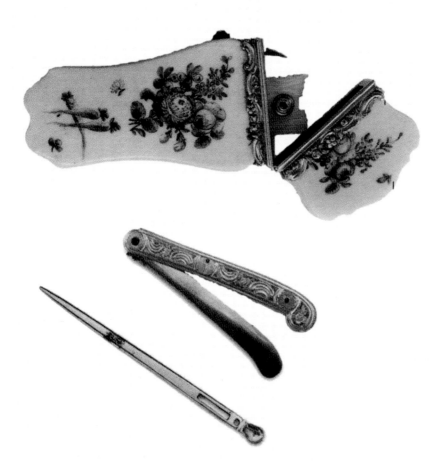

over a template. More widely-available silver would have been cut out from a sheet and shaped in a similar manner. Crescent-shaped strengtheners of copper or iron were soldered at regular intervals along the haft interior to prevent the soft metal from collapsing or denting *(plate 3.20)*. Three rivets were incorporated to hold the pieces together, one each for the blade hinge, the spring hinge and the tailpiece, the latter holding the haft

together and providing a firm base for the end of the spring. The rivet heads were covered with flattened coils of gold or silver wire or discs of gold or silver, stamped out (chased) with whorled or concentric circle designs and known as 'bird's eye' rosettes. The spring itself comprised a narrow sliver of iron, or hammered and tempered silver, that fitted along the back and coiled around the end of the haft where it was anchored centrally with a

Magnificent small pocket fruit knife, the haft of gold with bird's eye rosettes, decorated with flowers, scroll work and a tree with a squirrel beneath, c.1730, possibly English but the circular tang and fine decoration is more likely to be French
Plates 3.18 & 3.19

rivet. It exerted barely any pressure on the blade and merely acted as a stop to prevent the blade from being opened too far: this is known as a 'soft spring'.

Organic hafts were occasionally inlaid with gold wire in concentric whorls or bent into geometric shapes, known as *piqué posé* (*plates 3.23 & 3.24*). Metal hafts were engraved and carved with great skill and minutely detailed, to depict scenes, usually with birds and flowers, or with inscriptions of donation or ownership. Plainer hafts were occasionally engraved during the later 19th century (*plate 3.15*) when prettifying plainer objects became fashionable.

The blade would have been hammered prior to shaping and finishing in order to squeeze the atoms of gold or silver tighter together, making the blade harder

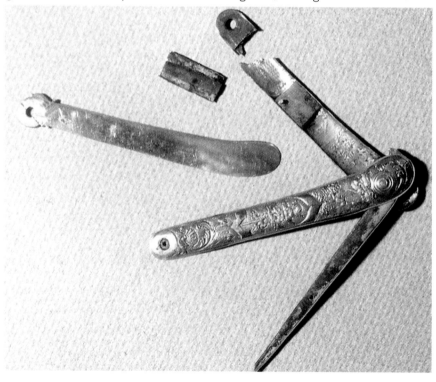

The same knife during a tiny repair which turned out to be a more complicated job! Note the iron strengtheners inside the haft.
Plate 3.20

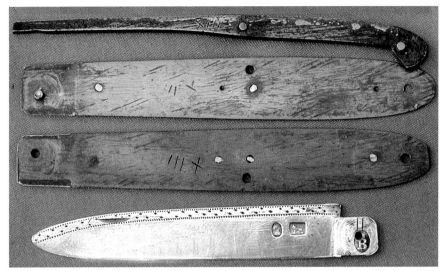

Components of two
English pocket fruit knives,
one assayed in 1805
showing the Roman
scratched-on numeration
of each part (II & XIII).
Plate 3.21

for better cutting and durability.
Note that the blade point still often
protruded from the end of the haft
until about 1770. This facilitated
opening the blade, there being no
risk of self-damage from such a
blunt point. Nail nicks were only
applied to steel and sharp-pointed
blades, which required near to total
enclosure within the haft.
Throughout the process each blade,
web, scale and spring was made for

an individual knife or fork and each
was marked with a series of small
cuts or scratches forming Roman
numerals *(above)*. This system of
numbering each part was traditional
and avoided muddling of individual
components. Handmade pocket-
knife components are still numbered
today so that each blade, spring and
haft component are made to be
assembled together.
Plate 3.32 shows some knives from

Two pocket knives of
French or English origin?
The left is of *Agennais*
form (style from Agen) and
the right, with its fine *piqué
posé*, could be either,
c.1750-70.
Plates 3.22 & 3.23

Rare piqué posé fruit knife, maybe English, c.1750 with scimitar-shaped gold blade. Its small size would have restricted it to cutting small and soft fruit such as grapes, which it performs very well. Below is a close view showing the fineness of the piqué posé silver and gold wirework and that it is still all intact. The box fits perfectly but would have been added c.50 years later.
Plates 3.24 & 3.25

this period and demonstrates that some people preferred a silver blade in a gold haft (although I have never seen a gold blade in a silver haft - perhaps it just looked too odd!). Blade and haft were normally made from matching materials. The all-silver knife (*plate 3.14*) was probably given at a funeral as a memento.

Hafting materials

Many media have been used to form the scales of pocket fruit knives. Tortoiseshell was most usually used for older knives up to about 1800 and from then only intermittently throughout the 19th century as cheaper nacre became more popular. Tortoiseshell was invariably

underlain with gold or gilt brass foil, carefully glued onto the liners before the scales were attached. The underlay gave a wonderful glow to the tortoiseshell. Ivory was also popular and was sometimes used during the late 18th century but it was often dyed green. 'Green ivory' was used as a hafting material, particularly during this heyday period for table and dessert knives. Natural or white ivory was less popular. Ivory with 'shakes' (covered with tiny capillary marks) was occasionally used but may have been considered too eccentric for general use. French taste and style also encouraged the use of nacre (mother-of-pearl) as a hafting

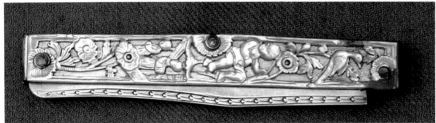

English or French? Both knives are unmarked c.1740-1770.
The knife, upper & lower left (showing both faces) has a definite French feel to it with its nacre scales sawn and carved with intricate *Chinoserie* decoration. The scales are laid onto gilt webs (liners). The lower right knife is probably English due to its squared ricasso and tang; with a chased silver haft.

Plates 3.26, 3.27 & 3.28

PAGE 63

material and some knives have been scaled with this material, usually underlain with gold foil to prevent corrosion salts from the iron-based mechanism from discolouring it. The nacre was sawn and filed in a mix of *Chinoiserie* and Rococo designs using birds, flowers and *amorini (above & below left)*. The brittleness of the material has often led to damage and subsequent restoration but there is no denying the supreme skill of French pearl cutters at this time.

In 19th century England, however, nacre soon dominated being a cheap and decorative material that ideally suited the haft of a pocket fruit knife and that could be decorated by carving, engraving or inlaying with silver or gold wire (*piqué* work). Nacre comes from several of the pearl oysters, the largest being the Golden lip pearl oyster *Pinctada maxima*. The most prismatic, first-quality nacre displaying pinks and greens, also comes from the Grey lip

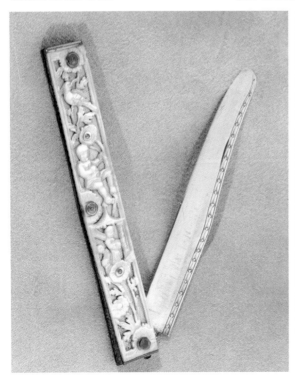

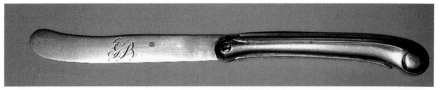

Typical all silver pocket fruit knife from an *étui* c.1750. Many such became separated from their containers over time. Below, a steel bladed example with Rococo decoration on gold scales; the webs have been made from lead, deceptively giving the haft more weight as if made of solid gold.
Plates 3.29 & 3.30

A page from Joseph Smith's *Manufactories* of 1816 showing the French influence still lingering in some parts of the Cutlery Trade: wavy-end bolsters and 247 & 248 have lock-back springs. 244 & 247 are "Spotted Knives" of stained cowhorn imitating costlier tortoiseshell.
Plate 3.31

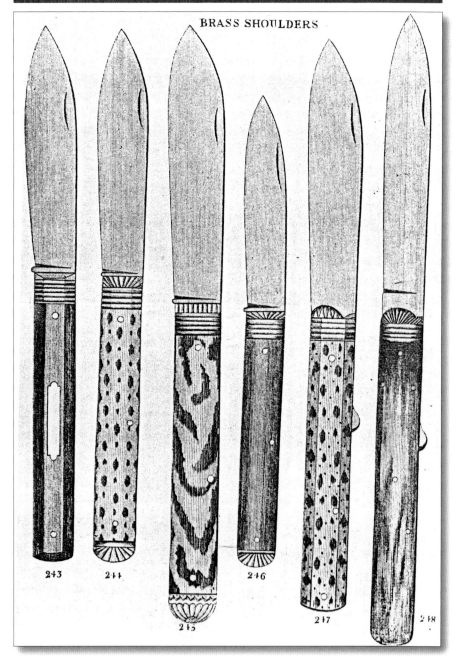

BRASS SHOULDERS

243   244   245   246   247   248

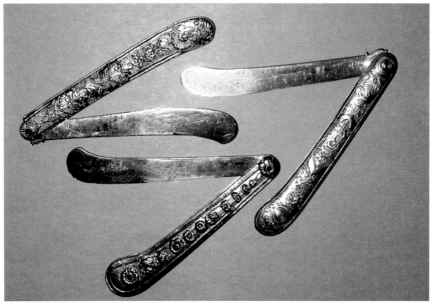

Three typical mid-18th century pocket fruit knives including two gilt on base metal examples (left). French influence is still strong at this time and due to their lack of hallmarks, they are difficult to differentiate.

French precious metal blades should normally bear some tiny hallmark at this time.

Plate 3.32

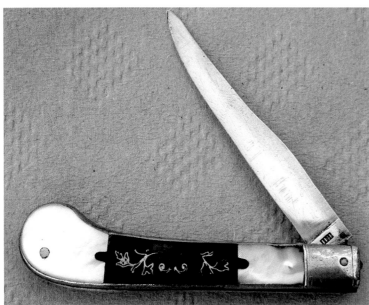

An unusual piece since the haft is typically mid-18th century English but the silver blade has an odd ricasso maker's mark and suggests that this blade may be a slightly later replacement from abroad.

Plate 3.33

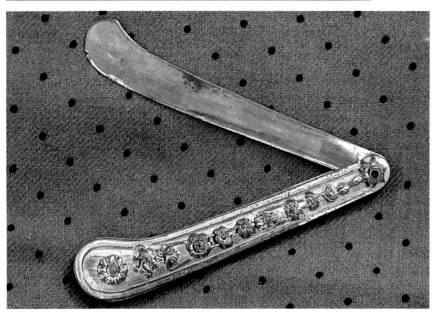

Gilt copper pocket fruit knife aping its golden peers. Circa 1730-70 but just as elegant. The spring, as such was more of a mechanism damper than a blade retention device.

Plate 3.34

Pocket fruit knives made before Sheffield's assay office opened in 1773, with stamped-on maker marks.

READ, GIBBS, PAGE, LAMPREY (see next page) from both Sheffield and London (Gibbs and T Gray).
Plate 3.35

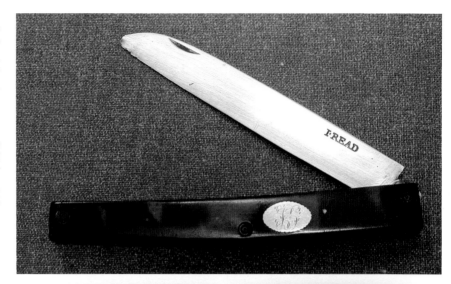

Plate 3.36

Plate 3.37

POCKET FRUIT KNIVES: 3 EVOLUTION OF ENGLISH FRUIT KNIVES TO C, 1770, THE PERIOD OF 'CONFUSION'

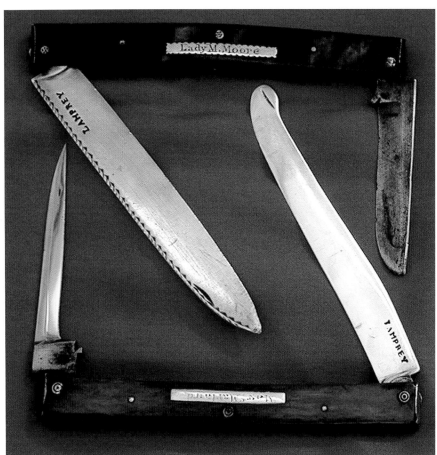

Selection of pocket fruit knives, with additional quill blades, c.1770.

The bottom right is a pocket knife with ivory scales and cut-steel bosses. *Plates 3.38 & 3.39*

Decoratively-styled pocket (steel-bladed) knives were likely used as the trend for precious metal blades grew in popularity. The silver bolster and rayed cap, also the fluted ivory scales show signs of French influence during the 1770s.
Plate 3.40

pearl oyster *Pinctada margaritifera*. The even more colourful Ormer and Abalone shells may have been considered too flashy for ornamenting English knives at this time, as they do not appear to have been used in this trade other than for inlaying French knives. Other hafting materials were dark woods, including ebony, also horn, bone and ivory (see above). Metal hafts of silver, gilt and gold were less usual at

this time when nacre predominated and these metals were reserved more for haft ornamentation during the late 18th and early 19th centuries. These are found as rosettes in the form of circles, rings, navettes, lozenges and sweethearts and were often minutely engraved and cunningly set into cut out areas and underlain with a minute layer of pitch or animal glue for adhesion (*plate 4.16*). Shields for ownership (next chapter) also formed part of this decoration but their purpose tended to be shunned at this time, owners' markings usually being blade-confined.

Fine pocket knife and silver-bladed fork by John Stephenson of Sheffield c.1760-70, who used the trademark LAMPREY. The back of the knife blade has been silver-spined to match the fork (above). The fork haft bears a circular shield engraved with the crest of Daly, the knife bears a similar shield with JD.

Plates 3.41, 3.42 & 3.43

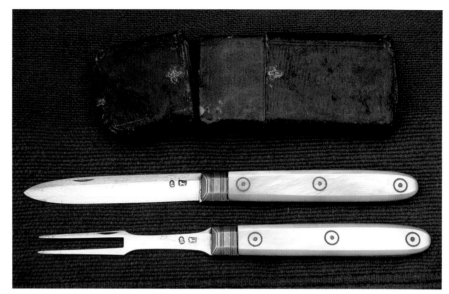

Even though this set was assayed c.1800, it shows the typical fine-grained and creamy-coloured nacre that was used for scaling early period pocket fruit knives.
Plate 3.44

Pocket fruit knife with pinchbeck-banded tortoiseshell case c. 1770. The lack of hallmarks and presence of a ricasso to the gilt blade points to a more likely English origin.
Plate 3.45

Blademarking or Quality control

Since there was nowhere for this Midland-based trade to have its precious metal wares assayed and marked until the end of August 1773, manufacturers began to stamp their trademarks on the blades of pocket fruit knives (and occasional forks) that they had made.

With the rapid industrialisation and increase in the cutlery trade, Sheffield produced directories of its traders, among them cutlers, who made these precious metal blades. They used their trade names as registered in period directories such as Sketchley's Sheffield Directory of 1774.

4 The 'Pistol-grip' period 1770-1790.

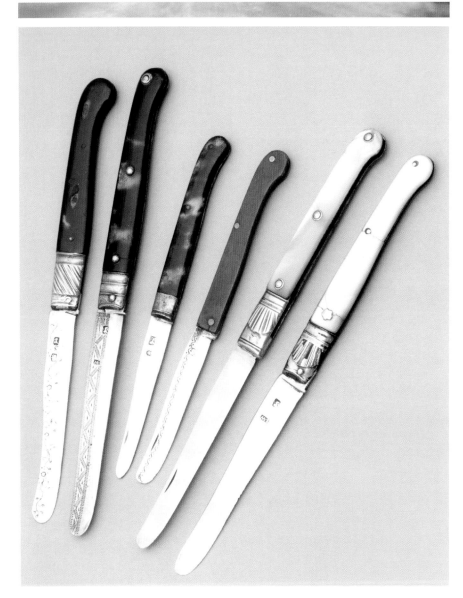

Sheffield-made pistol-grip and scimitar-bladed pocket fruit knives showing some period bright cutting patterns c.1770-1785.
Plate 4.1

Rare Sheffield-made
Berge fruit knife, c. 1790,
the ultimate in French
influence at a time when
English designs were
moving away from France.
Plate 4.2

As the popularity of pocket fruit knives increased in England and they were made in larger numbers, the styles began to break away even more from the influence of France. Occasionally, pieces were still made in the Berge style *(above)* and Messrs Gray and Colmore were still making and/or selling their French-styled wares. The majority of makers were producing fruit knives that were decidedly less French and reflected the style of 'things to come'. Pocket fruit knives were made principally in Sheffield and a few in Birmingham where there were no assay offices until 1773. Producers simply stamped or engraved their trademark (either their name or a word) on the silver blade or on the ricasso while some

were left blank if there was a risk of damaging such a small and delicate object *(plates 3.35 to 3.39)*[1].

With the expansion of the silver plating industries in Sheffield, in particular, a need was strongly felt for assay offices in Birmingham and Sheffield and on the 31st of August, 1773 offices were opened in both of these cities. The story relates that the choice of town marks was made in the Crown & Anchor tavern in the Strand, on the turn of a coin;

Footnote.

[1] *Where fruit knife blades were left blank, without any mark of assay or trade, this normally implies an English origin of pre-1773. By this time, French knife blades were gradually being marked with increasing frequency, even if only with the mark of the maker or sponsor. There are some instances, however, where differentiation of French and English knives is still difficult and their origin can only be divined through decorative style.*

Green ivory and silver striped *Berge* knife by of Eastcheap showing how French influence affected the more typical English knife below, by Joseph Creswick, c.1788. *Plate 4.3*

This non-hallmarked knife appears to be French c.1780. Its resemblance to period English pistol-grip knives is exact, yet the point is not central. The spine is gadrooned in English style - so did the French copy this one from the English? *Plate 4.4*

Sheffield won, so chose the crown while Birmingham was allotted the anchor as its assay mark.

Types

Early English pocket fruit knives continued in the traditional scimitar and pistol-grip shape although the blade tip no longer protruded from the end of the haft. Some were made with spear-point and/or scimitar blades but combined with square-ended hafts. These were the principal shapes of the time and continued as such until about 1785. Other knives were made with a small steel blade for shaping quill pens, at the opposite end of the haft in the manner of a *couteau-sans-clou*; the back of these knives was slightly bowed. Quill-*cum*-fruit knives were popular only until about 1830. Although the softer silver blades were always quite vulnerable, quill blades, by their hardness and thinness, were notorious for

snapping off if used for anything other than cutting and piercing. For this reason quill knives themselves were sometimes made multi-bladed.

Post-1785 fruit knives show further changes in their shape. The pistol-grip haft and scimitar blade were phased out in favour of the more versatile spear point blade and, as table-knives straightened out, so did the hafts for fruit knives. This basic pattern set the style for fruit knives for the next 150 years. The blade was now almost entirely enclosed within the haft, so a nail nick was normally added to the blade to assist with opening (*plate 4.10*).

Scimitar blades and pistol-grip hafts still continued to be made for a short while but only for all-metal knives. Some were plain and slim with soft spring mechanisms most likely made for period étuis, either solo or with other implements. Knives were also

made with decorated handles in both silver and gold (*plates 3.29 & 3.30*). The differentiation of French and English still tends to be blurred at this time, although the French examples are often minutely (and singly) hallmarked. Small French silver items (less than 1.5 ounces Troy) and gold (less than 1 ounce.) were exempt from assay but were obliged to bear a maker's mark. English pieces were now fully hallmarked although some marks were struck on the tang (ref. *page 86 & plate. 4.28*).

Introduction of folding fruit forks and the evolution of sets

The post-1785 era also saw the introduction of folding fruit forks to pair with knives. Earlier sets do exist

Unusual and unmarked fruit knife, c.1770
Plate 4.5

Single and steel-bladed pocket knife c. 1790, possibly French. Scales of nacre inlaid with engraved strips of silver. The style of decoration is more typical of a pocket fruit knife.
Plate 4.6

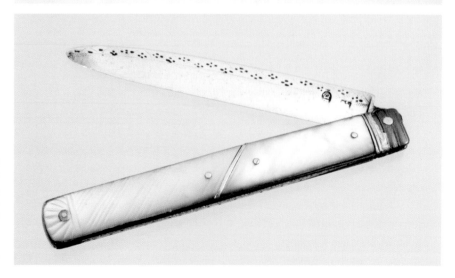

English pocket fruit knife, assayed in 1784, just before the duty on silver was levied. Note the French-influence of the single diagonal stripe of silver, normally found on Berge knives at this time.
Plate 4.7

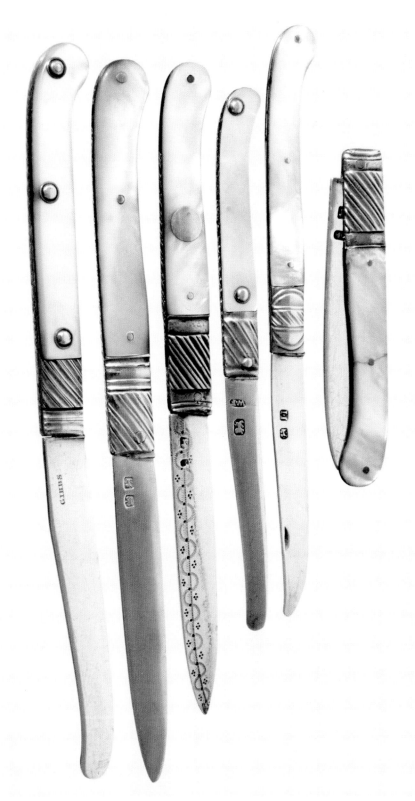

Nacre-scaled pistol grip pocket fruit knives showing a mix of scimitar and spear-point blades. The right-most of the open knives by John Ibberson, c.1775, unusually, has a nail nick since this style of haft facilitates blade opening. The closed knife shows how the blade is exposed for easy opening. *Plate 4.8*

Unusually small silver-hafted knife (2 inches/ 5 cm closed), c.1775, perhaps for a child. The hallmarks appear quite large on the small blade. *Plate 4.9*

before this time but are rare. Fork blades were two-, or occasionally three-tined but due to the difficulty in making such a small three-tined blade, combined with its resulting vulnerability, most fork blades were made with two tines (*plate 4.12*).

As the trend for bright-cut engraving became fashionable for period silverware it became the norm for the decoration of fruit knife blades, and forks received similar treatment along the entire length of the blade, giving them an eye-catching sparkle.

Box-shaped hafts on later 18th century Sheffield pocket fruit knives, c.1775-1790. The wavy lines on the top 4 knives' hafts is a typical pattern from this period. Note the unusual French style wavy bolster (top knife) and that the lower three knives' blades have been cut with nail nicks.
Plate 4.10

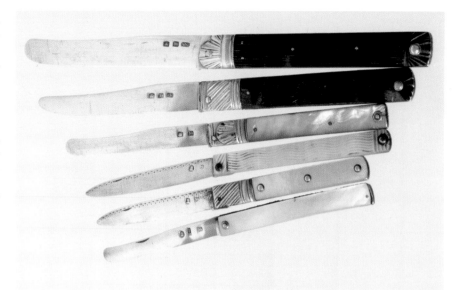

Knife-and-fork sets were housed in pasteboard or wooden hinge-lidded boxes, veneered with paper-thin leather (skiver). A small silver spoon, normally made and assayed in London, was occasionally added to a set but strangely was not made to fold in the manner of larger Campaign sets (*plate 5.14*). Instead it was just fitted into the box but was too small for the supping of fruit juices (*plates 4.13 & 4.15*). It might be a snuff-taking spoon, but its association with sets for fruit eating at this time would suggest that it was used for sprinkling the ever-popular nutmeg. Due to their less frequent use, forks in knife-and-fork sets tend to be in better condition, suggesting that elegant trend-setting in *alfresco* eating was not taken too seriously. In some instances the knife broke or wore out, leaving just the fork. Collectors tend to shun solo forks

Despite its rather worn condition, this knife-*cum*-fork by William Fox, c.1790 is a scarcity. The 'cut-and-stab' approach to fruit eating was evidently less elegant than using a knife and fork set
Plate 4.11

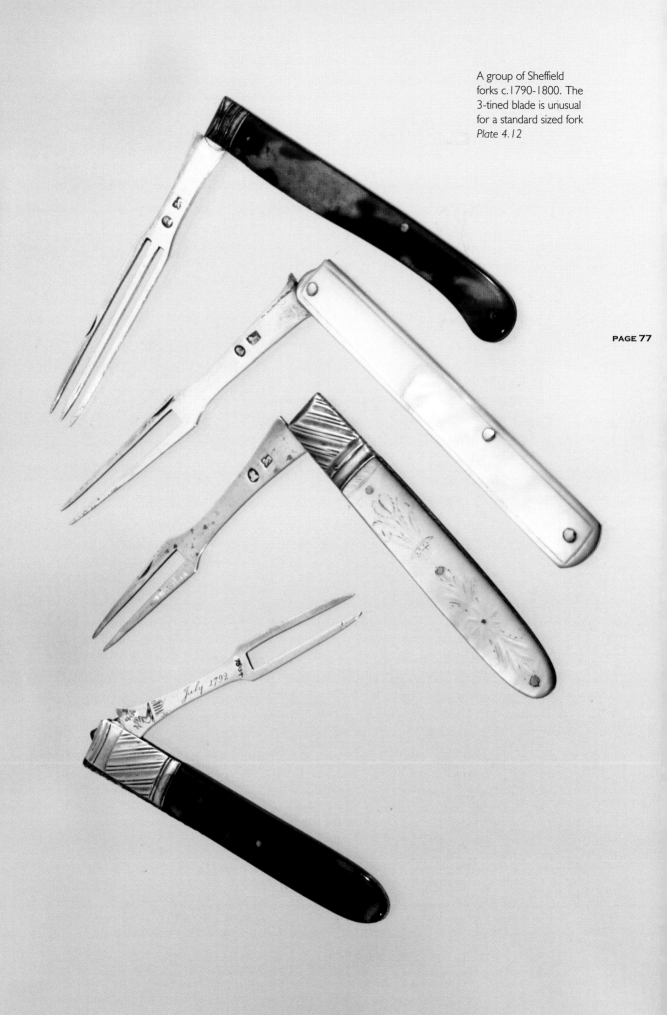

A group of Sheffield forks c.1790-1800. The 3-tined blade is unusual for a standard sized fork
Plate 4.12

July 1792

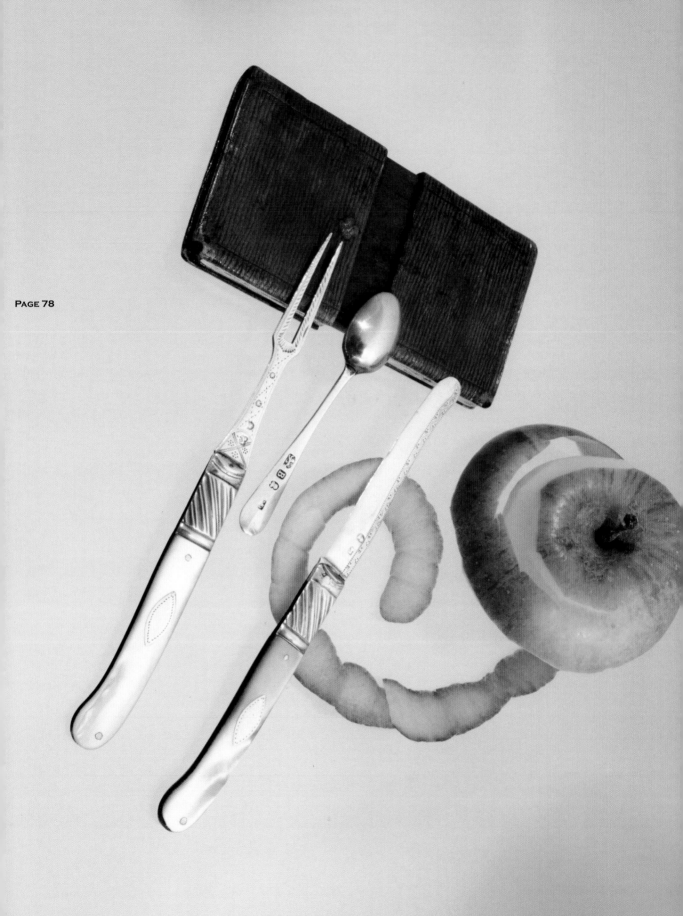

Boxes from this time
(c.1770-1800) could be
shaped like a book for a
three-some set - spoon
was assayed in London
1797 (George Smith)
- or the more usual
design below. Made of
pasteboard, often from
period newspapers, the
exposed parts were lined
with combed papers and
the exterior with stamped
leather
Plates 4.13 & 4.14

Another book box set entitled POEMS, assembled as a set c.1805, complete with a London-made spoon by JB, attrib. James Beattie, 1801. Note the slight disparity of duty marks: knife c.1790, fork c.1805 suggesting probable use of an earlier-marked stock item knife blade to complete the set.
Plate 4.15

as they suggest an incomplete set, yet they are scarcer than knives and, to some, are more decoratively appealing.

A few knives were made with a short fork blade at the other end of the haft. Although quite useful for picking up sticky sweetmeats they were probably supplanted by the more elegant matching knife and fork together. Although the example shown in plate 4.11 has had a 'busy' lifetime and might be shunned by some collectors, they are a scarce find.

Haft ornaments were set into the scaling materials using animal glue, which can often be seen around the edges.
Plate 4.16

A range of Georgian pocket fruit knives and forks showing typical haft ornamentation, c.1770 - 1800.
Plate 4.17

Hafts & materials

Hafts were generally left plain unless scaled with nacre, which was cheaper to replace if the decorative process failed. As it gained in popularity as a scaling material, nacre began to be decorated by carving and engraving. At first only the base of the haft was decorated by shaping with indents and then by engraving lines or chamfering along the edges, leaving the centre plain. Engraving eventually incorporated symbolic or abstract motifs (*plate 4.20*). The post-1785 period saw some of the bevelled hafts inlaid with silver or gold decoration in the form of pellets, circles, discs, sweethearts, navettes and lozenges. By using saws and shielding parsers, pearl cutters could cut out shapes in the haft to receive the precious metal ornaments. The metal ornaments were themselves usually decorated with tiny cuts from the engraver's scorper or drill tips to enable them to sparkle. These were placed into sawn grooves and depressions using animal glue, as traces of this substance have been found in hafts where the inlay has dropped out. This form of *piqué posé* decoration was popular at the turn of the 18th century (*above*).

An almost universal and significant ornament evolved at this time. Popularly known as a 'sunburst', it was applied almost invariably to nacre scales and consisted of alternating narrow engraved bands and broader wheel-cut lines, either in a circle or the more usual oval. (*plate 4.18, pages 82 & 83*) The design was used particularly on the reverse side of scales for the next 150 years.

Bolsterless knives and forks are occasional: these date c.1800, the bolsters are more vulnerable and liable to chipping (note repair to knife bolster). Both hafts have been wheel-cut to form 'sunbursts' (on both sides).
Plate 4.18

A range of unusual media were used as scaling materials c.1790 - 1810. This fork scaled with ivory-with-shakes, a material normally rejected by workers in ivory.
Plate 4.19

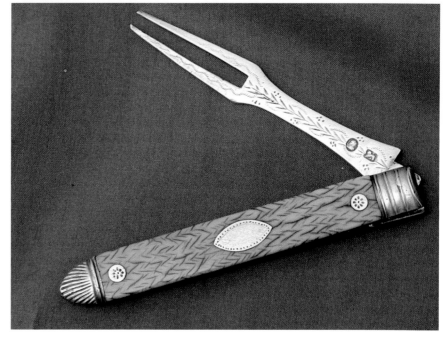

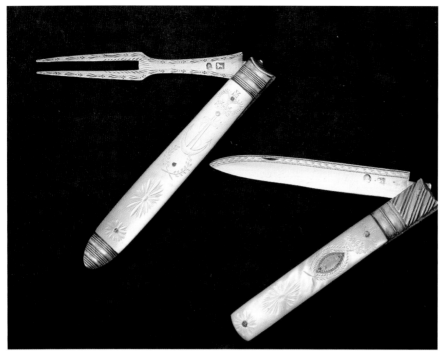

Wheel-cut and engraved sunburst patterns start to appear c.1790, along with patterns of patriotic symbolism extolling the Monarchy (crown), Hope (fouled anchor) and olive branches for Peace in difficult times when England was at war with France.
Plate 4.20

(*left*): Pocket fruit knife c.1790 with a non-silvered steel bolster.
Plate 4.21

(*right*): Still showing some French influence, a knife by John Roberts with bright-cut gilt haft banding and rosettes.
Plate 4.22

Inscriptions on knives at
this time are occasional;
rhyming couplets are
found on pocket knives
but are almost unknown
for fruit knives.
Plates 4.23 & 4.24

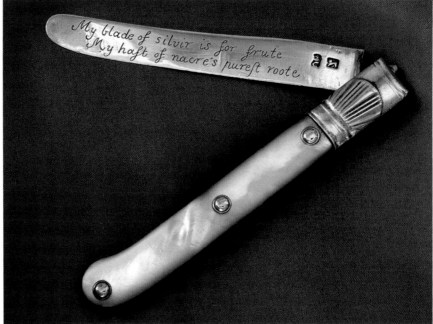

Ownership markings

Most post-1785 knife and fork
hafts normally incorporated a small
precious metal circle (c.1780),
rectangle or S-shaped shield
(c.1785-1810) in the mid haft *(plates
4.64 & 5.19)*. The shields were
let into the hafts by cutting out a
suitable depression in the nacre (or
scaling material) using a 'shielding
parser'. This was a bow-operated
drill bearing onto a protective iron
breast-plate strapped around the

operator's chest *(plate 8.49)*. The
blade comprised a sprung and
twin-bladed cutter with a bobbin
around the shaft which the bow
rotated, spinning the cutter within
the confines of a template clamped
over the scaling material, and cutting
out the required shape. Donors and
owners of pocket fruit knives and
forks eventually started to make use
of these shields and later knives from
about 1800 onwards record many
initials and sometimes a minute

Ownership markings
Fork shank marked "Mary"
and "July 1792" with a
crest.
Plate 4.25

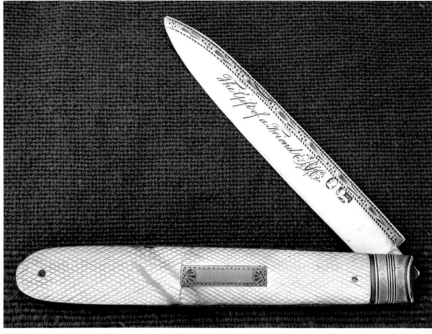

Inscriptions such as
this (c.1805) became
increasingly common on
post - 1800 knives. Note
that the shield is often
blank at this time.
Plate 4.26

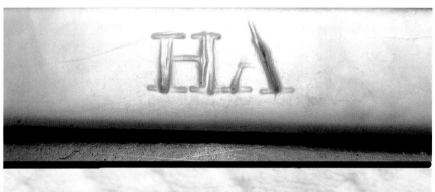

A mixture of ownership
markings for HA on a
Sheffield knife c.1785.
Plate 4.27

but charming message on the
blade. Ownership markings are an
important and interesting part of the
item's history (above). Later owners
have sometimes unwisely erased or
replaced such markings with their
own, immediately devaluing the
piece. Markings often show that
these elegant items were given to
women, a few even as Valentine
gifts (ref. *page 210*).

Georgian Period Hallmarking

After 1773 nearly all fruit knife (and fork) blades were hallmarked at Sheffield following successful assay. A regulation from the London Goldsmiths' Company stated that from 28th May 1790, exemption from hallmarking could only be applied to items that weighed less than 5 pennyweight, so that pocket fruit knife blades were now compulsorily assayed and marked. By this time nearly all blades were marked anyway, since the cutler/goldsmiths of both Birmingham and Sheffield would have been proud to show their wares marked by their respective assay offices. 18th century items from Birmingham are scarce, as the cutler/goldsmiths of Birmingham only starting mainstream production of pocket fruit knives after about 1800.

Progression of systematic hallmarking and positioning on fruit knife blades up to 1835.
Plate 4.28

Blades were sent in parcels to the assay office prior to assembly (in case they failed), bearing only the sponsor's (maker's workshop) mark. In Sheffield these were marked with the Sheffield crown, the sterling lion and the date letter for the year of assay. The term sponsor is used since in many workshops, the actual journeymen who made the components rarely added any individual mark to a small piece of silver. The workshop principal's mark alone was struck instead preventing the small surface area of the blade from being cluttered with marks. Hallmarks were rather large at this time, even for smallwork, and were hand-struck; only the essential marks – the sterling lion and the Sheffield crown were struck on the blade surface. The date letter was struck on the obverse side of the tang and the sponsor's mark on the reverse so that both remained hidden from view. These marks can sometimes be half seen by opening the blade three quarters (*plates 4.29 & 4.59*).

In 1780 a combination date letter and crown was devised for small wares and so, for a short while at least, the date letter became a 'blade mark'.

A duty tax had been levied on silver since 1720 (6 pence per ounce assayed and payable by the maker) since silver was a luxury material and those who ultimately purchased it could afford paying a bit more from the maker. In 1756 this turned into a kind of wealth tax but was repealed as the collecting of the tax was "vexatious and troublesome" and many smiths had devised cunning ways of avoiding payment. From the 1st of December 1784, the 6d per ounce assayed tax was re-instated and a duty mark was

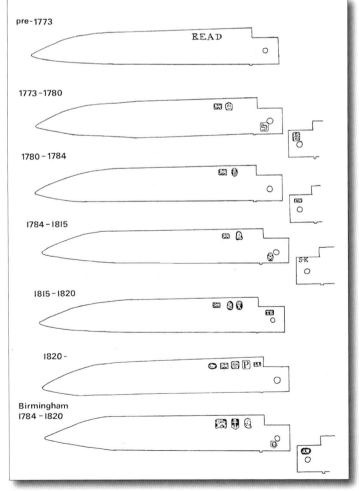

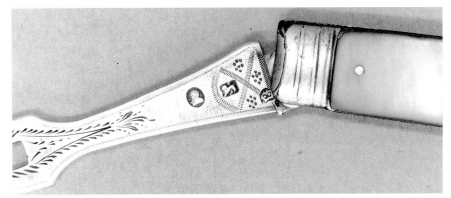

Tang-struck hallmarks just protruding showing the combination mark's crown struck more on the ricasso than the tang.
Plate 4.29

Series of tang-struck marks
Georgian knife tangs & blades showing the tang-struck combination crown and date letter marks for 1788, 1798, 1804 and (*below*) 1805. Note the oval duty mark for 1805, one of the proliferation years for pocket fruit knives.
Plates 4.30, 4.31 & 4.32

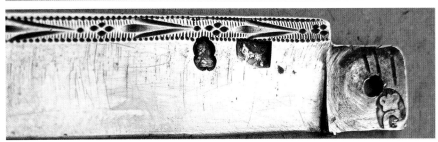

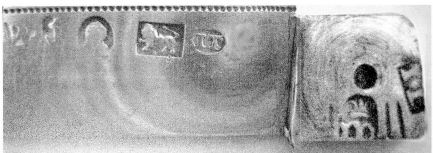

Curiously sponsor-marked blade by Joseph Taylor (of Birmingham) using his older I·T mark on the tang (Sheffield 1794) and his new oval cartouche IT mark on the blade, re-assayed in the same year (1794).
Plate 4.33

The tang marks can be occasionally obliterated by the hole for the hinge rivet.
Plate 4.34

Correspondence from M. Skelton relating to delay over the arrival of the new double duty mark, July the 13th 1797 and complaining about having to strike "The kings' head (duty mark) twice until proper marks are sent".
Plate 4.35

(below): Upper mark: the new double-duty mark within a double-cusped cartouche. *(lower):* the oval duty mark for 1805.
Plate 4.36

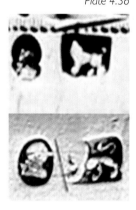

(right): Double duty mark using King's Head twice struck between July 1797 and April 1798.
Plate 4.37

Odd Hallmarking
Two blades with Sheffield assay for 1780. The upper blade has the normal hallmarks. The lower blade has the same marks but the combination crown and date letter mark has been inverted and a different (larger) sterling lion mark punch has inexplicably been used. This could be due to a temporary loss of the correct punch.
Plate 4.38

London—

Searchers Office 6 Octr 15

Sir

I have to acknowledge the Receipt of your Letter of the 4th Instant, and in Reply to observe that in a question where the Interest of the Crown is concerned I hardly think that any doubt can arise as to the Policy as well as the Propriety of adding some distinguishing mark on all Plate assayed at your Office since the 1st last, indeed if this is not before, the Crown must and most certainly will be daily defrauded by the Exporters claiming the high Drawback on their Plate, when actually the Duty paid to the Crown has been only 1/3—

The distinguishing Mark made by Goldsmiths Hall since I left is a notch at the bottom of the Kings Head (thus ^) that adopted by the Assay Office Birmingham is the changing the letter. The Authority for the different Assay Offices altering their mark does not come within my Province to speak on, but our only request is

right. For Sheffield (and Birmingham) the cartouche for this is elliptical, almost circular. In 1797, the duty was doubled and the duty mark changed again; an entry records this in the Sheffield Assay Book but not until April the 19th 1798 due to administrative delays (page 90). The cartouche was made with two or three cusps but this new mark did not arrive at Sheffield (or Birmingham) for about nine months. Some correspondence over the delay

Reply from the London Searcher Office, dated 6th of October, apologising for the "Unfortunate delay" in sending the new style duty punches to Sheffield. (*Letter illustrations courtesy of the Sheffield Assay Office*).
Plates 4.39 & 4.40

struck in addition to show that this tax had been paid.

The introduction of the duty mark (the King's head) meant that the combination mark was relegated to the tang since the duty levied on silver needed to be monitored. For this reason, only the duty mark and the sterling lion are visible on earlier Georgian knife and fork blades.

The changing shape of the duty mark, however, gives a clue as to when a blade might have been assayed. The early duty mark shows the King's head incuse and facing left. In 1786, the cameo duty mark was introduced which conformed to the style of the other hallmarks and with the King's head facing

is to be furnished with such Information from your Office so as to enable us to check any Fraud that may be attempted on the Revenue

The unfortunate delay that has already occurred will enable the Exporters of Sheffield Plate to practice the Fraud mentioned in the former part of this Letter without fear of detection—beckon whom the Responsibility will ultimately fall it is not for me to offer an opinion

I am Sir
Your obdt Servt
[signature]

To
J.W. Shelton Esq

Entry from the Sheffield Assay Office Day Book for April 19th 1798 and (top left) "New King's head 1st struck" having at last received the new punches from London. (*Courtesy of Sheffield Assay Office*).
Plate 4.41

Four Sheffield George III duty marks: incuse head (1784-1786) cameo in ellipse (1786-1797) cameo in cusped cartouche (1798-1820) excluding the oval (1805) and one tri-cusped duty mark of George IV for 1826.
Plate 4.42

Double-duty mark of two elliptical cameo marks used only between the 15th of July 1797 and April the 19th 1798 (for Sheffield and Birmingham).
Plate 4.43

took place (*page 88 & this page*) as the assay master found it tedious having to strike the old duty mark twice in lieu of the new single stamp, especially on smaller items. In 1805, an oval duty mark was used for one year due to another increase in duty, possibly due to the cost of the Napoleonic War, and then the two or three-cusped mark was used again (see below). Hallmarks became smaller and by about 1815 either the combination or sponsor's mark was struck on the blade itself. By the 1820s the hallmarks were mounted into a holding 'stub' and pressure marked into the blade using a special press (*plate 6.20*). Due to their reduced size and homogeneity, all the marks were stamped in a neat row on the blade thereafter. The cusped duty mark was again used and also during the reign of George IV, where it alternated with the oval cartouche mark once again but for no apparent reason.

(See plate 4.42 above for duty mark recognition and plate 5.45 for non-hallmarking of Georgian gold at Sheffield).

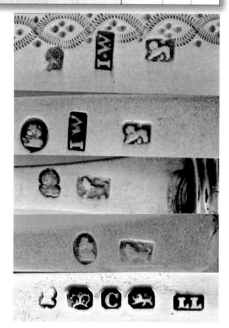

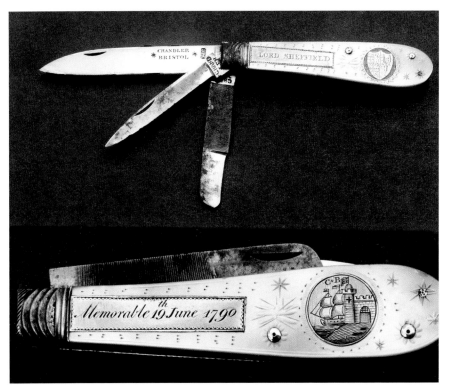

Unique pocket fruit knife, made by a Bristol cutler, William Chandler, to commemorate Lord Sheffield's whig election victory in 1790. Note the arms of the City of Bristol on the circular gold cartouche.
Plate 4.44

Unique knives

A very few Georgian knives were made for special persons. Lord Sheffield's name is recorded on a unique knife by a Bristol cutler, whose goldsmith's mark was not registered at the Bristol Assay Office. Walter Chandler of Bristol stamped a WC mark on the silver blade of a pocket fruit knife, which commemorates the "Memorable 19th June 1790", the day that Lord Sheffield, as the Whig candidate, was elected to parliament. A gold disc alongside has been engraved with the arms of the City of Bristol, which was the city's silver hallmark from 1700 – 1880. The obverse side of the haft shows his name on a rectangular shield alongside another gold disc bearing his coat of arms

(for John Holroyd) impaling that of his wife (Abigail Way). Chandler also engraved his name on the silver blade and stamped his normal cutler's mark on the ricasso of each of the two smaller steel blades. This piece must be unique, unless Lord Sheffield distributed a few of these to friends and supporters as tokens of his political victory.

Obverse gold shield of the above knife depicting the arms of Holroyd impaling Way.
Plate 4.45

Cutler's mark for William Chandler, hand-cut and showing his goldsmith's mark W.C struck sideways alongside.
Plate 4.46

Later 18th century blade ornamentation largely comprised wriggle-work, leading on to bright-cutting (right to left), c.1790.
Plate 4.47

Rare border pattern tool for producing zig-zag patterns, c.1800.
Plate 4.48

Decoration

Towards the end of this period, the outlines of folding fruit knives and forks were altered as the curved pistol-grip and scimitar blades were superseded by symmetrical hafts and spear-point blades. So that these new shapes would not appear too plain, knives and forks began to be more ornamented with engraved decoration.

Blades

Knife and fork blade decoration was applied by engraving, pouncing - using a spiked wheel, milled - using a wheel cut with decorative grooves under pressure, chased or stamped with a tracery of wrigglework or engraved bright-cutting along the upper edge of the obverse side of the blade, while fork blades were decorated all over on both sides. Early blades (c.1785-90) tended to be decorated with fine wrigglework in a single or double undulation using a chasing tool with a horseshoe end that had been cut with one 'unit' of the design. During the 1790s more oblique cutting of the metal, combined with twists and cabling in low relief, gave an added light-catching glint to the metal surface. Fork blades were even more elaborately decorated with similar wrigglework decoration, feather-edging or wavy bright-cut bands along the tines, whereas the central shaft of the blade was similarly edged or centrally-banded with an undulation of engraving or centred with a small central sunburst and emanating paired lambrequins along the blade; the ricasso was often decorated with a saltire cross of wrigglework or straight cuts, each quarter centred with four dots. There are many variations based on these designs.

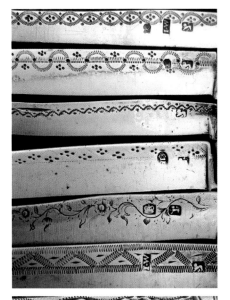

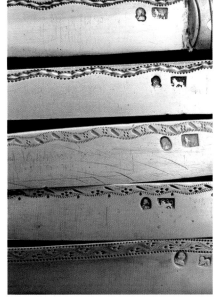

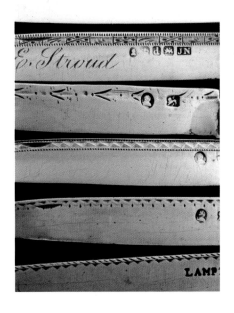

***Knife blade patterning:
1770 - 1840***

Interlacing wrigglework with (punched) dots, c.1780

Wavy & centred wrigglework with dots, c.1780

Wavy wrigglework with single dots, c.1780

Wavy wrigglework with dots, 1782

Wavy flowering stem, c.1775

Zig-zag wrigglework double border with cuts, c.1775

Pounce-bordered cable bright-cut, below milled wrigglework, c.1800

Pounce-bordered cable bright-cut, below milled wrigglework, c.1800

Wavy pounce-border with dots and cuts, c.1800

Wavy pounce-border with dots and cuts, c.1800

Straight pounce border with wavy wrigglework and teardrops, c.1790

Straight pounce border with dots and cuts, c.1840

Straight pounce border with leaves and dotted saltires, c.1825

Border of ermines, c.1790

Pounced border with alternating cuts, c.1790

Border of single cuts with pendent oval dots, c.1790

Border of single cuts with diagonals, c.1770
Plate 4.49

**Fork blade patterning:
1786 - 1816**

Pounce-edged band with alternating cuts, c.1800.

Pounce-edged band with thread-engraved border, c.1800.

Pounce-edged band, c.1800.

Looping wrigglework & botanical flowering stem, c.1790.

Pounced-edged bands with wrigglework and alternating dots, c.1790.

Ermine bright-cut on milled wrigglework bands, c.1810.

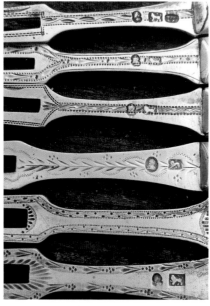

Pounced-border, interlace with sunbursts, engraved saltire base, c.1790.

Pounced border, sunburst with lambrequins, wrigglework saltire base, c.1790.

Zig-zag border, sunburst with botanical motifs, c.1800
Plate 4.50.

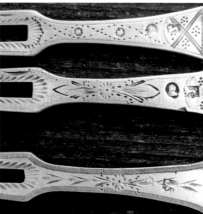

Bolsters

Not to be outdone by the French trend for decorating every part of a precious metal-bladed knife, English cutler/goldsmiths ensured that no part of such a knife should be left undecorated, giving the finished product greater appeal. Bolsters were decorated as soon as they were introduced into folding fruit knives in about 1770, although the occasional trend for 'bolsterless' fruit knives continued well into the next century. Early bolsters tended to be quite long, taking up to 30% of the haft length and were often gadrooned to match the spine decoration. Post-1785 examples tended to have the more conventional shorter bolster, about 15% of the haft length until c. 1815, when the longer bolster was revived for about 10 years. The bolster itself was made from copper or a copper alloy and soldered onto the base metal web or liner (ref. *page 255*) and was then decorated either with file work or die-stamped with gadrooned lines to match the spine pattern. Once decorated the bolster was then plated with applied silver or gold sheet.

French influence: another knife with a central haft stripe, c.1790.
Plate 4.51

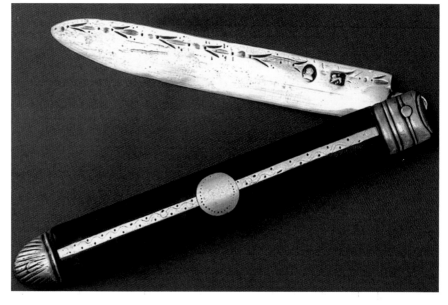

Springs and spinal decoration

Springs were coated with a silver spine in the manner of late 17th century French knives, to complete the fine finish of a piece. This comprised plain, bright-cut or chased thin silver sheet cut into strips, each strip then being soldered onto the back of the spring. The chased decoration on

Laurel wreath and variants - c.1770 - 1785.
Plate 4.52

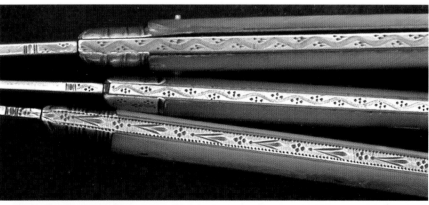

Gadroon - c.1780 - 1800 (lowest is c.1800).
Plate 4.53

Above: coiling wriggle-work, 2 variations and below, bright-cut c.1780-1800.
Plate 4.54

Below: engraved wreath variant and lozenge-cum-gadroon, c.1770-1780.
Plate 4.55

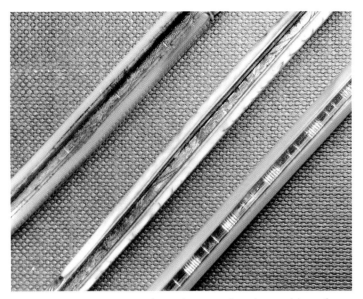

Undercut springs using filework, often copying the spinal pattern.
Plate 4.56

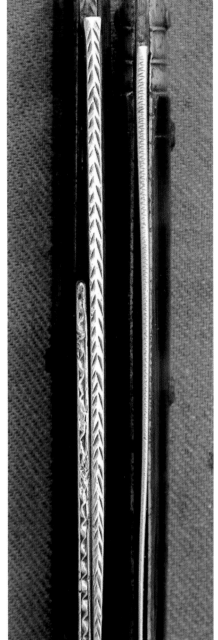

(Far right): Fruit knife blades c.1770-80 with leaf and wriggle-work engraved along the entire blade back. This may have been to test the skills of an apprentice but the fashion did not last beyond c.1790.

(Near right): The left hand blade of steel has been shortened and backed with a strip of patterned silver, matching the spring spinal decoration.
Plate 4.57

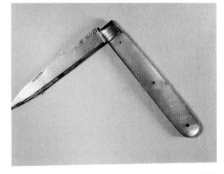

(Below right): Birmingham fruit knife by Edward Thomason c.1790, with an unusual applied steel edge. This feature may account in some way for the inverted hall-marks struck so close to the edge of the blade back.
Plate 4.58

the spine can also give an idea of period as it evolved throughout the next few decades *(plates 4.52-5)*. Early knife and fork spines were decorated with either a gadrooned, wriggle-worked or bright-cut engraved decoration, though some were left plain and a few earlier examples were chased with a laurel wreath pattern centred with two raised bands. At the turn of the 18th century, a series of transverse lines, like steps in repeated groups, began to be chased onto spines and this continued for a further 20 years. Cross-hatching was occasionally used and by the reign of George IV the combined 'steps' and cross-hatched design came into being and lasted throughout the Victorian and Edwardian periods. At times the spine pattern was continued along the entire back of a knife blade as well. More usually (and after c. 1780) it continued along the blade back for the first centimetre only *(plates 4.53-4)*. In finer examples the underside of the spring was decorated with filework often echoing the spine pattern *(plate 4.56)*.

Tang-struck hallmarks just protruding (for 1778) on a knife made by Robert Kippax and Company.
Plate 4.59

Reverses of many Georgian knife tangs all by RK for Robert Kippax and Co. showing the proliferation of knives his company produced c.1790.
Plates 4.60 & 4.61

Makers

Many of the silver smallworkers in Sheffield are assumed to have made fruit knives during the 1770 to 1790 period. Due to the partial marking of the blade at this time, conclusive results can be obtained through the dismantling of broken knives: many were made by Robert Kippax and Co. who worked as cutlers in Sheffield High Street. Kippax's R.K has been found on about 70% of tangs from knife blades made between 1770 and 1790. Other makers were John Winter, whose I.W is normally found stamped sideways on the blade itself, as was that of W.F for William Fox, James Tibbitts (I.T) and occasionally Joseph Taylor's IT (Birmingham) in a tight rectangle or oval, sometimes with an anchor (sponsor mark registered in both cities).

Conclusion

This was a time of elegance for English folding fruit knives and forks: scales were slim and not too heavy, they were modestly and elegantly decorated, as were the blades, or left plain. Precious metal caps, matching the bolsters, were added to the ends of many pieces. The end of the haft could be left unfinished and the pretty metal cap was glued or riveted onto the end

Two similar knives by John Winter c.1785. Despite their identical hafts and flat caps the further knife has a spear-point blade and with a laurel wreath spine while the nearer knife has a scimitar blade and a stepped spine (unusual this early); the hinge rivets also differ. Note Winter's sideways-struck sponsor mark on each knife, probably to distinguish it from that of John Watkinson.
Plate 4.62

(*plate 5.12*). The steel spring was quite slender in profile so that the mechanism was gentle and would not exert unnecessary pressure which could wear away the corners of a square tang too quickly. By contrast, later 19th century knives were made with thicker and harder spring mechanisms and could exert up to 40 pounds of pressure on the tang so that the tang corners were soon rounded off and the knife became difficult to use (ref. *pages 262-3*). A few Georgian knives and forks were even made with French-style (soft-spring) rounded tangs which made the opening of the blade a single action, smoother and easier, obviating wear and tear.

As the fashion for pocket fruit knives grew during the next period (1790-1815), the goldsmiths of Birmingham started to add folding fruit knives and forks to their more regular production of small silver items.

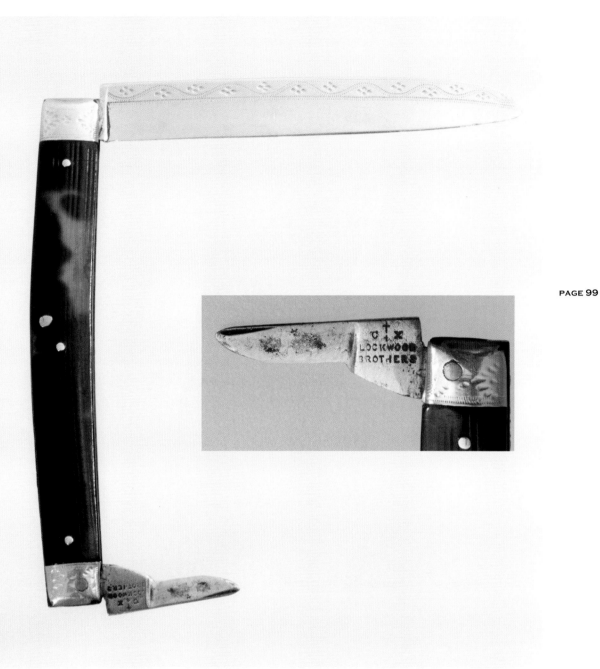

English gold-bladed fruit
knives are unusual as early
as this one (c.1770-1790).
The quill blade has been
replaced c.1820 but has
still been snapped off and
re-shaped.
Plate 4.63

Pistol grip-hafted knife and
fork set, 1780. Note the
crown bolsters and the
simple circular shields,
characteristic for pieces up
to c.1790.
Plate 4.64

POCKET FRUIT KNIVES: 4 THE 'PISTOL-GRIP' PERIOD, 1770-1790

5 'The Golden Age': 1790-1815.

An exceptionally finely-made gold-bladed tortoiseshell-hafted knife c.1800.
The shield engraved with the crest of Phillips.
Plate 5.1

A fine array of gold & gilt-
bladed fruit knives & forks
from c.1750-1815, plus a
French set c.1830.
Plate 5.2

D uring this time the styles and designs of Georgian pocket fruit knives and forks reached their zenith, and their greatest diversity both stylistically and in use of materials. The more regular production of gold-bladed knives, for example, made this a truly Golden Age for English pocket fruit knives. It was also a time when Britannia ruled the waves and was trying to keep herself and much of Europe out of the hands of Bonaparte. The Napoleonic campaign, particularly, initiated military trophies and possible symbols of England's watchfulness and business portrayed on hafts as engraved designs: fouled anchors symbolising hope, military trophies, bee hives or scythes and sheaves of wheat symbolising industry, standing herons symbolising watchfulness for enemies of England and doves holding olive branches suggesting a more pacifist approach (*plates 5.3-4, 6.6 & 6.8 & 6.27*). As haft makers and pearl cutters were chronicling these current events, the Royal Family were also symbolically depicted by crowns and by the Prince of Wales' triple plume armorial device whilst he gained popularity and fame as he grew to manhood; the plume is found on knives, particularly between 1790 and 1810 (*plate 4.18*).

Knife-and-fork sets

As this elegant vogue gained further popularity, knife-and-fork sets continued to be made in ever-increasing numbers and a few sets were even made as foursomes: fruit knife, fork, spoon and a steel-bladed pocket knife. (*plate 5.9*)

A new style of knife and fork that clipped together when not in use, also came on the market some time during the 1790s and was probably among the first to be made in this 'camping set' style. These were lined with copper (or an alloy) but with thicker than normal liners and were mounted with two to three nail-headed rivets standing about 2mm proud of the surface which clipped in two or three corresponding keyhole-shaped apertures in the haft liner of the pair (*plate 5.5*). This was also applied to campaign sets. Officers sent out to fight against the French might be given a parting gift of a steel-bladed pocket knife that clipped together with a silver folding fork and spoon and the ever necessary corkscrew. The spoon bowl was made to swivel

on the end of its haft rather than fold partly into the blade slot (*plate 5.14*). The spoons were ordered from London as very few spoons were produced in Sheffield at that time, whereas the silver fork blade, steel knife and corkscrew were invariably of Sheffield origin. A few campaign sets were even ornamented with decorated silver spines down the backs of the blades. For the more middle-class or less well-to-do officer, these were silver-plated, although

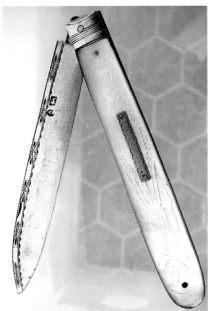

Symbolic items engraved with olive branches (for Peace) balanced with militaria c.1810 (*above*) and a large set engraved with scythes, rakes and be-ribboned wheat sheaves symbolising industry c.1800 (*below, left*).
Plates 5.3 & 5.4

An array of slotting sets c.1800, including a rare gold set (*above*).
Plate 5.5

(below): A Christmas present set, given in 1798 but hallmarked c.1796 using the elliptical duty marks (*see pages 89-90*).
Plate 5.6

(far right): Two honeyhive knives c.1800 & 1820 both symbolising industry. The left has been crudely hand-engraved: "The bee who steeps man's soul in sweet". See also plate 6.6 (next chapter).
Plate 5.7

such items did not normally appear until the post-Napoleonic period. Campaign sets were also produced as separate knife, fork and spoon, the corkscrew fitting into the knife's haft and the whole kept in a leather-veneered pasteboard or wooden box. Later 19th century sets were sometimes scrimshandered with personal details – regimental devices and dates of campaigns or battles (*ref. page 188*).

In his *Explanation or Key to the various Manufactories of Sheffield* of 1816, Joseph Smith shows, on one page, a range of pocket fruit knives and forks made in Sheffield at

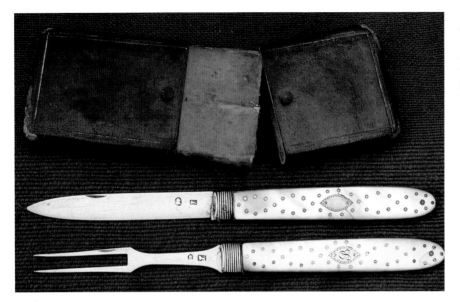

A matched set *semée* with rosettes, c.1790 (knife) and c.1800 (fork). Note the B on the fork's shield. *Plate 5.8*

A scarce four-piece set, including a steel-bladed pocket knife to match and London-made spoon by George Smith & William Fearn, 1792. *Plate 5.9*

that time. He interestingly includes some older styles from the 1790s that must have still been in current use (*plate 5.15*) and which include a knife and fork that clip together. He also illustrates other types of period pocket knife including some that still closely resembled those from France, especially the 'brass shoulder knives', many of which were made by George Patten, whose PATEN mark was registered both at Sheffield and Thiers, the cutlery centre of central France. A few knives were even made with French-influenced lock-back mechanisms – a raised lever, let into the spring of the knife, with a steel tooth at the pivoting end that locked into a corresponding notch in the tang and which prevented the blade from accidentally closing. A few of these are found on fruit knives and S. Colmore (*ref. plate 3.10*) favoured lock-back springs for his knives.

POCKET FRUIT KNIVES: 5 'THE GOLDEN AGE', 1790-1815

Some rare throwbacks to the 'French era' were also made at this time. *Réchange* bladed knives exist and comprise a pearl or horn-scaled haft, two steel blades and one of silver; later examples have a few additional tools (*plates 5.17 & 8.27*). The blade tangs clipped individually into a slot at the end of the knife haft and were kept in place by a sprung and pivoting lock. Even English *Berge* knives were made but conformed to the small size of English folding fruit knives (*plate 4.2*). Smith also lists 'Spotted knives' which were hafted with cow horn, artificially spotted to resemble tortoiseshell, but this may have been considered too lowly for the refinements of a precious metal-bladed fruit knife (*plate 3.31*).

Boxes

Individual knives and knife-and-fork sets were usually sold in boxes made of pasteboard *mâché*, often using

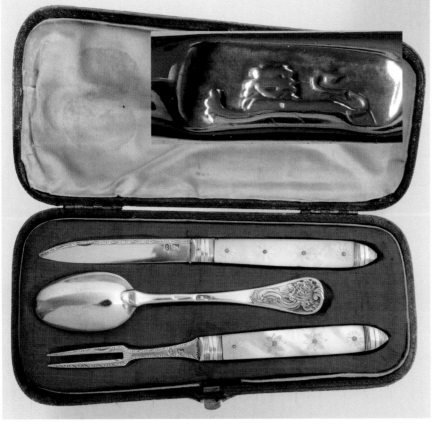

(above & opposite): Purse-type case, lined with green silk for a knife, fork & spoon set, the case catch engraved with the date - 1800.
Plates 5.10 & 5.11

A fine triple set c.1800 but with an earlier (Rococo) teaspoon, assayed in London, c.1750 (inset, sponsor mark rubbed) in a later case, c.1860.
Plates 5.12 & 5.13

Campaign set. Sheffield-
made, except for the
spoon bowl - London
1808.
Plate 5.14

(below): Plate from Joseph
Smith's *Manufactories of
Sheffield*, 1816. Note the
mix of contemporary
styles with some from
about 25 years earlier.
Plate 5.15

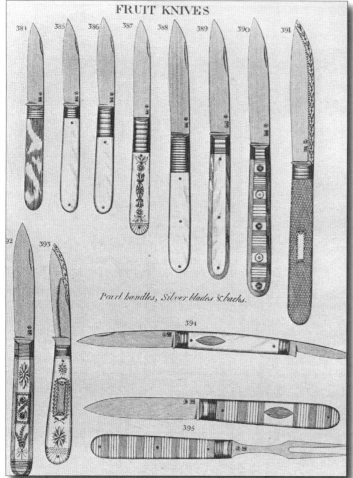

FRUIT KNIVES

Pearl handles, Silver blades & backs.

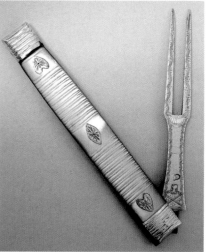

(right): Capped fork
c.1800. Note how the
bright-cutting is finer than
previously.
Plate 5.16

with skiver or wafer-thin morocco leather usually dyed in shades of red or green. Many had some impressed or gilt design around the border and a few were decorated all over. An impressed or gilt circle, star or shaped paper wafer was also added to ensure correct orientation of the lid.

For knife-and-fork sets, boxes were compartmentalised, perhaps with an extra space for a spoon, and some were charmingly shaped as books. Most boxes for sets were made from wood, carved in the base with appropriate shapes to hold the contents securely and with a

contemporary newspaper. Older examples tended to be painted black and moulded with raised designs, sometimes tapering. By 1800, boxes were generally rectangular in shape with pull-off lids and veneered

Rare English exchangeable bladed fruit-*cum*-pocket knife, c.1810, marked LOOKER of Leadenhall Street London, probably a retailer's mark as the assay marks are of Sheffield origin.
The wave-shaped shield of gold indicates an expensive item.
Plate 5.17

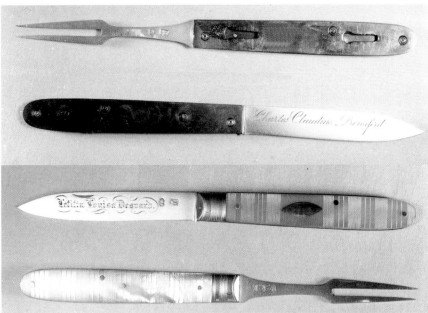

Two slotting sets c.1800, with ownership markings on the blades.
The upper set was (less usually) given to a man.
Plate 5.18

hinged lid. The interiors were lined with velvet and the lids with silk or white cotton lawn and, by the early to mid-19th century, had a pair of bands traversing the lid for insertion of a retailer's trade card (very scarce to find these!). Earlier boxes were fastened with a small hook and eye closure until about the mid 19th century when a spring-mounted button, similar to those found on small jewellery boxes, became the norm. Hinged boxes were also made for individual knives, although I have found one containing a single fork of the correct period which fitted exactly.

Other containers were based on contemporary and elegant dyed-leather purses with contrastingly dyed doe-skin compartments and fold-over and silver-edged lids that clipped onto a small silver clasp (*plate 5.10 & 5.11*).

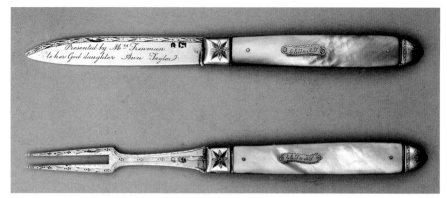

Another inscribed set c.1800, probably a Christening Gift complete with donation initials on the wave-shaped shields.
Plate 5.19

The cheaper end of the Georgian period market: smaller pieces, some decorated, with thinner blades and uncoated springs. The box for the small pair (centre) is typical with its gilt border c.1800. Note the gadrooned bolster for the costlier knife (lower left) and the smaller and cheaper fork (lower right), a style that was used c.1780 to c.1795.
Plate 5.20

Hafts, blades, bolsters & springs

Towards the end of this period, hafts began to be made slightly wider with thicker nacre scales, perhaps to make a larger area for engraving, and caps were gradually, but not completely, phased out. At the same time, hallmarks were slightly reduced in size and some sponsors' (makers') marks began to reappear on blades rather than being confined to tangs. Shields for ownership marks were still occasionally used and remained largely blank until around 1810-15. By the end of

the period it was much more in keeping to have a personal mark or inscription of donation engraved on the shield (*plate 5.19*) while longer inscriptions were engraved on the blade.

Blades themselves were invariably spear-pointed, most engraved with a frieze of bright-cut decoration along the upper side. By now wriggle-work had given way to heraldic ermine-style bright-cut decoration, bordered with dots.
Spring (spine) decoration mainly

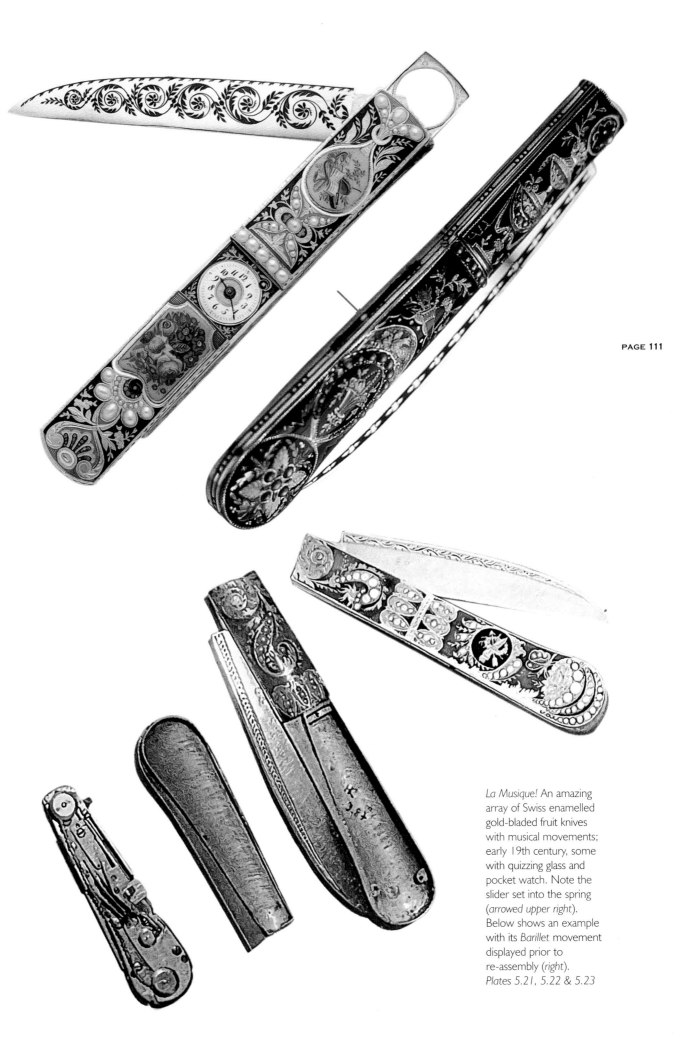

La Musique! An amazing array of Swiss enamelled gold-bladed fruit knives with musical movements; early 19th century, some with quizzing glass and pocket watch. Note the slider set into the spring (*arrowed upper right*). Below shows an example with its *Barillet* movement displayed prior to re-assembly (*right*). Plates 5.21, 5.22 & 5.23

A closer look at the knife from top right of the previous page with its *Barillet* movement exposed and a six tooth musical comb, operated by a fusee chain that connects to a tiny pull-down lug on the back of the knife and playing about 16 seconds of music. The panels, decorated with *champlevé* enamels and pearls. Swiss, probably Geneva, unmarked c.1810. (*Courtesy of Christies, South Kensington, London*). Plate 5.24

changed from diagonal ribbing (gadrooning) to transverse raised or indented steps, grouped in twos and threes or graded groups. Laurel wreath designs were still occasionally found, perhaps commemorating a victory over the French.

Cheaper pocket fruit knives

As the fashion for pocket fruit knives became more popular, their makers expanded their wares to suit those with less money to spend on such luxuries but who desired to imitate their peers. These fruit knives were slightly smaller than their superiors,

some bolsters were not silvered but made of steel rather than copper so that they might resemble silver before they rusted or dulled (*plate 5.20*). The silver blades were rather thinner and bendy so that not so many have survived. The nacre scales were usually left plain although some were lightly cross-hatched. The springs were not normally coated with decorative silver spines.

Musical fruit knives

At the other end of the market and for those with deep purses, these made ideal Grand Tour items

Another sensational Swiss musical fruit-*cum*-pocket knife, with an additional steel blade and watch under a sliding panel, with Geneva hallmark c.1810. *Plate 5.25*

– workmanship in miniature for the amusement of the rich. For some, these are the epitome of the pocket fruit knife maker's art although they can equally be regarded as being just too 'over the top'. They were made in Switzerland, normally Geneva or Zurich, from about 1800 to 1830. As Swiss watch and automaton makers were doubtless keen to exploit the market by selling their wares in as many different forms as possible they did not neglect to fashion exotic fruit knives as the *dernier cri* in souvenirs and doubtless caught the imagination of

many young Regency collectors on their Grand Tour.

Blades for such knives were made from gold; silver was probably regarded as rather too second-best for such first-class objects. Many such knives were, however, made with a second blade of steel housed in a parallel slot, in the manner of French pocket fruit knives. The haft designs of fruit and flowers might suggest that the steel blade was reserved for cutting flowers, although it probably had no special purpose and the whole item probably spent most of its life as a

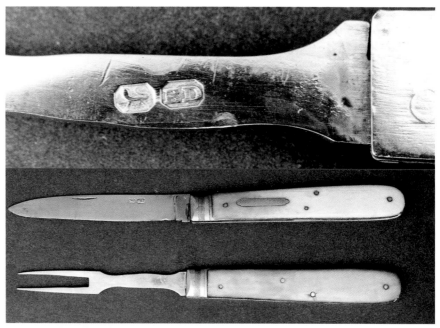

Another dubious set
appears on many small
knives bearing the
sponsor's mark for Samuel
(& William) Kirkby of
Sheffield, c.1815-20. The
George IV duty mark
should be in profile and
the 3 ensuing 'bat's wing'
marks are fake. He may
have kept his cheaper
items' prices down but
would have risked
prosecution.
Plate 5.27

rich man's conversation piece. The
gold blades were usually decorated
with a border of bright-cut engraving
or left plain; a few were decorated
with enamelling.

Decoration tended to follow neo-
classical styles of the later 18th
century. Hafts were ornamented
with urns and swags or with panels
depicting musical instruments, bows
and arrows, typifying the Arcadian
revival movement of the period,
and bordered with entire or split
pearls. Occasionally the two styles
were combined on the one haft
and separated by a row or frame
of pearls (_previous pages_). The
champlevé enamelling is always of
the finest quality, usually in shades of
blue including cobalt but occasionally
in polychrome. A few hafts were
decorated with swirls of split pearls
and translucent enamelling on a gold

guilloché background, a technique
beloved of later craftsmen such as
Carl Fabergé. Winding apertures
and watch movements were
often concealed beneath cunningly
integrated, sliding 'secret' panels so
that the overall line of the knife haft
remained unbroken. Such knives
have sometimes included other
useful items such as a reducing or
quizzing lens.

The most interesting feature,
however, is the musical movement.
The art of miniaturising a musical
box movement was not perfected
until 1796, when a certain Antoine
Favre of Geneva is recorded as
having invented a musical movement
that used a stack of tuned steel
teeth that were plucked by pins
set into a tiny cylinder powered by
a coiled spring. From this _barillet_
or spring drum and several other
musical mechanisms, cylinder
musical boxes were developed.
The _barillet_ movement for fruit
knives resembled the housing for a
clock spring and comprised a similar
hollow, disc-shaped cylinder which
contained a coiled spring. Winding
the movement caused the spring

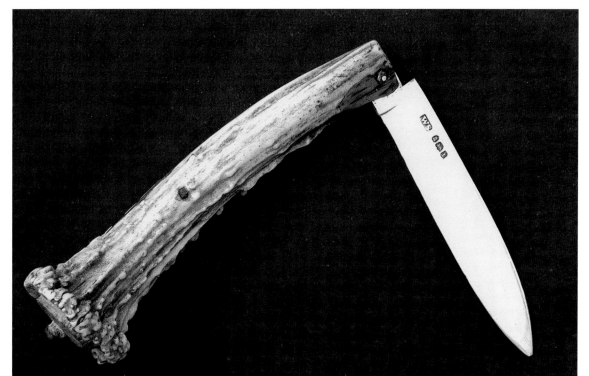

(above): A scarce staghorn-hafted fruit knife, the blade assayed in London 1804, most likely by William Stroud.
Plate 5.28

(left): The London goldsmith Hester Bateman over-stamped this Sheffield-made set, probably by John Watkinson, with her own marks as retailer, c.1797-8.
Plate 5.29

to coil tightly so that it would rotate the tiny cylinder, although its speed could barely be evenly regulated by a rather crude ratchet and pawl mechanism. A sliding pin along the back of the haft operates many such fruit knives. Pulling the pin downwards tensions the spring and as it unwinds, the knife plays the tune. Considering that most knives could only be fitted with 5 or 6 tuned teeth, that the notes might vary in speed due to the absence of a proper regulating device and that the music might have been all the rage in Geneva during the early to mid 19th century - you often have a tune that is hard to identify! If held in the hand, the music is barely audible and the knife should be placed onto a wooden box to act as a sounding board.

Apart from knowing that the movement design is based on Favre's 1796 invention, only one example has come to light with a single hallmark for the goldwork *(plate 5.25)*. None bear any maker's or sponsor's mark. Despite this mystery, and although some may have considered them as trifles in their day, musical fruit knives are now few in number. At auction they make well in excess of

Three blades marked with inverted crown combination marks for: 1817, 1818, 1819 (top to bottom).
Plate 5.30

Birmingham 'sliders'
(*upper*) Two knives by Joseph Taylor, assayed in 1791.
Plate 5.31

(*middle*): Reverse sides of above knives to show slider mechanisms.
Plate 5.32

(*lower*): Scarce set of knife and fork by Samuel Pemberton c.1800.
Plate 5.33

£15,000 depending on the condition of the enamel casing and the musical movement. (See also Chapuis & Loup, 1919).

Contemporary Fakes

Period fakes are rare – pocket fruit knives were hardly important enough, in their time, to attract a forger's attention and yet a few do exist. Plate 5.26 shows a slotting knife and fork pair whose blades are made of a white metal resembling silver. The sponsor's mark on each blade is BD, who is not listed in any directory, and the skinny sterling lion alongside is decidedly 'wrong'! The style of the bone-scaled set puts them at c.1810-1830.

Another possible fake may just be a series of mis-struck marks but is found on many knives made by Samuel and William Kirkby. Apart from the S.K mark and a rather crude George IV duty mark, the remaining set comprises a repeated trio of 'bat-wing' marks. Maybe the

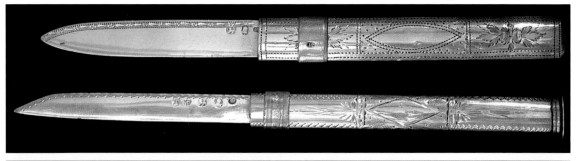

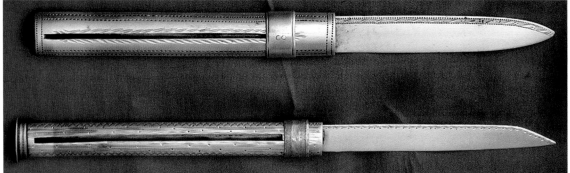

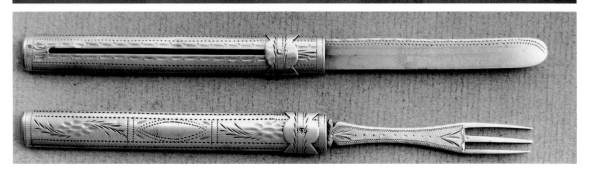

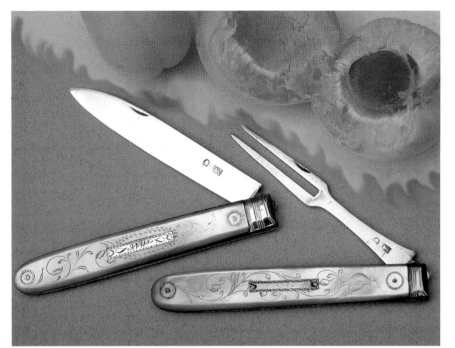

Later Georgian decoration
incorporated birds and
scrolls among
the inlaid circles and
rosettes c.1810.
Plates 5.34 & 5.35

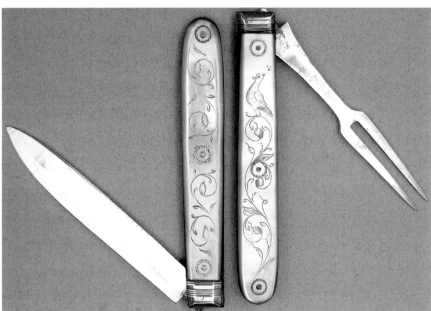

hallmarking stub (for they belong
to the 1820s, ref. *page 138*) was
sloppily loaded the day his parcel
of blades was marked but then the
marks would hardly appear to be
all the same (*plate 5.27*). Many
examples have been noted.

Hallmarking and Makers

The makers of pocket fruit knives
still continued to be centered in
Sheffield, while those in Birmingham
largely made other small silver items.
Joseph Willmore and Joseph Taylor

were more renowned for making
snuffboxes and vinaigrettes, yet their
marks are most often found on early
examples of Birmingham pocket fruit
knives, especially those with sliding
blades and made entirely from silver
(*see opposite page*). Alexander
James Strachan (mark: A.J.S) was
a London goldsmith, whose gold
boxes were 'of the finest' at the
time, has also been recorded as
having made at least one pocket
fruit knife. (*plates 5.47 & 5.48*)
The knife is of top quality with a

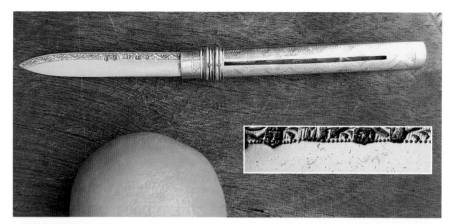

Gilt sliding knife by Matthew Linwood, Birmingham 1792. Note how the border decoration has almost defaced the hallmarks demonstrating that the blades were sent for assay prior to decorating in case they failed the Assay.
Plate 5.36

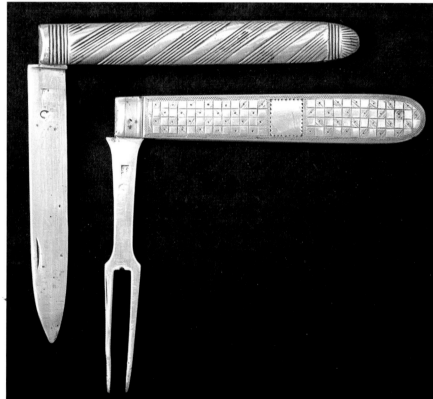

Silver-hafted Sheffield fruit knife & fork engraved *á la mode* as for nacre scales. Knife c.1790, fork c.1800.
Plate 5.37

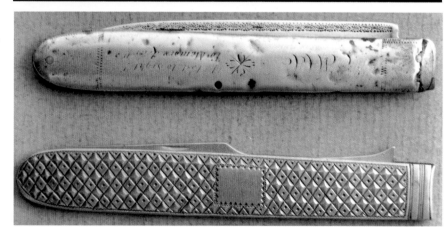

(upper) Unusual remembrance fruit knife, well-worn but with part of inscription still legible - "To Memory dear" c.1800.
(lower) Beautifully-engraved cross-hatching pattern on a fork haft c.1800.
Plate 5.38

cast foliate bolster and cap, assayed in 1811 (his mark was registered in 1799). The knife is unusually bladed with 18 carat gold in the old tradition since lower grades of gold had been permitted for assay by Act of Parliament since 1798.

The date letters for Sheffield were

POCKET FRUIT KNIVES: 5 'THE GOLDEN AGE', 1790-1815

irregular in sequence until 1824. Between 1796 and 1823, Roman letters were used and from 1815 to 1823 the letters were duplicated. The Assay Office inverted the crown, to avoid confusion, say for 1819, when the letter V was used to avoid duplication with 1798. The inversion is noticeable only in the combined (crown and date letter) mark. Even when the stub-marking system was adopted in the 1820s, some confusion still arises between the 'C' date letter for 1811 and 1826 (refer next chapter, *plates 6.17 & 6.18*).

For more information on duty mark changes refer to previous chapter.

Metal-hafted (& sliding mechanism) fruit knives

At a time when hafting materials were at a decorative zenith, metals for hafting could appear plain unless beautifully engraved or chased.

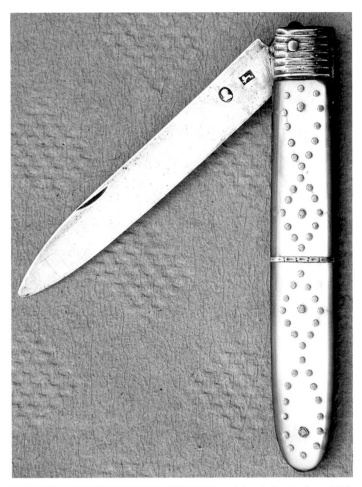

At first the Birmingham smiths produced some of their earliest pocket fruit knives in silver or gilt but with sliding rather than folding blades. This breakaway from the conventional folding knife seems to have been unique to them. The haft was made in the manner of a period needle case, from one piece

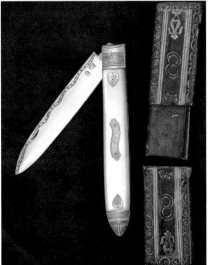

(above): Fruit knife c. 1790 scaled with nacre off-cuts and decorated with *piqué clouté.*
Plate 5.39

(far left): Bolsterless fruit knife with fine cross-hatch engraving.
Plate 5.40

(left) Boxed fruit knife with heart-shaped rosettes, c.1800.
Plate 5.41

Presumed to be experimental, this crowned version of the sterling lion appeared briefly on Sheffield silverwares, including pocket fruit knives, during 1807.
Plate 5.42

Fruit knife c.1805 (note the oval duty mark for that year) with a lozenge-filed bolster.
Plate 5.43

Cheaper-type fruit knife with plain nacre haft, c.1810 decorated, perhaps by an apprentice to show his skill with the pouncing wheel.
Plate 5.44

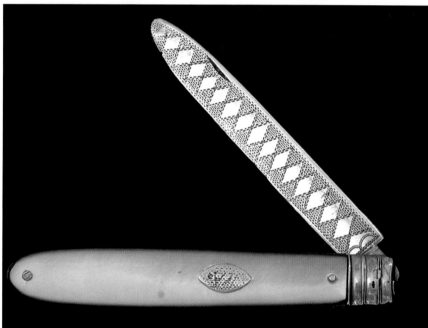

of folded silver sheet decorated with bright cutting or wriggle-work then soldered along one side and cut with a slot along the other. The silver blade was mounted onto a bed of lead with a pair of rivets that connected to a separate and decorative silver collar. The collar could be moved up and down the haft slot, extending or retracting the blade as desired (*plates 5.31 to 5.33 & 5.36*). In time, the hafts became

dented inside people's pockets and the mechanisms rather stiff, or even jammed. Those that have survived often demonstrate this problem which may explain why the vogue for these sliding knives (and a few forks) was rather short-lived; they appear to have gone out of fashion in about 1810.

Conventional Georgian fruit knives and forks were sometimes hafted

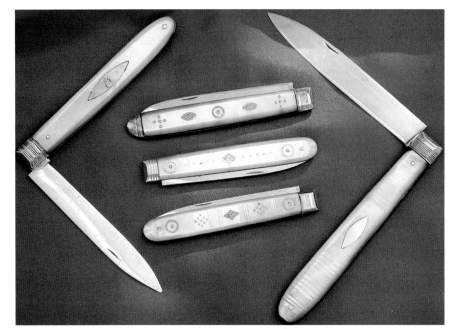

PAGE 121

Sheffield gold-bladed fruit knives in standard and smaller sizes: c.1790-1810. The smaller size may have been due to keeping down the cost of such an item. Sheffield was not granted a license to assay gold until 1904 so all of these knives are unmarked.
Plate 5.45

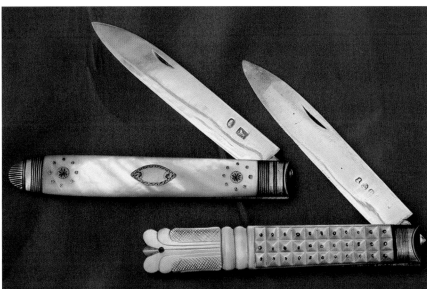

Two silver-gilt Sheffield fruit knives c.1810 and 1825.
Plate 5.46

with silver and decoration similar to that found on the more regular nacre hafts (*plates 5.37 & 5.38*). During the next period the silver hafts began to take on a more individual style.

Hallmark rarity

Some fruit knives and forks were subjected to experimental or unusual hallmarking. In Sheffield, the sterling lion mark was given a crowned head for a short while in 1807, although there is no apparent record of this in the Assay Office files. This may have been restricted to small items as it has not yet been noted on largework. Pocket fruit knives have been found with this mark and it may have been an attempt to shift the Sheffield crown to the more visible hallmarks on the blade. The new mark may have resembled too closely the London crowned lion mark, which was used from 1544 to 1549 when the Goldsmiths first introduced the sterling standard as a deterrent against silver debasement. Whatever the reason no correspondence with the Sheffield Archive or the Assay Office in Sheffield has solved the mystery

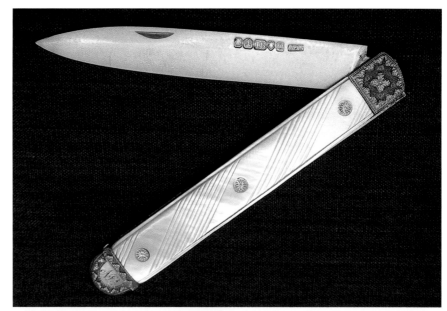

PAGE 122

Individual 18 ct. gold-
bladed knife by the
London goldsmith A J
Strachan, more famous for
fine gold boxes, 1811.
Plates 5.47 & 5.48

surrounding the (very) temporary
existence of this mark. Only a few
items have been found struck with
the crowned lion (*plate 5.42*).

Gold and gilt blades

Why have a gold blade? The
physical properties of gold (as of
silver) include a softness which
makes the metal unsuitable for blade
making. Gold can also be annealed
and hammered squashing the

component atoms closer together
and creating a physical hardness so
that it can hold a fairly sharp edge
and be capable of cutting even citrus
fruit without bending or breaking.
Gold has traditionally been the metal
of kings and queens; pocket fruit
knives and forks bladed with gold
or silver gilt were made for those
who could afford them and wished
for something non-tarnishable and
costlier than mere silver.

English gold-bladed fruit knives

These date from the mid-18th century (*ref. plate 3.15*). Early examples are very scarce and only started to appear in numbers during the 1790s in exactly the same styles as their silver counterparts. The only differences are that the spring spine was normally left plain in a gold-bladed knife (or fork) and that many single knives were made slightly smaller than their silver counterparts (*centre of plate 5.45*), probably to keep the retail price down. They show very little wear and may have been kept as items of social snobbery to 'flash about' rather than use. A few sets were made and even fewer slotting sets have turned up (*plate 5.55*). None were hallmarked unless assayed in London and most were made in Sheffield, having the greater production at this time. A few probably came from Birmingham although differentiation is not possible. When the Assay Offices opened in these towns in 1773, neither was deemed 'worthy' of needing gold assaying facilities since production was so small. Birmingham, however, soon required gold assay facilities due to the production of fine snuffboxes, and in 1824 an Act was passed in Parliament permitting the office to assay gold. Sheffield production was still small and the city did not receive permission to assay gold until 1904! Most gold-bladed knives were made in and around Sheffield and these are totally unmarked. Not even a sponsor's mark was permitted and some may have resorted to sponsor marking the tang. Many makers doubtless found this frustrating and even produced their own (illegal) designation punches, such as a 9ct stamp, which was found on a knife dating (stylistically) from the 1880s (*plate 7.68*).

Gilt items were subject to the normal silver hallmarking laws and

A similar item from Sheffield but with a striped bolster, rayed cap, domed rosettes and diagonal bands of engraving *à la Française* c.1800.
Plate 5.49

PAGE 124

Superb enamel-decorated knife with 18ct gold blade, c.1810, retailed by S J Phillips of London. The decoration is typical of French *Empire* period and the French provincial census mark (eagle's head - *below*) suggests a French origin, yet the knife was fully hallmarked in London, 1810; the sponsor's mark has been struck too lightly to be legible. *(Courtesy of Messrs Woolley & Wallis, Salisbury)* *Plate 5.50 & (below): 5.51*

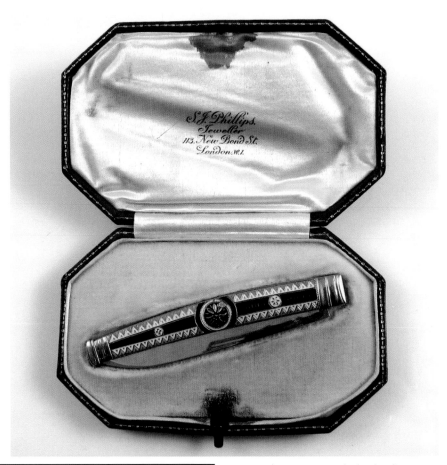

were therefore marked in the same way as plain silver. A few knives were made with blades of polished brass and a few meaningless pseudo-hallmarks were stamped onto the blade. These could be classed as contemporary fakes except that the haft workmanship on some is too painstaking and they were possibly made as gold imitations for those with shallower purses (*plates 5.53 & 6.29*).

Gold knives in France
Gold-bladed knives were also produced in France during this period but I have yet to see one earlier than c.1770. Some beautiful examples were made in the *Berge* style with nacre hafts striped with gold bands and with banded gold caps (normally bearing a tiny assay mark). The blades were finished with grooved backs or with raised borders and were slightly raised centrally along the backs, always matching with the blade of steel, itself coated with a soldered strip of gold sheet (*plate 2.56*). The gold caps were laid onto shaped wooden underlays, themselves glued onto a sliver of underlying nacre, presumably to avoid the risk of accidentally cracking the scales should such a knife be dropped (*page 34*). The nacre scales were generally engraved with cross-hatching, and inlaid with gold bands or gold rosettes. Nacre scales were occasionally inlaid with carved slivers of gold and abalone shell, mixing beautiful natural colours with the more subtle tints of the

This pair has been bladed with 9 or 14ct gold by Thomas Mortimer, London 1806. He later worked with Hunt & Roskell who supplied the later box c.1850. The shields have been engraved *L'amitié* which was a fairly common period friendship token.
Plate 5.52

A brass-bladed knife with pseudo-hallmarks imitating the fine quality of its gold peers by being beautifully made, c.1815 "All that glitters".
Plate 5.53

Sheffield gold knife c.1790-1800 with typical large engraved rosettes.
Plate 5.54

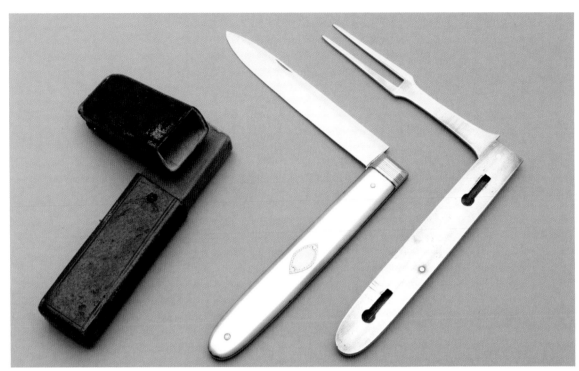

Clipping (or slotting) sets in gold are extremely scarce, this Sheffield set dates c.1790-1810.
Plate 5.55

Knife and fork set in silver, the rosettes enhanced with engraved stars. The slightly outward bowed hafts are indicative of c.1800-1810.
Plate 5.56

nacre (*plate 2.36*). For those who required something even more luxurious, knives were also made with enamelled hafts in neo-classical or Arcadian styles, often bordered with tiny split pearls and frequently bearing the renowned names of TOURON and DELAUNAY (*plates 2.41 & 2.50*). If gold knives came from Paris, then a different set of

punches was used to differentiate gold from gilt but many were assayed at Orléans and even smaller provincial towns where there was no provision for a set of punches to distinguish precious metals. Gold knives were also made to double with steel-bladed knives and the two were housed in a special green case of shagreen or *galuchat*. Individual

gold knives have also turned up – one stamped with the name of GAVET: Parisian cutler ("to the King") - a very fine example hafted with plain ivory and ornamented with huge golden rosettes (*plate 5.58*). The tang is U-shaped rather than right-angled so that the blade glides in an out of the haft in a smoother motion than usual, known as single-action.

Gold and gilt knives and sets continued to be produced during the 19th century, including one set, complete with a folding spoon. The knife has been made in the *Berge* style and the fork and spoon are spring-backed; all have been capped with tiny gilt scallop shell caps and fitted into a handsome *galuchat* case marked with the retailer's name of TOURON, *24 Rue de la Paix, Paris*, c.1830 (*plate 7.89*).

Although this is a quill knife c.1790-1800, the haft was originally made for a fruit knife. The maker has added a decorative spine that curls around the haft base and halway up the blade slot to compensate for the shorter blade.
Plate 5.57

Luxurious and large gold-bladed knife by Gavet of Paris c.1815 and below a Sheffield silver-bladed fruit fork by William Coldwell c.1815. Note the similarity of the fork haft and that both have soft-spring mechanisms with rounded tangs to ensure a smoother opening and closing of the blade in a single-action.
Plates 5.58 & 5.59

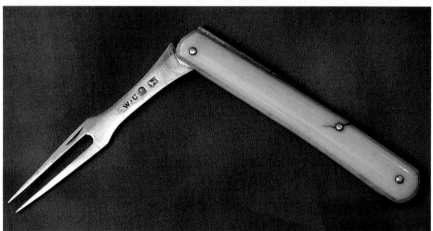

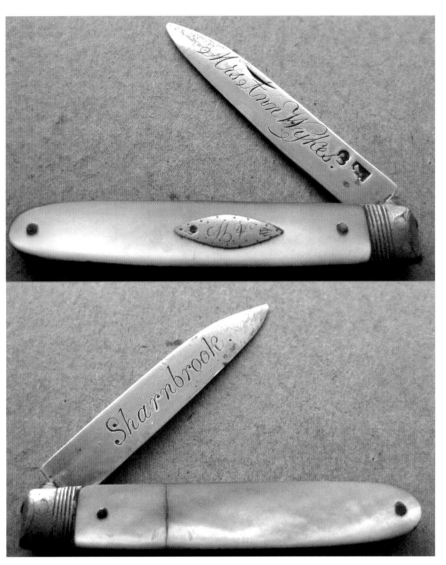

A rather worn and plain fruit knife c. 1800, the blade lavishly inscribed (some might say defacingly) with the recipient's/owner's name: Mrs Ann Wykes of Sharnbrook.
Plates 5.60

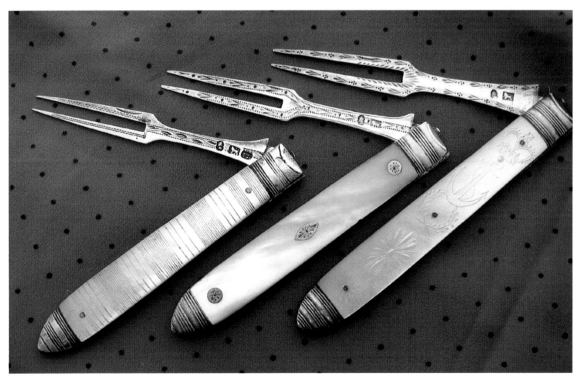

Three typical Georgian period forks, c.1800 engraved with bright-cut decoration.
Plates 5.61

A normal size fork placed between a larger-sized fruit knife and fork, c.1790.
Plates 5.62

Georgian capped knife, struck with the double-duty mark, Sheffield, 1797. Note the box imitating the design of tortoiseshell and the interesting scallop design on the corner which adds an eye-catching flash to the blade.
Plate 5.63

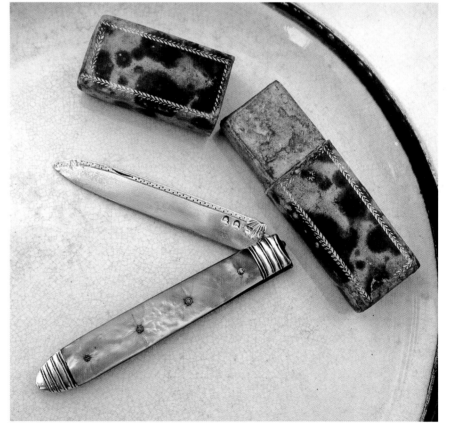

Silver-hafted neo-rococo set by Joseph Taylor c.1816. Strangely these were assayed in Birmingham, yet there is no anchor mark. The cusp in the base of the assay (lion) cartouche is the only differentiation. In Sheffield the cartouche was rectangular until 1918.
Plate 6.1

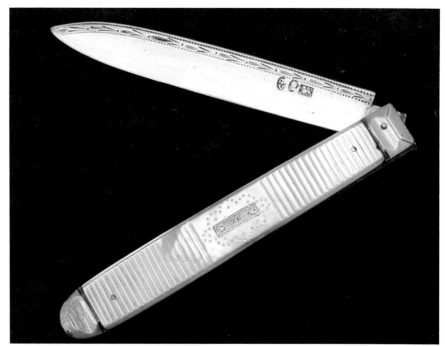

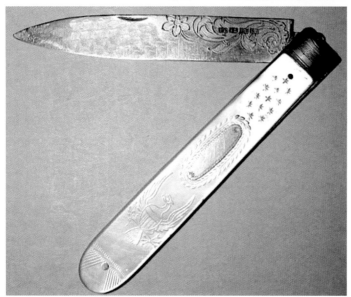

The engraved stripe-bellied eagle and 13 stars may have had some American connection. The knife has been stamped with 4 sponsor's marks in place of normal hallmarks, I.L for Joseph Law c.1825.
Plate 6.3

This period is fundamental to the change in decoration, particularly of the haft. The Birmingham goldsmiths become more productive in pocket fruit knife making: some became successful enough to start larger businesses.

Gradual changes in taste touched the not-quite-so-humble pocket fruit knife. As Regency styles blossomed, the gentle elegance of the neo-classical was modified and then replaced by the coming fashionable influence from the Middle East.

Pocket fruit knives did not really show this influence until the mid 1820s when botanical motifs were engraved into nacre hafts although decorative feathering of the haft base started in about 1810 (*plate 6.27*). *Piqué* work continued to thrive but in this case using numerous studs or pins to form geometrical patterns or designs such as lozenges or butterflies. Bright-cut engraving of *piqué* rosettes was no longer required and the pins were too small anyway. This pinwork was often combined into carved and domed areas of nacre or ivory, diagonally or vertically cross-hatched (*plates 6.4 & 6.5*).

Pearl cutting

As nacre had become the prime scaling material due to its cheapness, ease of carving and engraving quite apart from its physical appearance, it was used for scaling 90% of pocket fruit knives and forks As decorative styles changed again the role of the pearl cutter became increasingly more important and continued to progress throughout the 19th century. Sheffield, in particular,

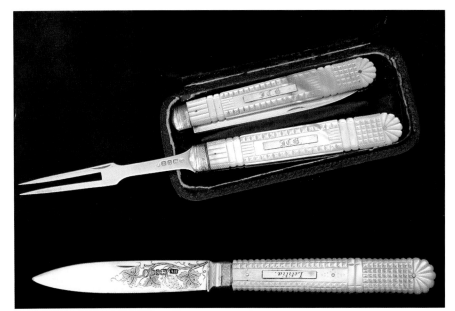

Aaron Hadfield was a leading manufacturer at this time: the set (1827) and the single knife below (1838) typify his craft. *Plate 6.4*

PAGE 133

became a centre for this craft, and although those who practised the craft were part of a production chain, biographical records are scant. None appear to have signed their work except for commissioned or exhibition knives. Yet certain styles and designs, characteristic of certain pearl cutters are apparent on many knives and forks and were used by the coterie of knife makers.

Pearl cutters were often linked to silversmithing firms but a few seem to have traded exclusively in nacre at this time until they or their descendants started silversmithing. Pigot's *1829 Sheffield Directory of Professions & Trades* lists two pearl cutters working for the firms of Atkin, Oxley and Law (mark LL) and Joseph Mappin and Son (JM, registered as a plate worker in 1833 and but not as a silversmith until 1848 J.M). In 1834 Pigot again lists pearl cutters for Mappin and for Atkin & Oxley (A&O) but without Joseph Law, as well as John & Henry Hardy (not registered as a silversmithing business until 1898), John Roberts (JR in 1844) and William Staniforth (WTS [son] but not until 1902), suggesting that the pearl cutting trade was growing.

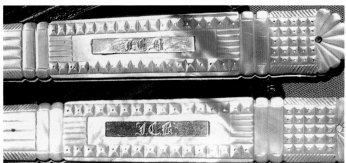

Nacre scales became thicker and broader, creating a larger area for decoration and lessening the risk of damage during riveting. The thicker and larger scales enabled pearl cutting, metal inlaying and carving to reach new heights of excellence and style as the century progressed, with even more challenging shapes appearing as fashions changed.

Close-up of Hadfield hafts showing the painstaking precision of his pearl cutter's workmanship. *Plate 6.5*

Haft decoration

Prior to moving on with their designs, pearl cutters re-iterated some patterns for pocket fruit knife scales in use about 20 years before. Nacre scales were cut with transverse stripes that were continued onto the copper bases of bolsters (as web extensions), particularly when longer bolsters were revived (*plates 6.9 & 6.10*); others were cross-hatched. Cross-hatched (quilted or domed) scales were often centred with silver

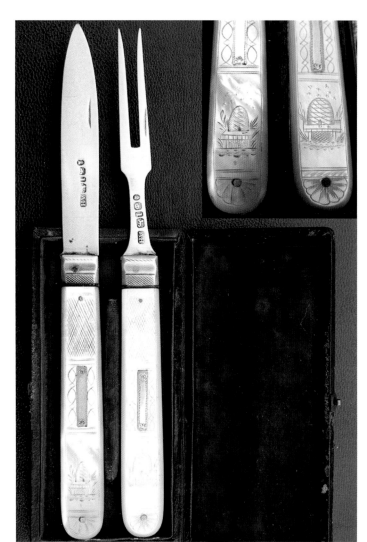

The fine quality of Aaron Hadfield's workshop is again shown in this fine pair engraved with beehive motifs, possibly depicting commerce, 1833. The slight disparity of the engravings suggests the possibility of a different pearl cutter for each piece.
Plate 6.6

Blade types and decoration

Blades remained largely undecorated until the end of this period and were still the preserve for later patterns of bright cutting. By the 1830s, the Botanical Era began to spread its tendrils and fruit motifs onto blades as well as hafts. Sansom, Hadfield, Atkin & Oxley and the Nowill family were some of the better makers who followed this decorative trend and produced some exceptionally fine items. Blade shapes also altered as the point was occasionally swaged forming a short double-edged point. Swaged blades were made with a long groove (or 'French nail nick') running from ricasso to swage, replacing the more conventional crescent-cut nail nick, since there was no room for it on a double-edged blade (*plate 7.14 & 7.47*).

Bolsters

Between 1815 and 1830, bolster patterns and dimensions varied greatly. The long bolster of the 1770s and 80s was reintroduced to pocket fruit knives as bolsters on steel-bladed pocket-knives became longer once again. The firm of Barlow (Sheffield) appears to have been one of the instigators of this style and the Barlow name appears on several engravings of such pocket-knives in Joseph Smith's 1816 *Key* (*plate 6.11*). Many other makers would also have contributed to this temporary style change as well so that the term 'Barlow Knife', as it has been frequently called, is a misnomer for fruit knives as no known examples were made by Barlow.

Bolsters were still made from copper or copper alloy and then silver-plated. They were decorated by die stamping in a press, with either a few or many transverse grooves

wire studs, known as *piqué clouté*, particularly noticeable on thicker scales which were less vulnerable to damage during manufacture (*plate 6.4*). Feathered and Anthemion-shaped bases (*plate 6.27*) appear to have marked the beginning of these changes in style and many knives in this style were exclusive to Thomas Sansom who registered his mark in 1808 but didn't start fruit knife production until c. 1815. Post 1820s nacre scales gradually developed a more geometric style leading to the beginning of the Botanical Era during the reign of William IV (1830-1837). Engraved vine and other botany-related motifs started to trail along both haft and blade, and other fruit motifs followed during the reign of Queen Victoria.

Bouquets of flowers and baskets of fruit started to appear during the 1810s but more commonly post 1820: (*upper*) by John Nowill, 1827 with a scallop shell cap; (*lower*) c.1810.
Plate 6.7

(*plate 6.9*). By c.1825 longer bolsters were gradually retired and by the 1830s short bolsters were entirely back in fashion again. Haft decoration influenced even more the form of the bolster decoration as bolster styles gradually moved on from Georgian neo-classicism to an organic complex of differing styles throughout the rest of the 19th century.

Metal-hafted knives and forks

The style of silver-hafted knives and forks broke away from that of their nacre-hafted cousins at this time, following those used for pocket quill knives. Joseph Taylor of Birmingham and William and John Nowill of Sheffield were both exponents in the production of knives and forks with cast silver hafts depicting rococo-revival shells, flowers and scrolling leaves (*plate 6.1*). Both the Nowill and Law families of Sheffield also produced fine silver-hafted knives die-stamped with Arcadian motifs – shells and anthemia, the central panels decorated with standing figures of period wild-fowlers, hunters or the classical figures of Flora or Ceres (*plates 6.14 & 6.15*). These same haft patterns were also used in the manufacture of quill

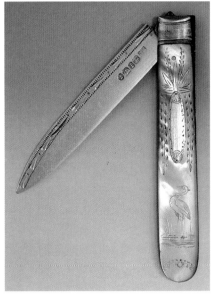

Knife by Samuel Kirkby, 1829, the haft engraved with a heron, perhaps symbolising England's watchfulness for enemies in the post-Napoleonic period.
Plate 6.8

knives. A few were even produced by silver-plating onto die-stamped pewter hafts (*plate 6.16*). These styles and techniques may well have influenced the future production of pocket fruit knives in America.

Fruit knife blades were also incorporated into period and earlier apple corers. From the early 1800s a silver tubular apple corer with a scoop blade at one end might also have a silver fruit blade at the other. Each could be unscrewed, turned and screwed back into the handle. These tended to be made more by the Birmingham makers than Sheffield, typically by Joseph Taylor.

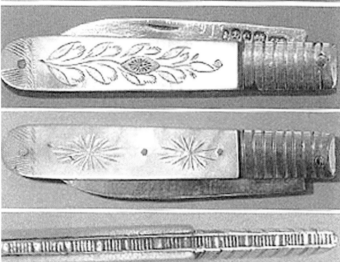

The partnership of Henry Atkin & John Oxley produced many fine fruit knives and forks. This knife would have been one of their cheaper standard items. At this time, the long bolster was revived for about 10 years perhaps following the popularity for the 'Barlow' knife (*next page*).
Plate 6.9

A similar style of knife by Thomas Nowill, 1823.
Plate 6.10

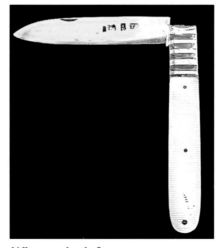

What to look for

Although the finest of pocket fruit knives and forks are only occasionally encountered in The Trade or on the Internet these days, some superstars can still be found. Good condition is obviously important and desirable and yet some items of unusual design or which commemorate an historic occasion are still rejected by some collectors, due to a small crack in the nacre or a crease in the blade, who prefer condition to historical interest.

Pocket fruit knives were made in different sizes from small and cheaper items about 2-3 inches (closed) to the more expensive (up to six inches). A few giants (up to 9 inches: *plate 5.62*) were also made but are rare. The cheaper items were bladed with thin silver sheet and tend to lack the silver coatings to the spring and bolster (*plate 5.20*). Nacre or bone scales were left plain, or might be more crudely or rudimentarily engraved.
[For more detailed information, see last chapter.]

Plated blades

As the silver-plating industry continued to gain strength from the need for low cost combined with elegance, the cheaper end of the pocket fruit knife industry began to produce full-sized items bladed with German Silver (cupro-nickel-zinc alloy) and then plated with silver. Plated pocket fruit knives of this type began to appear during the 1820s and continued to be made for a further 70 years (*plate 6.25*). Close plating of blades also continued but was later subsumed by the cheaper electroplating technique. Close plating was always vulnerable along the cutting edge of the blade and where damaged or worn away, has produced unsightly patches where the blade subsequently blackened due to its carbon steel composition. It could equally oxidise underneath the silver envelope leading to raised sinuous lines in the silver due to the gradual spread of the underlying oxidation products from the carbon

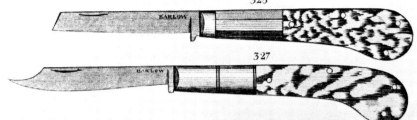

Page from Joseph Smith's *Manufactures of Sheffield*, 1816 showing two pocket knives marked BARLOW with their characteristic long bolsters. *Plate 6.11*

steel blade. The need for plated pocket fruit knives continued during the ensuing years and is discussed in greater detail in the following chapter.

Makers

A handful of makers became quite renowned for making pocket fruit knives, as well as other small and fancy items. Larger firms produced catalogues of their wares, suggesting that they were making a great many pieces to tickle the fancies of romantics and aesthetes, but I have never seen a vendor's catalogue showing pocket fruit knives older than c. 1890. The diversity of patterns at this time, was immense. Among the many makers of pocket fruit knives during this period was Thomas Sansom [TS] a typical exponent of the feathered and anthemion base, later incorporating Doves of Peace and olive branches into his designs during the 1820s. Aaron Hadfield [A.H] also known as Hatfield, produced items of the finest quality and is probably the most desirable maker from this time. He also produced some cheaper knives. His styles were often similar to those produced by the partnership of Henry Atkin and John Oxley [A&O] and it's likely that they shared the same pearl cutters. Both of these firms deserve mention for their production of blades engraved or chased with vine motifs and nacre hafts cut with geometric and quilted designs, inlaid with fine *piqué* work. The equally renowned Nowill family

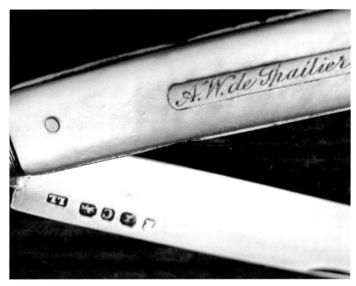

of Sheffield cutlers also made pocket fruit knives. Thomas [TN – c. 1790/1800], Joseph [IN - c. 1810], John I [J.N – c. 1830], William [WN – c. 1840] and, later, John II [JN – c. 1880] produced fruit knives of generally good quality but usually of a plainer or more restrained design. In Birmingham the firm of George Unite [GU] specialised in small silver fancy items, the pocket fruit knives and forks that came from his workshop being normally of finest quality. He seems to have created a particular type with a haft slightly reminiscent of a violin (*plates 6.28 & 7.36*).

Hallmarking (1815-1830)

Striking a full set of hallmarks on the blade gradually became the standard during this period, as hallmarks for

As the 19th century progressed, ownership markings became more commonplace on blade and shield, perhaps denoting an upsurge in fruit knife popularity. *Plates 6.12 & 6.13*

Two neo-classical silver scaled knives with die-struck motifs depicting a wild-fowler, by Aaron Hadfield 1828 and (right) a standing figure of Flora, by Thomas Nowill 1824. Note the increased use of anthemia and scallop shells at this time.
Plate 6.14

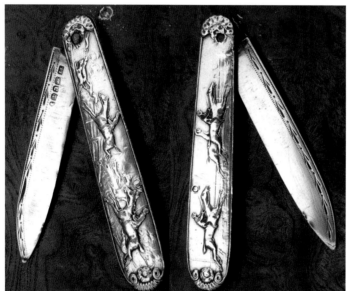

Front and back of silver-scaled fruit knife with die-struck equestrian motifs: Joseph Law, 1824.
Plate 6.15

smaller items were made even smaller than before. By 1820 the hallmarks were grouped together in a stub and mounted into a hallmarking press. A piece that had passed the assay test was placed in the press and the sides closed together by turning a weighted ('fly') handle (*plate 6.20*).

Spherical weights, attached to the turning handle allowed easy control and balance of the press during the delicate process of hallmarking. The result was a neat row of evenly spaced hallmarks of the same depth which could all be fitted on the blade (*plate 6.17*). Many knives have been

found struck with the date letter 'C' or 'c' as a full set on the blade, and collectors have often debated whether this might be for the year of 1811 or for 1826, since the two date letters are so similar. This date letter is often found on knife blades by LL or AH who must have both sent large parcels of blades for assay during the year. The answer is 1826 since the duty mark is a typical George IV smaller size whether in an oval cartouche or tri-cusped. Also the marks are in a neat row indicating stub marking, and the sponsor mark of LL for Atkin, Oxley & Law was not registered until October 1824. The earliest mark for Aaron Hadfield (or any other AH mark variant) was registered in March 1818.

Britannia hallmarked set

Another hallmarking rarity was discovered when I was offered a fine knife and fork set struck with Britannia Standard hallmarks from Sheffield, 1823 (*plate 6.30*). During that year, a parcel of only four blades made from 95.8% (Britannia Standard) silver was submitted for assay by the sponsor, Aaron Hadfield. Since Sheffield possessed no small-work Britannia hallmark punches, the Assay Master was obliged to use the large-work punches instead. This he did by hand-striking with great care so as not to distort the shank or blade of either piece, and only singly struck each hallmark, which is why they appear rather shallow and faint, particularly the huge Britannia mark as wide as the fork's shank! The inversion of the U, on the fork, may be another example of Matthew Sayles' apparently slipshod hallmarking as he was Master from 1809-1833 *ref. page 140*. In contrast, the smaller sponsor's mark has been deeply (double) struck, being a normal small-sized punch, whereas the Assay Office punches were struck only after the sponsor had submitted the blades for assay with his own mark already present.

Further problems with duty marks

The George IV duty mark was made smaller than that of George III to conform to the size of the other stub-mounted marks and is quite recognisable on its own due to the slightly narrower dimensions of the head (*plate 6.17*). During the king's lifetime the duty mark was often portrayed in a tri-cusped cartouche, similar in style but still smaller than that of George III. By the time of William IV's reign (1830), the George IV duty mark was still being used (the new King's head mark was late in arriving again), so the duty mark was struck sideways, perhaps to denote the former monarch's demise but there is no actual record of this fact. William IV's duty mark was made slightly bigger and more circular, rather like the George III duty mark from 1786-1797 and it lacked the earlier king's collar and laurel crown.

New punches for each year were ordered from the Stamp Office in York. On receipt of these, the old ones were supposedly returned. Somehow Sheffield seems to have had problems with the late arrival of duty punches at significant times (e.g. doubling of duty, the death of monarchs). A collection of plaster impressions of duty marks shows that William IV's head was not actually struck until 1835 and there are some hallmark sets with the new duty mark being struck only in 1836 (see next pages)! Bradbury's *Guide to Marks of Origin*...., known as the

Another neo-classical knife, the haft adorned thickly with oak leaves die-struck in pewter then plated with silver: Joseph Nowill 1829. *Plate 6.16*

(*Above*): Three sets of stub set hallmarks, all in a neat row and all from the workshop of LL for Atkin, Law and Oxley. There is always debate whether the letter C is for 1811 or 1826? 1811 marks would be slightly larger and less in a neat row. LL was registered in 1824. *Plate 6.17*

(*Left & lower left*): 1826 (letter c) seems to have been a bumper year for production in Sheffield and yet it is often mistaken for 1811 (letter C) when tang-marking was in its heyday. *Plates 6.18*

Another from the LL partnership: a scarce multi-bladed compendium 1823 with a fruit knife blade included. The steel blades bear the cutler's mark for Thomas Nowill.
Plate 6.19

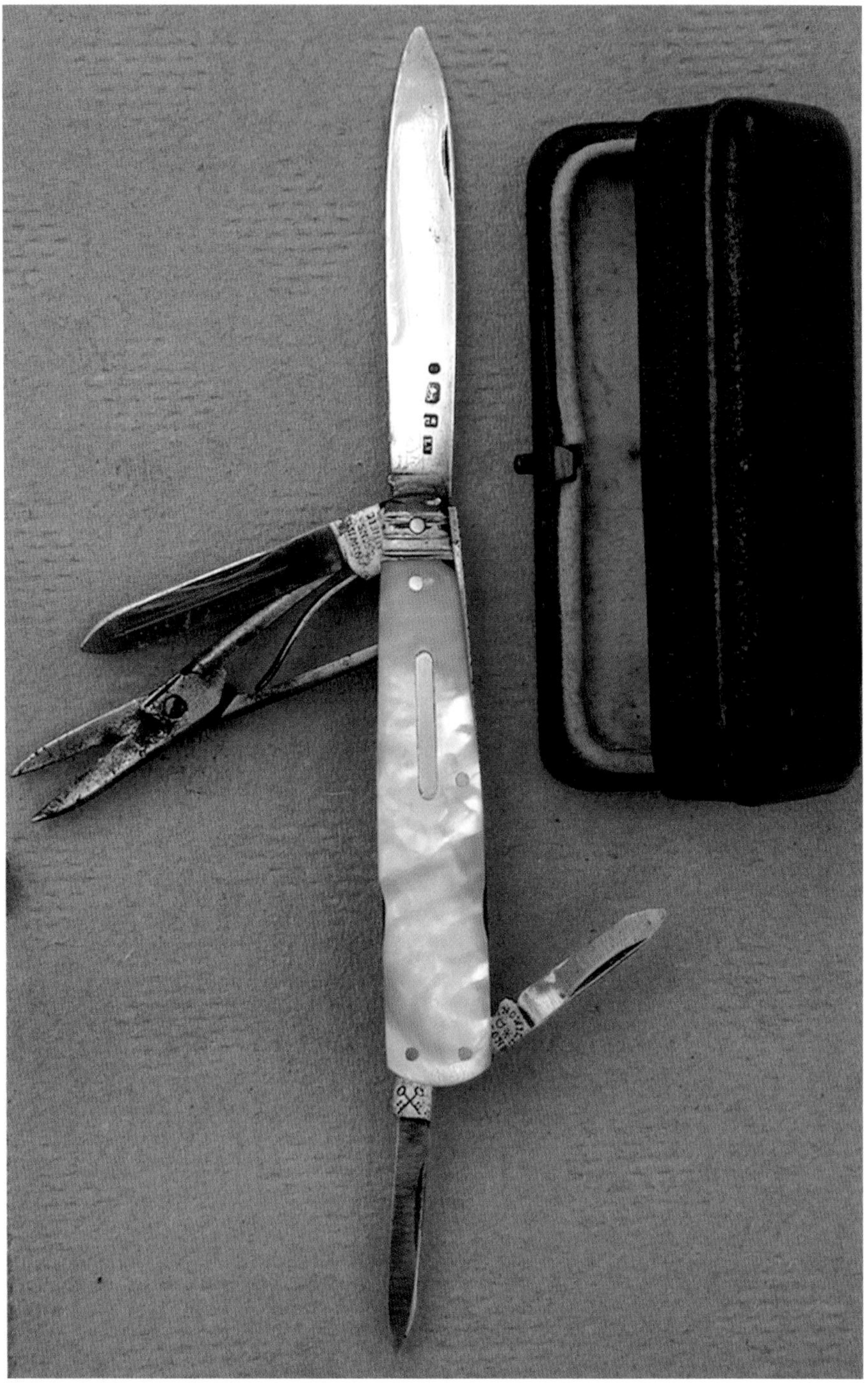

"Little grey book of hallmarks", also shows the changeover to William IV in 1835.

The assays were carried out by the father and son team, Matthew and Lewis Sayles, and there is correspondence to bear out that their work was sometimes lax. The striking of the duty marks from 1830 onwards, both upright and sideways, does lend some credence to this! A chance search in 1869 revealed an accumulation of 40 years worth of previous duty punches. Perhaps the Sayles family had stored these away against the eventuality of the next monarch's duty punch being late in arriving. To bear this out, when William died and Victoria became Queen in 1837, her duty punch was not issued and used in Sheffield until 1840!

The late Billy Ibberson standing by two old fly presses for hallmarking at Sheffield Assay Office. *Plate 6.20*

Birmingham suffered even more problems with duty marks, since the city never seems to have received a William IV smallwork duty mark and continued using the George IV duty stamp (right way up) until 1839/40 in Victoria's reign! According to Crisp-Jones (1981) a largework punch impression, which arrived in 1838, clearly shows William IV with his neck bare, but the smallwork punch closely resembles George IV's with his collar, rather than William IV's bare neck. In fact a small work punch was provided but items bearing its impression are curiously scarce! (*plate 6.21*) The problem of late issue for duty marks seems to have affected nearly all the provincial assay offices following the accession of both William IV and Victoria.

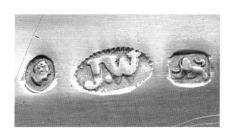

William IV small-work duty from a vinaigrette lid (courtesy of the Birmingham Assay Office). *Plate 6.21*

Conclusion

The end of this period formed a transition of style as Victoria came to the throne in 1837 and the new series of styles and design patterns continued to evolve and become even more adventurous.

Most unusual knife
combining a cheaper
silver-plated bright-cut
bordered blade with an
extravagant cast floral
bolster and spine and floral
rosettes. Owner's marking
of H P on shield and
engraved date (presumed)
of 1821 on ricasso.
Plate 6.22

POCKET FRUIT KNIVES: 6 LATER REGENCY TO PRE-VICTORIAN. ROCOCO AND NEO-CLASSICAL RE-VISITED, 1815-1837

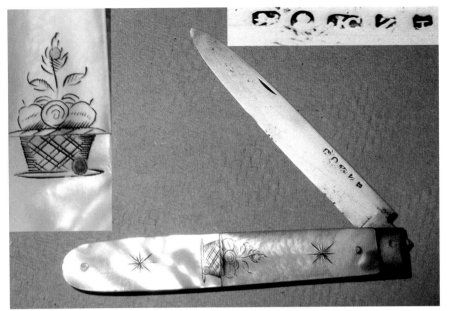

Silver-bladed knives, scaled with nacre off-cuts, are quite scarce. This, by James Collins, Birmingham, 1823 the join cunningly concealed by the edges of the fruit basket. *Plate 6.23*

Another fruit knife with nacre scales made from off-cuts, c.1820 and presented to a Master of Foxhounds, perhaps in memory of a loyal hound Corser, whose portrait is engraved on the other side but rather obscured by rivets. Note the steel rather than silver blade. *Plate 6.24*

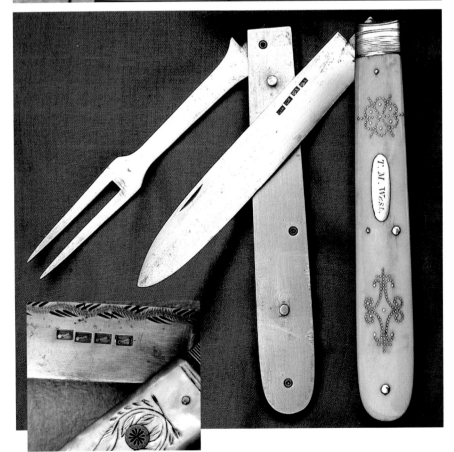

A fine and large slotting set with repeated marks of 2 rows of pellets, similar to those from the 'tadpole mark' workshop (inset, on a brass blade), c.1830. The above set with blades of German Silver, ivory scales superbly inlaid with *piqué clouté* work. *Plates 6.25 & 6.26*

Modified neo-classical.
Squared anthemion-ended knives and forks seem to typify the work of Thomas Sansom (1828 and c.1810) combined with feathering (*centre*) or a peace motif of a dove and olive branches surrounding the central shield. Aaron Hadfield also seems to have used this style later on (1840) but less often than TS.
Plate 6.27

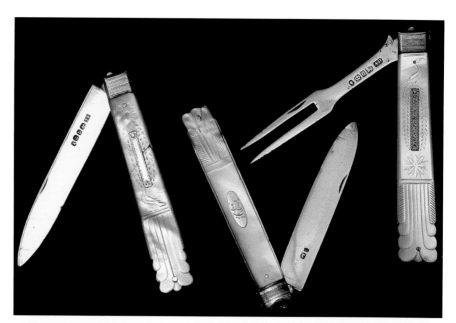

PAGE 144

Another 'signature style' but this time for the renowned Birmingham goldsmith George Unite whose mark was first registered in 1832.
Plate 6.28

A finely-made knife with a brass blade and haft mounts. The fine decoration suggests that it may well have been made (c.1830) to imitate a gold-bladed knife.
Plate 6.29

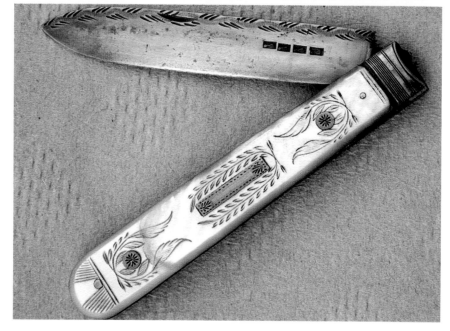

POCKET FRUIT KNIVES: 6 LATER REGENCY TO PRE-VICTORIAN. ROCOCO AND NEO-CLASSICAL RE-VISITED, 1815-1837

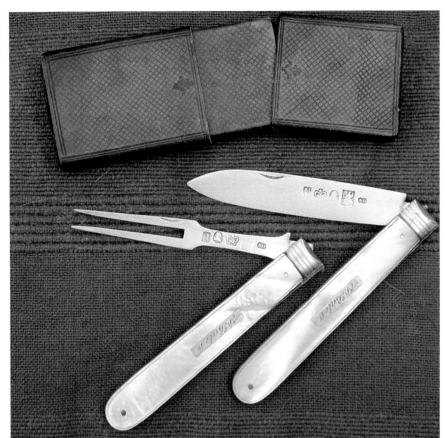

A fine-quality set by Aaron Hadfield 1823 and presumably made by commission in Britannia standard silver. The Sheffield Assay Master lacked any small-work punches for this standard and resorted to using the large-work punches which explains the larger sized marks in relation to Hadfield's normal-sized sponsor mark.
Plate 6.30

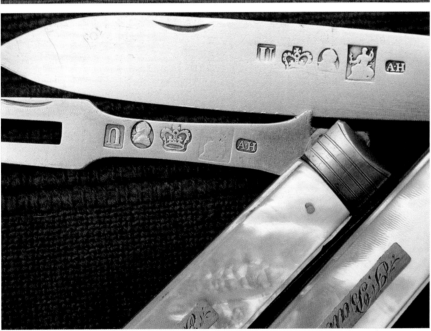

Problems with duty marks - upright or sideways?

A series of duty marks for Sheffield (top to bottom): 1829, 1835, 1836, 1837, 1838, 1839 (twice). Sheffield seems to have been dogged by the tardy arrival of new duty marks from London, following the deaths of both George IV and William IV! Note how the head is often stamped sideways for the years after each had died (except for 1836 and 1838). This may have been due to inefficiency of the assay masters in returning the expired punches to the York or London Stamp Offices. *Plate 6.31*

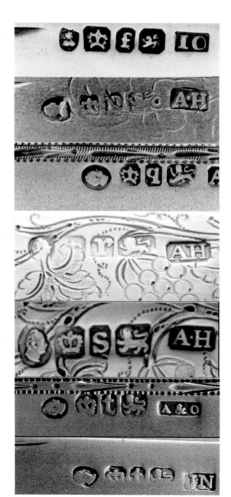

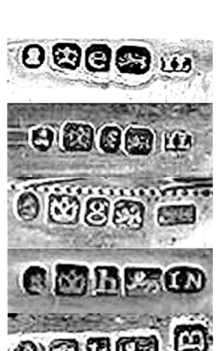

(far left): A sequence of Sheffield duty marks from 1823 to 1842. Note how the George IV duty mark was sometimes tri-cusped, sometimes oval. Bear in mind that George IV died in 1830 and William IV in 1837.
Plate 6.32

(left): William IV's accession Year 1830.

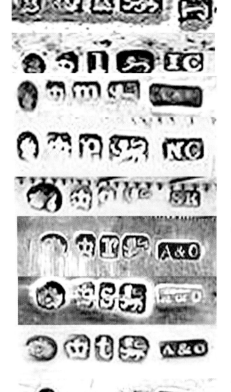

Still using Geo. IV duty in 1836

Victoria's accession year. First use of Will. IV duty mark, the year he died!

Victoria duty mark first used in year 1840

PAGE 148

Birmingham also had its problems with late duty marks. This knife assayed in 1838 shows a George IV duty mark. The Victorian duty mark also eventually appeared in 1840.
Plate 6.33

Series of hallmark sets from the Late Ted Kleinman's Birmingham fruit knife series. Note how the duty mark for George IV remains unchanged throughout the reign of William IV (1830-1837) and how Victoria's head doesn't appear until between 1839 and 1840.
Plate 6.34

1824

1829

1831

1832

1834

1838

1839

1840

1841

1842

Late Georgian knife by
Aaron Hadfield, 1826.
Note the renewed use
of the rosettes and circles
at this later date and
the flatness of the nacre
scales, compared with the
chamfered and curved
surfaces of the 1790-1810
era.
Plate 6.35

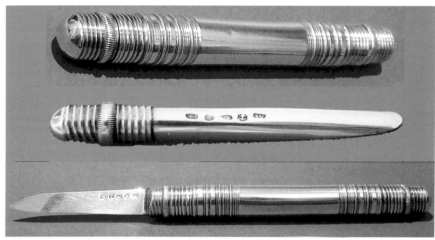

Fruit knife blades also
made an ideal adjunct
for apple corers, this
by Joseph Taylor of
Birmingham 1820. The
similarity of the W versus
w for 1794 and 1820 is
confusing but the marks on
the knife blade appear to
have been stub-mounted.
This was harder to achieve
on the corer with its
curved surface and when
stub marking was in its
infancy, so the handle set
of hallmarks were hand
struck.
*(Courtesy of Daniel Bexfield
Antiques).*
Plate 6.36

Slotting knife and fork sets are fairly common during the 1800s. By 1826 they are less usual and for the next 50-60 years are quite scarce until the locking format of the 1890s and early 1900s.
Plate 6.37

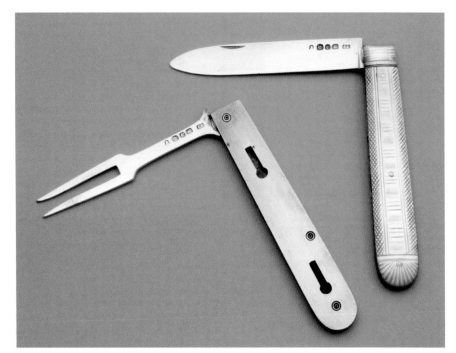

Cheaper end of the range fruit knives were rarely scaled with tortoiseshell. This example by Thomas Nowill, 1823 also shows a slight indentation of the haft so that the blade could be picked out more easily – an unusual refinement for a cheaper knife.
Plate 6.38

7 The extravagance of the Victorian period between 1837 and 1890

A glittering array of
Victorian decoration
centred with the
Queen & Prince Albert.
Plate 7.1

Souvenir pocket fruit knife commemorating the Great Exhibition of 1862, the Crystal Palace depicted on the obverse scale. Probably by Martin & Hall but over-stamped by Henry Wilkinson & Co who may have retailed these at the event. (*below*): The reverse side of the haft.
Plate 7.2

PAGE 152

During the first fifty three years of Queen Victoria's reign, the designs for pocket fruit knives and forks continued to evolve and took a noticeably bolder upturn in decorative style and overall quality. Some changes were subtle: fork blades becoming slightly curved along the inner edge, slightly shorter in length and with the tine points less needle-sharp than previously. At the same time, forks gradually started to decline in numbers as, presumably, matching sets started to decrease in popularity. By the 1900s forks were quite scarce.

Decoration was the buzzword at this time and haft designs, particularly, must have tested the skills of pearl cutters, who created the most astonishingly decorated nacre scales. Even as early as 1855 haft styles began to herald the approaching Aesthetic and Arts & Crafts movements (*plate 7.40*).

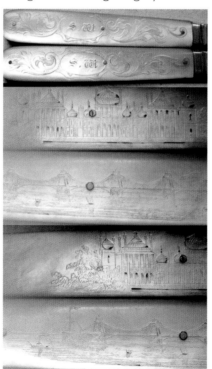

Commemorative items are scarce enough, let alone a set! These by Aaron Hadfield, 1850 showing Brighton's Pavilion and Chain Pier, both completed in 1823. These scenic items, like that of the Crystal Palace were probably made as souvenirs for visitors to the Great Exhibitions of 1851 (Hyde Park) and 1862 (Crystal Palace).
Plate 7.3

Early Victorian haft designs followed on from the William IV period, favouring botanical; including (not surprisingly) fruit motifs: trailing vines, decorously heaped fruit and the inevitable cornucopia which enjoyed a vogue during the mid century, particularly as it formed a conveniently and aesthetically curved base for the end of the knife (*plates 7.9 to 7.11*). Cornucopias were

Early Victorian pocket knives (left) by Aaron Hadfield 1840, still a leading name in fruit knife manufacture at this time with tulip-shaped haft, forecasting the Aesthetic and Arts & Crafts movements.
The lower knife by Joseph Mappin & Son, 1841, decorated in the more retro-style of William IV knives.
Plate 7.4

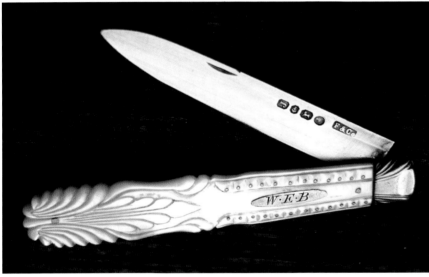

Typical Victorian knife by Foxall & Co of Birmingham 1858, combining neo-classicism (Anthemion terminal) with quilted *piqué clouté* work.
Plate 7.5

Part of nacre haft showing fine engraving of Cyclamen flowers, c.1860.
Plate 7.6

carved and engraved into both haft and blade, adding a touch of the continuing neo-classicism.

Organic knives

During the 1850s-70s ivory or bone was also used to make an entire knife, even the spring. The ivory blade was often stamped or engraved with the words FRUIT KNIFE, to prevent abuse. Bone examples were also produced to cater for the cheaper end of the market (*plate 8.39*) and some examples have been traced back to the 1820s. Tortoiseshell was revived as a scaling material for all types of pocket fruit knife, contrasting beautifully for those made with ivory

blades. Such hafts were rarely left plain and were frequently inlaid with cabled silver wire and fragments of highly prismatic ormer shell nacre to form birds perched on branches, with leaves and fruit. (*plates 7.13, 7.69 & 7.70*)

A few knives were made with blades of nacre (*plate 7.17*) but were probably too fragile to have survived in any quantity and are scarce. Towards the end of the century and later, souvenir knives were also made with horn blades (*ref. plate 8.39*).

Metal-hafted knives and inter-purchasing

Metal-hafted knives and forks continued in production and, during

Another masterpiece from Hadfield's workshop, 1840. The *piqué clouté* work is exceptionally fine and its undulating symmetry would have have been difficult to achieve on such a fissile substance as nacre.
Plate 7.7

A different style of haft by Hadfield's Birmingham rival, George Unite whose mark overstamps that of a Sheffield maker (maybe Hadfield), also assayed in 1840 and in Sheffield where Unite also registered his mark. The standing heron continued as a likely emblem of England watching her shores after the Napoleonic campaign.
Plate 7.8

the middle of the century, still adhered stylistically to the neo-classical / rococo revival mix of the 1820s (*plate 7.18*). By the 1880s they were decorated in more period taste with scrolling vegetation engraved into the metal surface or cast from moulds in deep relief. Components were occasionally assayed in different offices! Knives could be assembled, both blade and haft, by the same maker but marked at different assay offices. James Fenton, for example, registered

sponsor marks at both Sheffield and Birmingham and an example is shown bearing the anchor on the haft and the crown on the blade (*plate 7.21*). This disparity of marking seems to have been quite acceptable and suggests inter-purchasing of hallmarked blades and hafts between makers in order to complete orders. Sets often show a disparity of dates, with a fork blade assayed a few years earlier or later than the knife (see **hallmarking** *pages 157-8*). At this time the original sponsors' marks were more frequently over-stamped by those of the retailers (see *opposite page*). Although sliding knives were phased out by the 1820s, Victorian examples can occasionally be found, usually from the Birmingham manufactory of Hilliard and Thomason (*plate 7.26*). More unusual metal-hafted pocket fruit knives have come to light recently, echoing the styles of the later 18th century with slightly scimitar-shaped blades and scrolling pistol-grip hafts. These are quite small in size, being several inches when closed, but show a great elegance and neo-classical style, dating between c.1840 and 1890 knives of this Georgian revival style are scarce (*plate 7.22*).

The cornucopia was a design favoured during Victoria's reign, at first engraved, 1840, and later carved (*below*). *Plate 7.9 & 7.10*

Overstamping

Larger firms also had shops and sold pocket fruit knives into the retail trade and directly to the public. They evidently purchased blades and hafts from each other, probably to complete last minute orders. Sometimes the original sponsor's mark was overstamped with that of the retailer (*plates 7.28-30*) but instances of differing sponsor marks on silver hafts suggest an occasional laxity with over-stamping: for thinner gauge blades this laxity would have been a necessity! This can lead to a confusion of marks, even more for those with differing date letters (*see previous page*), and can be most confusing to present day collectors.

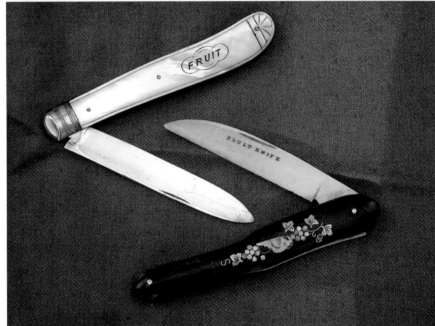

Cornucopia sets are always most appealing: this set by George Unite 1860.
Plate 7.11

(top right): Victorian forks are less common than Georgian and may signify a gradual downturn in making sets: *(upper)* by Harrison & Howson, 1842 *(lower)* by Gervaise Wheeler, 1840.
Plate 7.12

(right): Unmarked fruit knife, c.1870, the other comprising a bone blade and horn haft prettily inlaid with ormer shell chips and silver wire: both knives clearly labelled for their intended purpose.
Plate 7.13

This confusion is further exacerbated by the continued sharing of pearl cutters. There can be identical hafts with blades bearing differing sponsors' marks; a specific haft design was not always unique to one sponsor! The actual blade-making and knife assembly would not have been sub-contracted out so that the actual 'making of the knife' *per se*, was still specific to one particular workshop and one sponsor's mark. [For illicit 'marriages' of haft and blade refer to chapter 10.]

Hallmarking & duty marks (to 1920)
The Victoria head duty mark was only slightly quicker in arriving at the Sheffield assay office than those of former monarchs. William IV's head continued to be struck sideways as the duty mark at Sheffield until 1839-40 and the same for Birmingham although their mark was always upright. During Victoria's reign, the duty mark remained in the traditional oval cartouche until 1862, when the shape was altered to a square with canted corners, so that its shape would conform to the

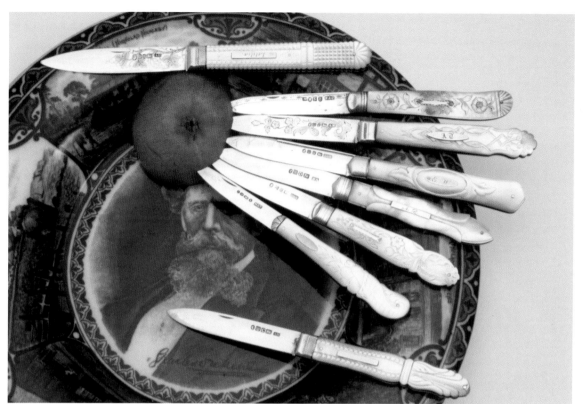

style of the other hallmarks (*plate 7.32*). By late 1862, the square cartouche had become established but in Birmingham the Queen's head remained in an oval cartouche until 1890. This was also when the duty mark was removed from all small items, leaving just the assay lion, date letter, office and sponsor's marks on the blade.

At this time, some Sheffield makers spread their business further afield as demand increased, and they registered marks at other assay offices including London, Birmingham and even Chester (*plate 7.33*) (though no fruit knives have yet been recorded from an actual Chester-based sponsor). The Sheffield and Birmingham assay registers record only the original works address but none of their outlets. Examples from assay offices further afield are even scarcer, but a later example was found in a collection, made by Charles Lamb, and hallmarked in Dublin in 1907

(*plate 7.31*). None have yet been found from any of the Scottish assay offices, Newcastle or Exeter despite occasional confusion between the 'tight rectangular cartouche' surrounding the assay lions of both Sheffield and of Exeter. A few of the larger Sheffield firms, such as Thomas Bradbury, had outlets in London, and for a short period (at least for several later 19th century dates) he had the added cachet of having his blades marked in the capital (*plate 7.34*). Knife-and-fork sets from this time

A fan of knives from 1838 to 1868 showing typical early to mid-Victorian haft and blade decoration. The fourth knife down has a 'French' nail nick & swaged blade (enlarged on another knife below).
Plate 7.14

Engraved fruit designs on both haft and blade, by J Y Cowlishaw, 1855.
Plate 7.15

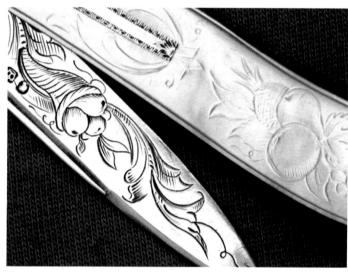

A Victoria & Albert knife by Walker & Hall, 1875. J E Bingham was the principal of the firm and his mark was only superseded by the familiar W&H pennant in 1894.
Plate 7.16

Unusual nacre-bladed knife c.1890.
Plate 7.17

often show a disparity of hallmark date letters and since parcels of blades sent for assay were often enormous, the hallmarking of so many blades could have extended over St Dunstan's day (19th of May) and the annual change of date letter. There are many examples of knife blades and fork blades bearing sequential year dates indicating this

or that older assayed stock was still in assembly during the next assay year.

Makers during this period.

The manufacture of pocket fruit knives reached new heights at this time. A handful of workshops produced the finest knives – Aaron Hadfield (continuing), Martin & Hall, Henry Wilkinson, J&J Bell, John Oxley and Henry Atkin, now as individual firms. One of the more remarkable was that of John Yeomans Cowlishaw whose JYC mark should be familiar to even novice collectors. Knives, at this time, were top quality using the foremost of pearl cutters (*plate 7.40*) and his workshop produced some of the finest mid-19th century knives. He became a pillar of the Sheffield community but died by his own hand in 1894, following the death of his wife. His workshop continued to produce fine pocket fruit knives until about 1900; quality then declined to the level of the mass-produced cheaper items, perhaps due to demand and the loss of their principal. The mark was changed to J.Y.C sometime between 1903 and 1907; both marks ran concurrently for a few years although the mark with the stops was smaller and confined to smaller wares only (*plates 7.44 & 8.38*).

Martin & Hall also continued making fine pocket fruit knives so it seems odd that these were totally absent from a complete catalogue of their wares, c.1890, which came up for auction in 2005, although table fruit knives were included.
In Birmingham, George Unite and occasionally the partnership of Hilliard & Thomason, continued to produce wares that rivalled Cowlishaw's in quality of both design and finish.

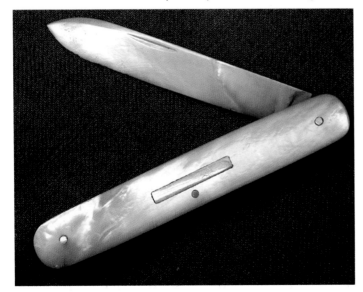

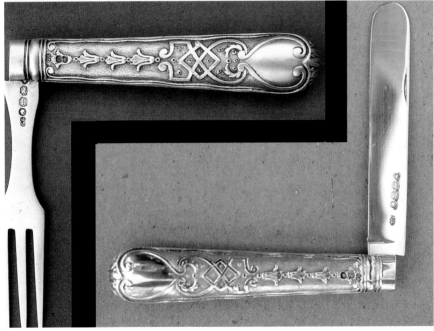

Silver-hafted knives were often lavish in style and a variety of designs were revived throughout Victoria's reign: neo-classical (*left*): 1856, neo-Rococo (*right*): 1889 by Brookes & Crookes and a Celtic/Tudor mix known as Elizabethan 1863 (*below*) by George Adams, London. *Plates 7.18 & 7.19*

Plated examples

Few collectors seem to realise that pocket fruit knives and forks were also made with blades of base metal such as brass, to resemble gold, and a white alloy of nickel, copper and zinc, known as 'German Silver' and electroplated with silver. This is rather unusual, considering that fruit-eating was still something of a luxury and yet many plated folding fruit knives (and a few sets) were made during the 1840s when the newly discovered process of electroplating silver onto German Silver largely superseded the more expensive silver fusion-plating onto copper. The whitish metal blade had the added advantage of being less noticeable when the silver plating wore away with use.

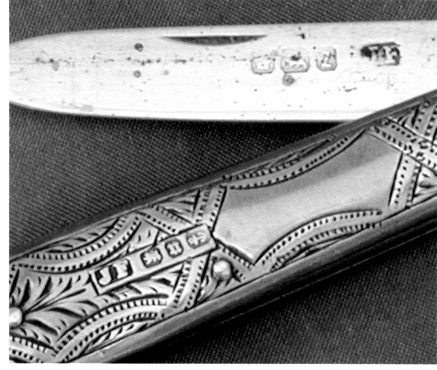

(left to right): Knives that sold at the Army & Navy stores in London were additionally stamped with an A&N retailer's mark: made by Cowlishaw 1898 with a hammered finish, keeping in touch with the Arts & Crafts movement. The stylised ivy leaves of the centre knife are more in keeping with Aestheticism, by Hilliard & Thomason, using Chester office in 1864.
Plate 7.20

(above right & right): A knife assayed at Sheffield 1892 (blade) and Birmingham 1894 (haft), both by James Fenton whose mark was registered at each office.
Plate 7.21

The basic construction was the same as for any spring-backed folding knife: the blades were made from blanks of German Silver, shaped by machine stamping and then plated with silver by electro-deposition. Some blades appear never to have been plated – no trace of silver having been found even in such crevices as the nail nick or the pseudo-hallmarks. Hafts were made largely from nacre or bone but, so far, there has been no record of tortoiseshell being used on a plated knife. Cheaper mother-of-pearl was invariably used and many hafts were scaled with off-cuts of that material (*plates 7.51 & 7.53*). The joins in such knives were either disguised or engraved to give the product a

better finish. Although each knife and fork was likely destined for a less discerning market, much skill and attention was still lavished upon it. Plated hafts were made in a different way and many were used in conjunction with silver-bladed knives. The haft was made from base metal, usually brass, and then coated with solder. A thin sheet of silver was applied and the silver was bonded

Small gilt knife by Francis Higgins, London 1846. Note the scimitar blade, reminiscent of the 1770-90 period, perfectly fitted in a Hunt & Roskell box. *(Courtesy of Daniel Bexfield Antiques).*
Plate 7.22

Unusual scroll-ended knife by Edward Hutton, Sheffield, 1889.
Plate 7.23

PAGE 161

Four cusp-ended knives, 1844-1873, decorated with fine engraving, mainly from Henry Atkin's workshop. The significance of the Prince of Wales' feathers motif can only guessed at since he was only 3 or 4 in 1844 when this knife was assayed.
Plate 7.24

PAGE 162

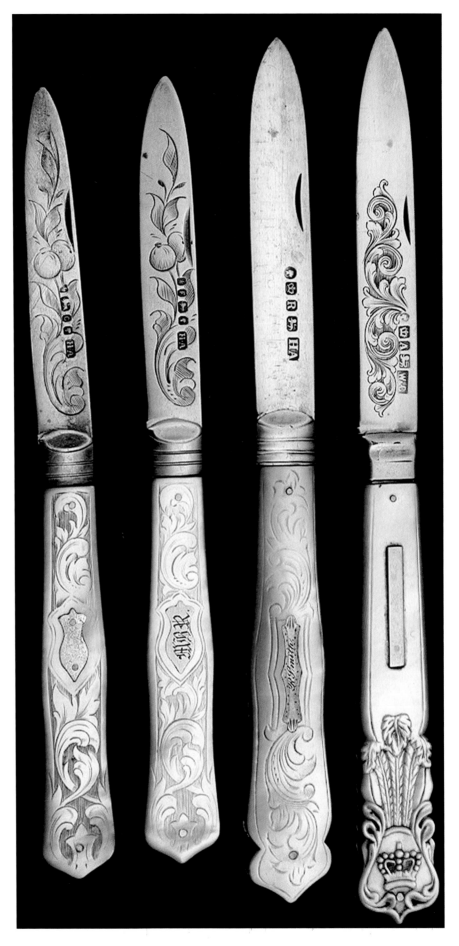

POCKET FRUIT KNIVES: 7 THE EXTRAVAGANCE OF THE VICTORIAN PERIOD, 1837-1900

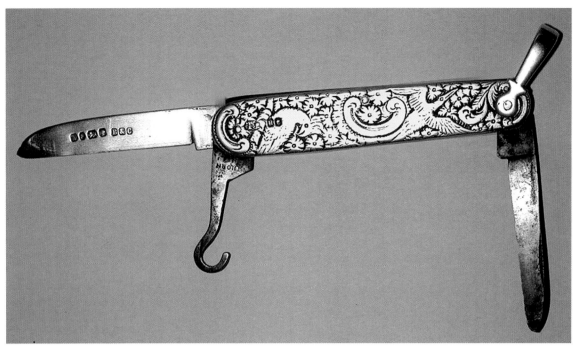

to the solder in a similar manner to the close-plating technique but using a gas flame instead of a heated iron. Decorated hafts were made from die-stamped sheet silver, bedded onto solder and using just enough heat to melt the solder and make an effective join. This proved to be highly successful and even the detail of finely-decorated hafts is normally still visible. This process was also used for the coating of the base metal bolsters on earlier knives until about 1840, when the process was gradually replaced by cheaper electro-deposition or the use of German Silver for cheaper knives.

Plated folding fruit knives and forks are scarcer than their silver-bladed peers. This apparent paucity may be due to their smaller profit margin, considering the labour involved in their making and assembly. Only a handful of Sheffield silversmiths appear to have made plated knives. Others continued to produce cheaper knives, smaller in size with uncoated iron bolsters, uncoated springs and thin and easily-flexible blades.

Sponsors' Marks for plated blades

The firm's mark only was stamped on plated blades, as there was no need for an assay to be carried out. Sponsors split their corporate initials into a row of separate punch marks so, at a glance, they would resemble the hallmarks found on silver (*plates 7.55 to 7.57*). In order to distinguish plated wares from those made of silver, the makers often altered the typeface of the letters from Roman to Gothic. The usual **A&O** mark of Henry Atkin and John Oxley would be altered to a separated **A&O**. J.Y. Cowlishaw's JYC mark was represented with his silver sponsor's mark besides several device marks, although later knives from his workshop show that he changed to separate gothic letters c.1880/90 (*plate 7.52*). Meaningless device marks, such as the helmet used by Atkin & Oxley or the gothic M used by William Briggs (*plate 7.54*), were usually struck alongside the sponsor's initials but have since confused both collectors and dealers – several have thought

Combination fruit-*cum*-pocket knife with button hook by Brookes & Crookes, Sheffield 1873. *Plate 7.25*

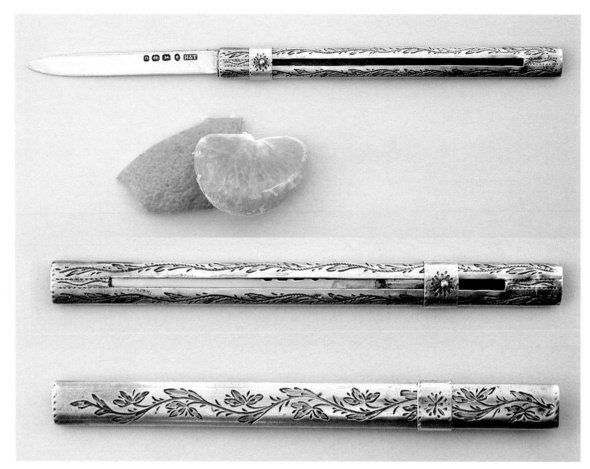

Much later sliding fruit knife
by Hilliard & Thomason,
Birmingham 1852.
Plate 7.26

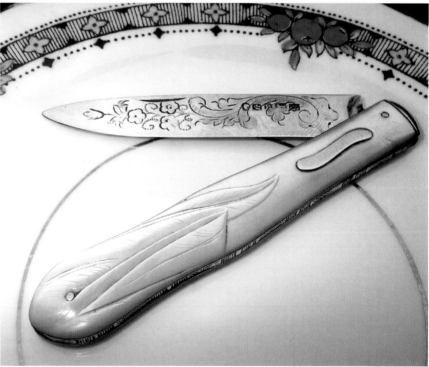

Another superb knife
by Martin, Hall &
Company, Sheffield 1858.
The folded-leaf design
is also a typical 'forerunner
design' of the coming
Arts & Crafts movement.
Plate 7.27

that a knife with the 𝕸 mark had been assayed in London in 1767! Other marks commonly found on silver-plated German Silver blades include the Tudor Rose, fleur-de-

lys for John Nowill and the gothic S, which usually stands for "and Son/s" but if it appears on its side can be considered as another device mark. Inexperienced dealers and

collectors are still misled by these marks, ascribing them to some rare provincial assay! Some device marks actually resemble silver hallmarks – versions of the sterling lion passant - while the 'town' marks of Birmingham and Sheffield were also used. John Gilbert's electroplating firm in Birmingham used the mark J.G alongside a recumbent anchor, presumably to

Over-stamping
Over-stamps by Hilliard & Thomason (left) even partly obliterating the sterling lion (1911) and by Harrison Brothers & Howson (below left) over-stamping Henry Wilkinson & Co. on a fork blade in 1866.
Plates 7.28 & 7.29

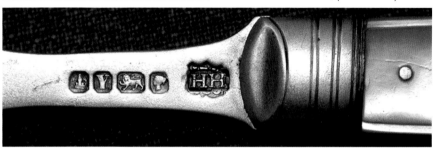

(below left): Another over-stamp but by J Y Cowlishaw onto another mark. Note how the scratched Roman numerals have been superseded by a stamped number on the tang at this time (1861).
Plate 7.30

(below): A scarce Dublin-assayed fruit knife by Charles Lamb. Although the date letter is post-Victorian (1907), the style of the haft has barely changed from the 1870s.
Plates 7.31

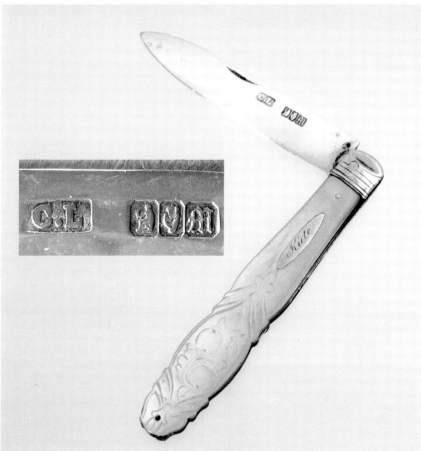

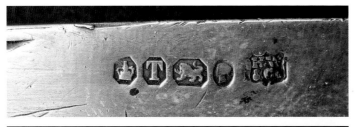

Changeover in cartouche for the Victorian Sheffield duty mark between 1861 and 1862, from oval to square with canted corners.
Plate 7.32

Use of other Assay Offices
The Chester office was used fairly frequently from c.1880-1910, in this case by Hilliard & Thomason in 1898.
Plate 7.33

(below): London was favoured, particularly by Thomas Bradbury of Sheffield who had a large parcel of blades assayed there in 1877-8
(lower): The upper blade by Francis Higgins in 1860.
Plate 7.34

avoid a disagreement with the Assay Office (*plate 7.56*). The style of his knives suggests a date around 1820-30, although they probably date from around 30 years later. (*ref. fork in plate 7.51*)

A few carbon steel blades were close-plated with silver but using a thinner silver envelope than that devised by Colmore (*ref. pages 55 & 56*). Each blade was dipped in molten solder and then a thin envelope of silver was heated, using a hot iron, to re-melt the underlying solder. The silver soon wore away from the cutting edge, with use, revealing the carbon steel blade – also detectable with a magnet. A few carbon steel blades were also electroplated but the softer and much thinner plating was not made to last.

Continental finer-quality plated knives and forks are rare - the majority were made with electroplated steel blades.
Some plated knives still bear the engraved names and initials of their original owners indicating that cheaper gifts were as well received as the more costly.

Gold blades

Gold-bladed pocket fruit knives and forks are extremely scarce from this period. Gilt items abounded, especially when produced as sets, but gold seems to have been abandoned, probably due to the lack of assay facilities in Sheffield and therefore the lack of quality control, which may have discouraged patronage of such otherwise costly pieces. Even Birmingham, with its gold assay facilities introduced in 1824, saw very few blade parcels for folding fruit knives submitted during this period. (*Refer also to 9CT mark, plate 7.68*).

Knife-and-Fork sets

Production of knife-and-fork sets gradually dropped to an all-time low towards the end of the 19th century, but prior to this gradual decline, they were still being made to the highest standards. Although they are slightly scarcer than Georgian, Victorian sets reflect the amazing standards of pearl cutting and design already mentioned. Forks from this period show that makers were still trying to turn this less fashionable trend around by producing wares of superior quality. Period catalogues show that many of these, with their finely carved nacre hafts, were among the most expensive items (*plate 8.24*). A few sets were made, even in pairs, combining knife and fork blades apparently situated at

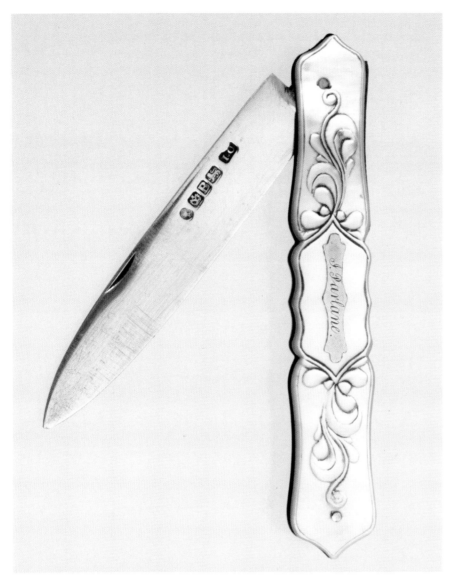

Typical Victorian bolsterless
knife with cusped ends
and fine scroll-carving,
by John Oxley, 1845.
Plate 7.35

either the same or opposing ends
of the haft, although if perfectly
symmetrical they could simply be
clipped back-to-front! (*plate 7.61*).

Steel-bladed knives
From the later 18th century
onwards, small single-bladed steel
pocket knives were produced,
matching the size and shape of their
silver-bladed cousins. Whether
these were used for fruit or for
some other purpose is unknown
but it is certainly quite likely that
they were either cheaper substitutes
for those who had less money but
wished to impress a young lady, or
for those who found the precious
metal blades too flimsy. Steel-

bladed knives appear to have been
as popular in France. Smaller and
dainty French lock-back steel-bladed
knives with gold ornaments are
occasionally found contained in rigid
pasteboard boxes veneered with
green-stained *galuchat* (stingray
or dogfish skin). Nacre hafts were
carved into various shapes including
hands or small animals, such as the
stylised loach fish shown (*plate
7.84*).

Stainless steel was not discovered
until the early 20th century, yet
these carbon steel blades are still in
remarkably good condition although
many have lost their original
polished finish.

A fine Victorian knife in its case. This design was much favoured by George Unite of Birmingham, 1851.
Plate 7.36

Another fine Victorian knife in its case, by Alfred Taylor of Birmingham c.1860.
Plate 7.37

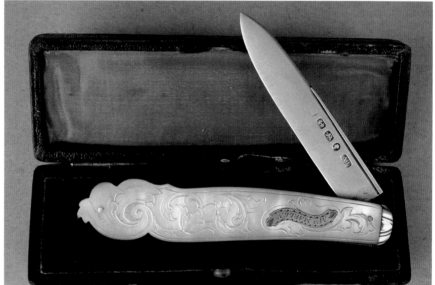

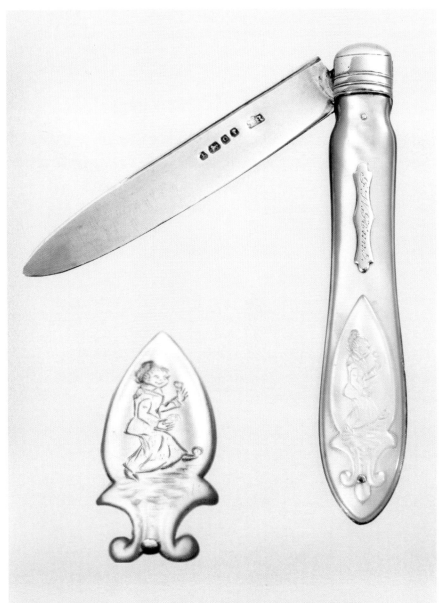

A rare piece by Thomas Royle of Sheffield, 1881. Royle registered his sponsor's mark in 1851 but his production of fruit knives was small. This knife with its raised leaf-shaped cartouche and smiling Japanese girl is most unusual.
Plate 7.38

Large families were quite usual for well-to-do Victorians. The much-loved Mrs Baker would have been delighted with this fine ear-of-wheat knife from her eight loving children & husband in 1874. The haft design reflecting aestheticism and with a fine strap-worked bolster.
Plate 7.39

One for a father, assayed in 1855 but not presented until 26 years later. The haft is just magnificent and shows an incredible 35 year advance to the Arts & Crafts and even Art Nouveau movements. Unsurprising that such a fine piece should come from the Cowlishaw workshop.
Plates 7.40

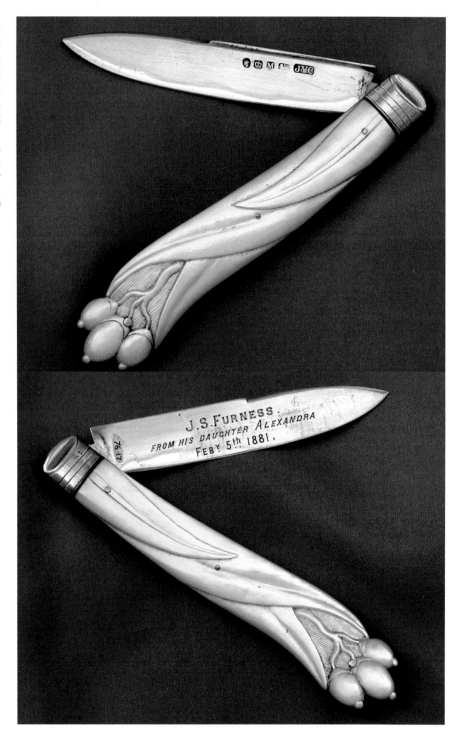

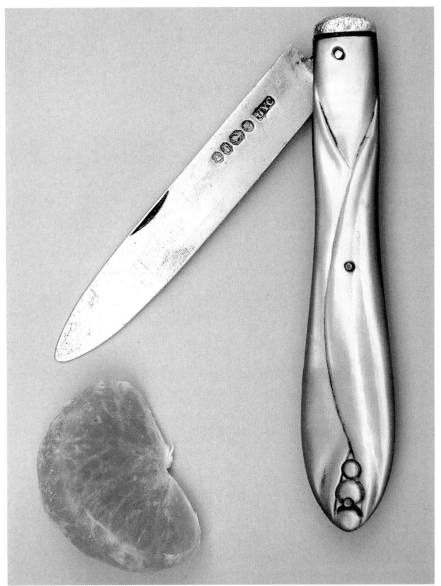

A similar design, reflecting Art Nouveau trends about 40 years earlier. This knife apparently from Cowlishaw's workshop, 1861, but over-stamping Henry Wilkinson & Co. This and the previous design were used by a *côterie* of Sheffield's finest producers of pocket fruit knives.
Plate 7.41

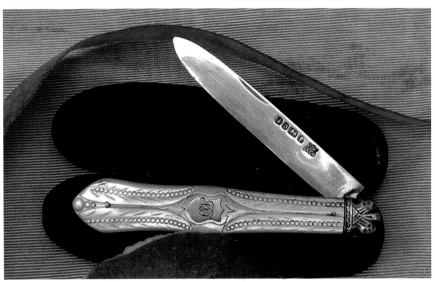

Pearl cutting often incorporated this beading effect into a haft, this by Henry Wilkinson & Co., 1871.
Plate 7.42

J Y Cowlishaw
The Cowlishaw workshop produced many fine pieces throughout the latter part of the 19th century. Although JYC took his life in 1894, the firm continued without him. The JYC sponsor mark was altered c.1905 to J.Y.C although the original JYC mark was still occasionally used. However, without its principal, the company appears to have been forced into producing many smaller, cheaper knives as well.
Plate 7.43

(right): Alteration of JYC marks.
Plate 7.44

1904

1905

1907

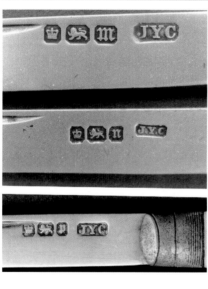

(right): A finer knife in silver, 1899.
Plate 7.45

Fine knife by Cowlishaw, 1866, again showing a variation of the rather Art Nouveau 'peapod' design.
Plate 7.46

Two more knives from the Cowlishaw workshop: the upper with a French nail nick and swage to the blade and an acanthus cartouche surrounding the ownership shield, 1855. The lower beautifully engraved with an acanthus leaf on the bolster and with vines trailing along the blade – a typical fruit knife motif from this period, 1864.
Plate 7.47

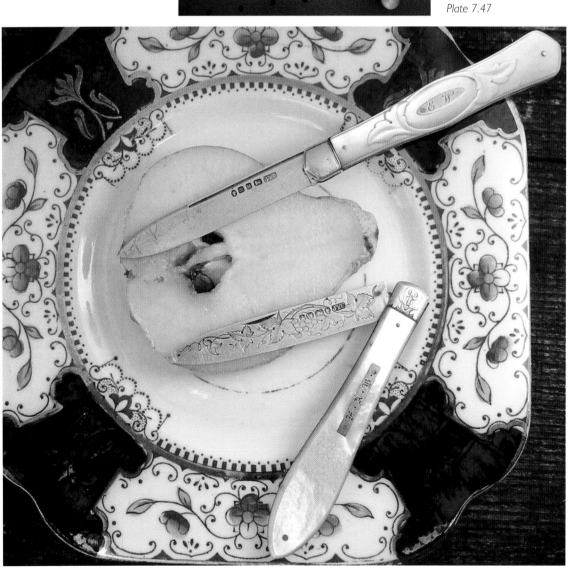

A smaller-sized onion-
based knife by Francis
Clark, Birmingham 1845.
Plate 7.48

Owners' markings were
all-important: the quality of
this shield engraved: AMY
is superior to the pearl
cutting.
Plate 7.49

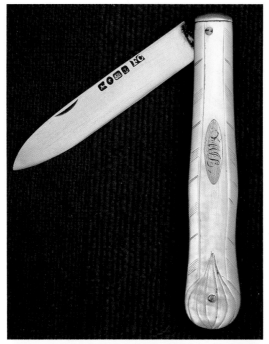
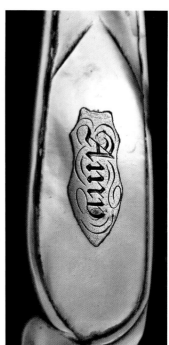

Small purse-sized
pocket-*cum*-fruit knife
c.1880, gold haft inlaid
with cut precious
stones by Fabergé
workmaster Gabriel
Niukkanen, typical of
Russian pre-revolutionary
extravagance.
Plate 7.50

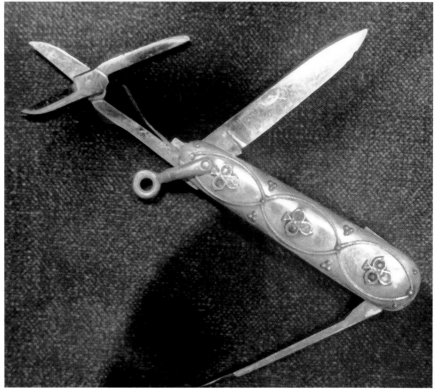

Plated bladed pocket fruit knives.

A range of German Silver-bladed knives and scarcer fork, some with silver electro-plated blades. (L - R) by John Gilbert c.1840, knife and a fork by William Briggs c.1830-40, Dove of Peace knife by Henry Atkin (alone) c.1850 - these two knives' hafts have been made up from nacre off-cuts, knife by Atkin & Oxley, c.1825-30.
Plate 7.51

Plater's mark of J Y Cowlishaw includes a Tudor Rose device, c.1860-70.
Plate 7.52

Although some have become rather scruffy and would be shunned by many collectors, these plated knives are still a valuable source of information: the lower knife with its worn electro plated blade reveals the underlying cupro-nickel alloy; another hafted with the same material (above) and another plain nacre-scaled knife (above) both by Thomas Marples & Son c.1870; one by J Y Cowlishaw (above) with engraved nacre, as good as a silver example and (top) a knife by an anonymous maker who used the three repeated 'tadpole' marks as his trademark, c.1820-50.
(inset): Close-up of William Briggs' mark including the gothic M which has sometimes deluded people into identifying a London assay for 1767!
Plate 7.53

Two sets of platers' marks struck repeatedly to imitate period hallmarks, c.1830, showing rows of diagonal raised lines and 2 rows of pellets: neither of these marks has yet been ascribed to any known plating firm.
Plate 7.54

More platers' marks on pocket fruit knife blades
Arthur Worrall Staniforth.
Plate 7.55
John Gilbert & Co.
(Birmingham).
Plate 7.56

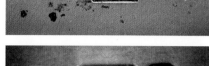

Thomas Marples & Sons
with additional
Fleur-de-Lys mark.
Plate 7.57

Close-plated blades on
knives this late (c.1860)
are quite scarce. The haft
comprising nacre off-cuts
and banded with pewter,
by J Stevenson & Law
with quatrefoils and
trefoil marks.
Plate 7.58

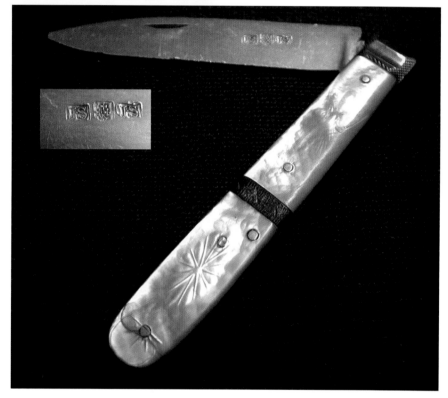

Fine plated knife c.1850 with a previously unknown plater's marks on the blade.
(*inset*): The ricasso (enlarged) from the quill blade of this ornate knife, has been stamped with the cutlers' marks of William Nowill, suggesting that the hitherto unidentified plater's mark of the fleur-de-lys, rose and gothic S (sideways) may have belonged to this maker.
Plate 7.59

A scarce Prince of Wales
commemorative fruit knife
but of plated German
Silver c.1850 by WDA.
The Phoenix mark is
loosely attributable to
Waterhouse & Company.
Plate 7.60

Boxed double set of
detachable fruit knife and
fork, with ivorine scales,
1885.
Note how the fork blades'
positions can be reversed
for each pair.
Plate 7.61

Pocket fruit knife typifying
Victorian decoration, by
Aaron Hadfield 1851,
combining clusters of *piqué
clouté*, engraving to the
'violin-style' handle and a
neo-baroque flame design
on the blade.
Plate 7.62

Three 19th century knife & fork sets: (*lowest*) by Aaron Hadfield 1836 with oak sprig decoration, (*mid*) by James Fenton 1863 carved with longitudinal fluting and (*top* - mark rubbed) 1870.
Plate 7.63

Scarce three-some set by J Y C, 1860. Note how the spoon has increased in size to a normal teaspoon and now made in Sheffield rather than in London.
Plate 7.64

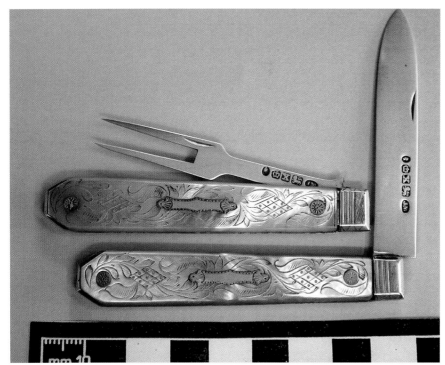

A fine early Victorian set by Joseph Mappin 1865 showing tang wear, unusually, to the fork so that the blade 'sits up', rather than the more usual wear to the knife tang.
Plate 7.65

Fork and knife tangs (of above set) showing the rounded fork tang (left).
Plate 7.66

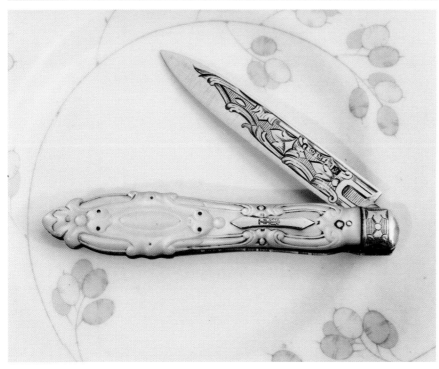

Magnificent knife typifying the Victorian Baroque, by Martin, Hall & Company, Sheffield 1855.
Plate 7.67

A scarce 9-carat gold-bladed Victorian knife c.1880 and showing how the anonymous (Sheffield) goldsmith stamped an illegal 9CT mark on the blade, rebelling against the gold ruling for Sheffield at this time. Gold was permitted to be assayed and marked in Sheffield but not until 1904.
Plate 7.68

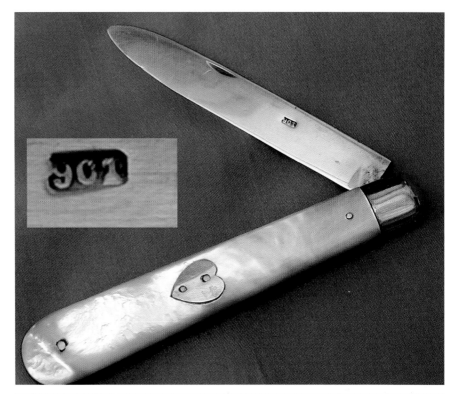
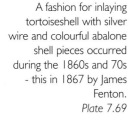

A fashion for inlaying tortoiseshell with silver wire and colourful abalone shell pieces occurred during the 1860s and 70s - this in 1867 by James Fenton.
Plate 7.69

A similar but bolsterless example from Birmingham by Hilliard & Thomason, 1867 (again) and perhaps given as a Valentine gift.
Plate 7.70

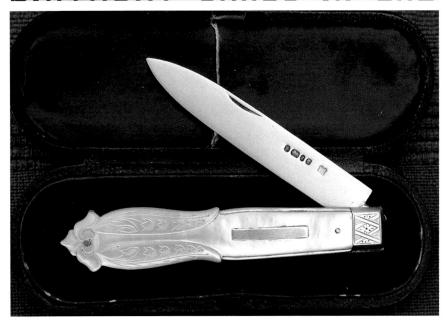

A knife in its box by another of the best makers at this time, Martin & Hall, 1876, incorporating lilies-of-the-valley into the base of the nacre haft.
Plate 7.71

An anonymously (unmarked) Sheffield knife c.1860, the nacre scales rather amateurishly scratched "In Sheffield's town was I once made, Both pearled haft & silver blade / A Londoner would waste his life attempting to make such a knife", revealing the long-standing rivalry between cutlers (especially) of each town.
Plate 7.72

Cased knife by John Nowill 1841, with unusual scrolling cap and rayed bolster, a pattern that he used fairly frequently.
Plate 7.73

Sharing pearl cutters? Two
knives with identical ears-
of-wheat hafts
(*top*) by Henry Wilkinson
& Co., (*lower*) by T. Ashton
& Son, both 1858.
Plate 7.74

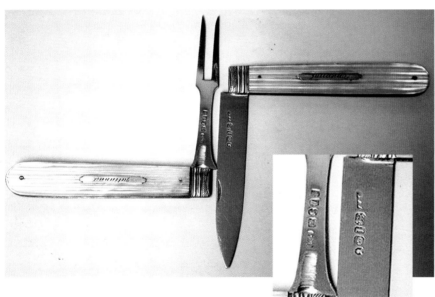

Another dichotomous pair:
the knife from Sheffield
by Atkin & Oxley, 1833,
the fork from Birmingham
by George Unite, 1834.
Both date letters are
coincidentally L!
Plates 7.75

Knife and fork set by
Edward Thomason, 1829.
The cross-hatched design
for nacre scales was
continued into the early
Victorian period.
Plate 7.76

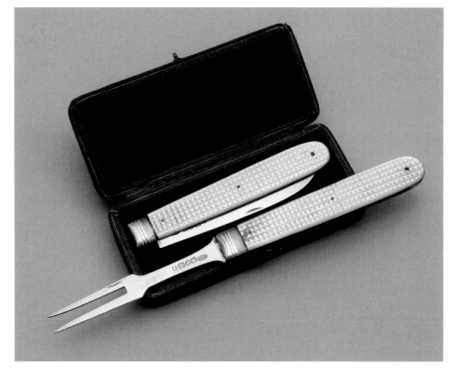

Late Victorian knives and
pairs gradually came to be
housed in these clipping
leather purses, reminiscent
of money purses,
at this time.
Plate 7.77

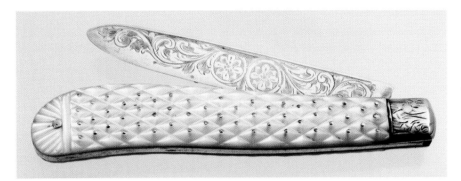

These pocket fruit knives elegantly decorated with 'quilted' nacre carving and centred with silver wire *piqué clouté*. This type of ornamentation was particularly popular during the 1860-1890 period. *Plates 7.78 to 7.80*

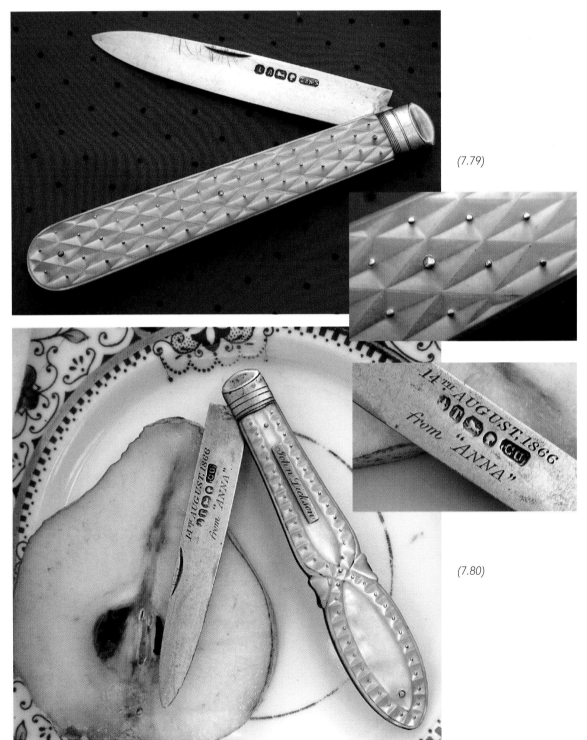

(7.79)

(7.80)

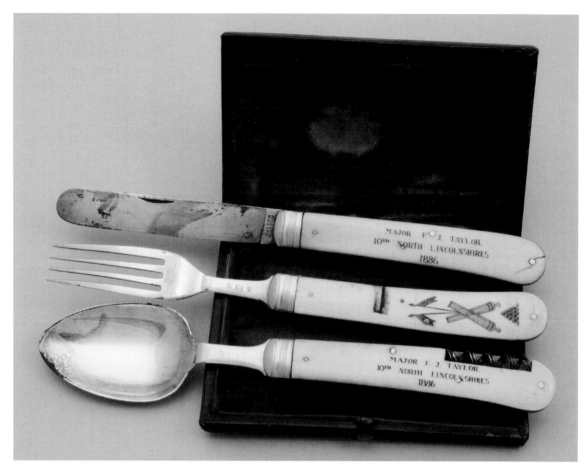

Close-plated campaign set by Joseph Mappin & Co. c.1850, the ivory scales scrimshandered with the later owner's details. The corkscrew has been attached to the spoon rather than the knife for this set.
Plate 7.81

Later French pocket fruit knives

Nineteenth century French pocket fruit knives began to diversify in style between 1810 and 1820. Spring-back knives, especially *Empire* pieces gradually became more popular superseding the springless *Berge* knives.

Many smaller-sized knives were made twin-bladed as before with a blade of precious metal doubled with one of steel but both blades were situated at the same end of the knife, each operating on its own spring. A few appear to have been made with reduced-size steel blades, for quill cutting, but the majority were made with twinned blades. One has been found coupled with an English fork blade (c.1790) which pre-dates the knife blade by some 50-60 years. It probably replaces a long-broken steel blade or may have been altered in a hurry to

be more fruit fashionable: the possibilities are endless (*plate 7.86*). The elegant haft has been inlaid with bees or cicadas in *piqué posé*, closely resembling those, symbolising immortality and resurrection, that had been a part of the Royal Houses of France since the 5th century AD and which device Bonaparte adopted to conjoin his new Empire to the old kings of France.

Nacre was still a popular hafting material at this time and was often carved with period roped borders or engraved with a silver thread border, sometimes inlaid with precious metal wire in the manner of *piqué posé*. This manner of decoration was still popular, especially for decorating tortoiseshell scales – an art at which the French were still unsurpassable.

19th century French pocket fruit knives
Despite its scimitar blade, this fruit-*cum*-quill knife dates from c.1840, by C or G F. The crown-shaped bolster of German Silver (cupro-nickel alloy) is typical of the period. Superbly inlaid with silver wire stringing and scrolling plant motifs, this type of knife would normally have a steel blade exactly matching the silver but despite the apparent age of the quill blade, the spring on that side does not curl around the base and compensate for the shorter blade (see below), suggesting that the pen blade may substitute for the lost original.
Plate 7.82

Beautiful French multi-bladed fruit knife with more conventional twinned silver and steel blades: the steel blade stamped ROBIN Langres, the matching silver blade by O M with a snake between the letters. The worn Minerva head mark alongside bears a tiny number 2, denoting .800 silver. The finely silver-inlaid haft contains an additional slotted set of silver tools under the tortoiseshell scales - an ear pick and a cigar piercer, c.1850.
Plate 7.83

PAGE 190

Silver with a sponsor mark in a lozenge (diamond shape) denotes a post-1797 assay (see French chapter 2).

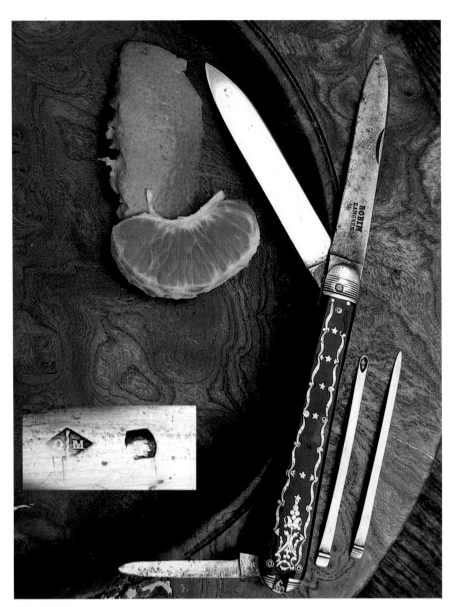

Conclusion

This fruit knife period, along with the preceding two, lasted one hundred years and represents the heyday for pocket fruit knives and forks. During the next century their gradual demise slowly brought about a decline in quality and the gradual disappearance in production of these charming items.

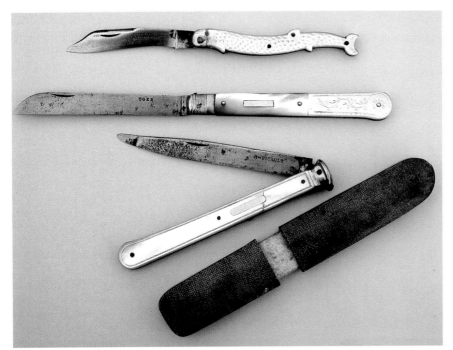

Three mid-19th century steel-bladed pocket knives, doubling as fruit knives: (*top*) by Dutrone and modelled as a stone loach fish; (*mid*) by Oger with a nacre-scaled haft terminating in a roundel; (*lower*) by Picault of ?Langres and beautifully made with gold mounts and cable-stringing with a lock-back mechanism, housed in a green-stained shagreen (*galuchat*) case.
Plate 7.84

Two matching steel-bladed fruit/pocket knives with scales of blonde tortoiseshell, underlaid with gold leaf, and inlaid with brass wire cabling by Sauvagnat; bolsters of German Silver, mid 19th century.
Plate 7.85

Unusual fruit knife by MF c.1850, the tortoiseshell scales stunningly *piqué posé* with silver bees or cicadas, which were a regal and Napoleonic symbol. The steel knife blade has been replaced in antiquity by an English fork blade decorated in period style to c.1790.
Plate 7.86

Another and more conventional two-blade knife by C or GF and with very fine *piqué posé* stringing and inlay work laid into tortoiseshell (enlarged below). The Minerva Head mark shows the silver to be of second grade (.800) with a number 2 in the mark below her chin. The maker of the steel blade is clearly marked Richard at Besançon but whether the goldsmith and cutler or retailer both worked in Besançon is open to conjecture.
Plate 7.87

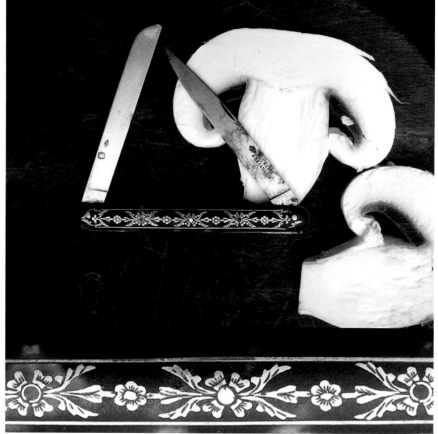

Magnificent *Berge* knife in the retro-style of the Empire by the renowned cutler/goldsmith Gustave Marmuse, 26 rue du Bac, Paris c.1850. The blades have been hollow ground (concave surfaces) and marked with a stylised seahorse (cutler's mark), his GM with a mermaid sponsor mark is also on the silver blade with the tiny Crab mark for post-1839 small silver. The scales of thick tortoiseshell have been beautifully inlaid with tooled gold panels. Note the green-stained rayskin case, with a typical early 19th century steel hinge, which fits into a red felt case with purse clips, probably from the early 20th century.
Plate 7.88

A highly luxurious French set. Although these were made c.1830 when Touron was at 24 Rue de la Paix (Paris), they still show the previous influence of the Empire period. With steel and gilt blades mounted in the *Berge* style. They were retailed by Touron in the luxurious *galuchat* (shagreen) and gilt brass case. Maker's mark of JP in a lozenge with an ermine tail above may have belonged to the Parisot family who were contracted by Touron at this time.
Plate 7.89

8 The declining years, 1890–1940.

Four cheaper-quality mass-produced knives, made over a 60 year period. *(left pair):* 1862, *(right pair):* 1926 & 1925). *Plate 8.1*

Some inventively-styled knives were still being made although this delightful fish by William Webster, 1894 may have been 'married' with a replacement blade by Charles William Fletcher, 1909 - the hinge rivet intended to form the eyes has just missed; yet it may still be an inter-purchase to complete a hasty order.
Plate 8.2

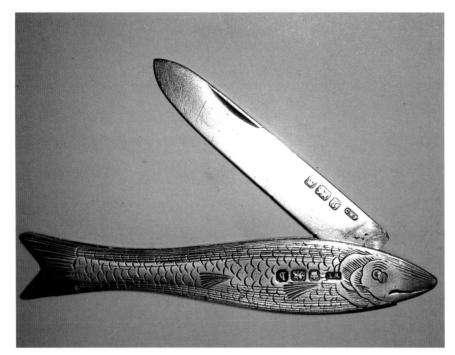

Victorian scroll engraving was still practised as a decoration to enhance Edwardian silver knives, this by John Nowill & Son, 1903 and 1904 (haft): a typical sequential-year-marked piece.
Plate 8.3

Although the approaching *fin-de-siècle* saw a huge revival in the decorative arts with the coming of the Arts & Crafts and Art Nouveau movements, pocket fruit knives received little of this stylistic attention. Up to this time, one can trace their gradual development before the artistic blooming of this period and yet only a few were actually decorated in period fashion. Perhaps tiring, at last, of this type of trinket, those with money were gradually relinquishing the folding fruit knife leaving them to the poorer middle and lower classes that sought to better themselves by using such dainty accoutrements.

A plethora of rather dull, small and cheap items were produced instead, many of them scaled with nacre, either left plain or rather crudely engraved with repeated or similar designs as the number of skilled pearl cutters presumably declined or whose skills were contracted into producing other and more costly wares. Blades were often thin and flexible, spring spines were left bare and bolsters were plain and no longer plated with silver.

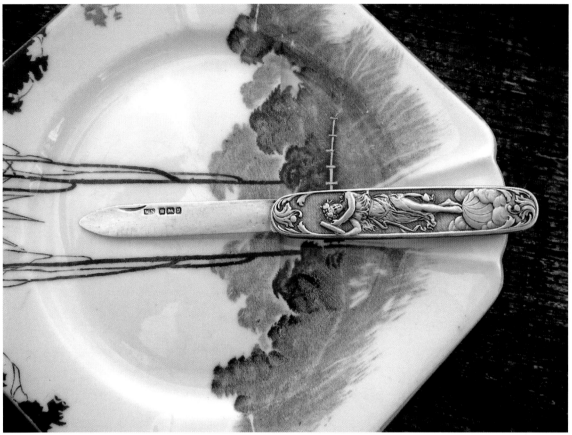

Despite this apparent abandonment of quality, there were still makers who strove to fulfil the need for pocket fruit knives and produced finer examples, but in general, although period catalogues from manufactories still show some finely made knives, these were mainly from the preceding period. Only a few reflect the amazing new designs of the times that were lavished on other everyday objects. For most pocket fruit knives only a continuation and slight development of styles from the High Victorian period, were made. Waning numbers of finer examples were still beautifully shaped and engraved and a few were made with new style indented scimitar blades.

Many of the pocket knife and cutlery firms, such as Parkin and Marshall (**PM**) and Dixon (**JD**), list samples ranging in quality and price from 2/6d (12.5 p) to 21/- (£1.05) (*plates 8.24 & 8.47*). Even the cutlery

giant Joseph Rodgers produced some well-made, if rather plain, examples, the firm's Cross and Star trademark being stamped alongside their sponsor's mark of **JR** (*plates 8.25-26*). Among their production of exhibition and collectors' pocket knives, Rodgers also made a few special fruit knives with silver wharncliffe blades. Wharncliffe is a suburb of Sheffield and the local baron, who was a patron of Rodgers at that time, gave his name to a beak-shaped blade that he designed in the early 19th century for whittling.

Extra Tools

For some, a pocket fruit knife now needed to be more multi-functional. Silver blades were occasionally incorporated into multi-bladed pocket-knives, in the manner of late 17th century French knives. However, for those who used fruit knives as elegant

Exceptional fruit knife to show that a few, at least, were decorated with Art Nouveau motifs stamped onto the haft: depicting a terpsichorean figure bestriding the globe, by William Needham, 1907. *Plate 8.4*

Art Nouveau style is rare on fruit knives although this small pocket knife may well have been used for fruit. The silver haft may be French and bears London import marks for 1902.
Plate 8.5

accompaniments to *alfresco* eating, slim, curved and blunt-pointed blades with a specific fruit-eating function were occasionally added. These were pippers ('seed picks' in the USA), to remove the pips

from citrus fruit; nut peeler/picks that were similar in appearance but more robust to delve into nut shells. Some knives were sold in a larger box with accompanying (rigid) nut picks, suggesting that fruit

Ferns and scrolls are quite usual during the early 1900s and a revival of the scimitar blade but with a noticeably notched or clip point, by John Hunter, 1902, hallmarked *au verso*.
Plate 8.6

Tools for fruit knives abounded in the early 20th century, many with patent numbers: *left*, a nutpick or nut peeler; *below*, (*right clockwise*): a toothpick in haft, grapefruit saw, pointed pipper blade (with purse case), patent orange peeler and a saw-ended blade.
Plates 8.7 & 8.8

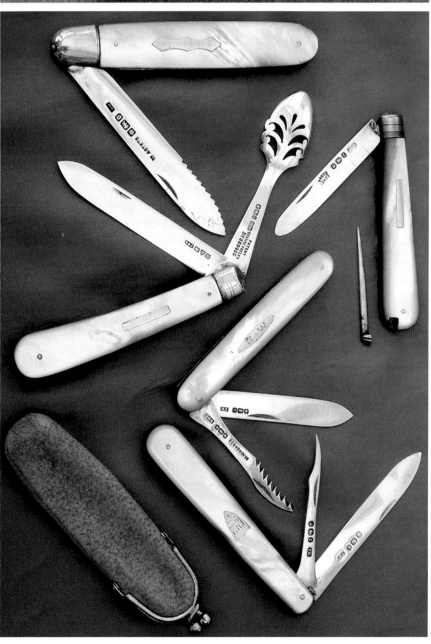

Illustration showing "Levi's complete specification" in the Patent Register, 1895, for his toothpick in fruit knife haft.
Plate 8.9

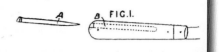

13,423. **Levi, S. H.** July 12. 1895

Pocket knives.—A toothpick A is provided as an attachment to a fruit knife. When not taken out for use, it fits away in a socket B in one of the scales of the knife handle, with its head flush to the surface of the scale.

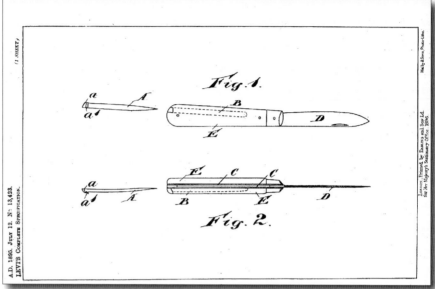

eating was popularly accompanied by nuts (*plate 8.10*). There were also variously-shaped saws to cut into tougher-skinned fruit, such as grapefruit and several types of orange peeler blades. All of these tools were integrated into fruit knives during the period between c.1880 and 1910 (*plates 8.7-9*) and appeared individually, or as part of

a knife, in period trade catalogues (*plate 8.24*). These tools were also individually patented, the patent number frequently being stamped on the blade. Tool knives with exchangeable blades, one in steel and one in silver, have turned up in the *lame de réchange* style and although these are usually mid 19th century, some have a later-added

A full boxed set comprising fruit knife, two nut peelers and apple corer, by Hilliard & Thomason, of Birmingham 1890 and retailed about 30 miles further north by H. Pidduck & Sons, Hanley (Stoke on Trent).
Plate 8.10

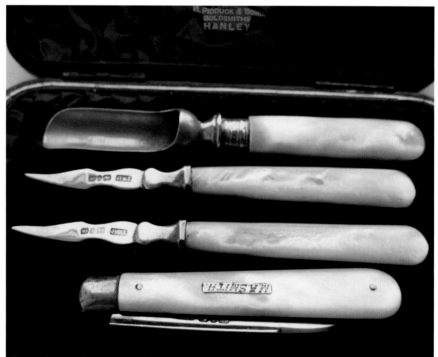

The hovering bird & butterfly motifs are typical of the styles used to adorn pocket fruit knife hafts and blades alike from Sheffield & Birmingham.
These range in date from 1890 to 1902.
Plate 8.11, 8.12 & 8.13

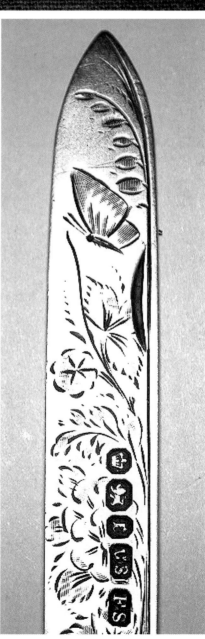

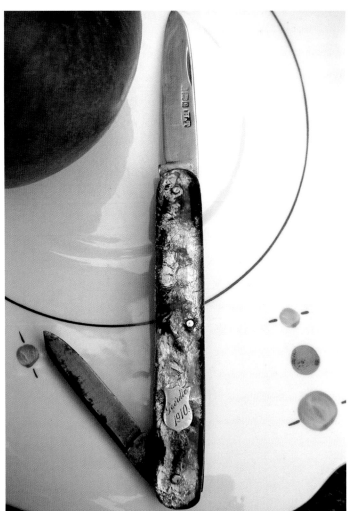

silver blade (*plate 8.27*). By the mid 1890s a toothpick in the form of a short silver spike was occasionally added as a sliding tool fitting under the scales at the base of the haft; the knife's major blade was marked with the patent registration number for this additional tool[1].

[1] [Footnote] 13,423 Levi, S.H. Pocketknives, 1895 – a toothpick is provided as an attachment to a fruit knife. When not taken out for use, it fits away in a socket B in one of the scales of the fruit knife handle, with its head flush to the surface of the scale.

Change of blade material

With the discovery of stainless steel by Harry Brearley of Thomas Firth's Company and the production of the first ever stainless steel blades in 1914, the silver blade was sometimes replaced by one of stainless steel: it was both tougher than silver and not blackened by fruit acid. From this time, therefore, period catalogues frequently listed their pocket fruit knives with

(above): Fruit knife by Hilliard & Thomason of Birmingham and assayed in 1902. Enamelled fruit knife hafts are very scarce at this time since the decorative trend for Art Nouveau seems to have had little influence on fruit knife decoration. The enamelling has been underlaid with precious metal leaf.
Plate 8.14

(right): Brightly-coloured celluloid hafts in check with brass filings or 'tiger stripe' *(below)* typify the more interesting pocket fruit knives during the Art Deco period: these are both 1926, by William Needham.
Plates 8.15 & 8.16

The advent of stainless steel brought about a gradual decline in the manufacture of softer silver blades although electro-plated carbon steel blades were sometimes made as well. (*lower knife*). The upper knife's trademark for 'Everklean stainless' shows a knife grinder as its logo. *Plates 8.17 & 8.18*

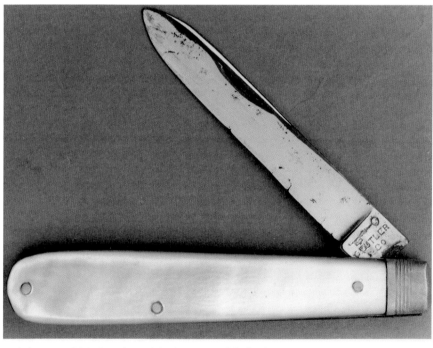

stainless steel blades alongside those with traditional silver (*plate 8.53*). The hafts of both types were almost invariably scaled with nacre or precious metal. The use of stainless steel gradually superseded the softer silver as blade material. Silver and gold were still used to scale pocket and smoker's knives but after about 1930 only a few decorative fruit knives were bladed with silver in the traditional manner.

Haft decoration

Traditional designs from the 1870s and 80s still persisted, including the fine *piqué*- worked hafts, but many were still engraved, typically, with designs of a flying bird or a butterfly, a small sailing boat, or bamboo stems that echoed the revival of Chinoiserie designs during the Edwardian period (*plates 8.11-13 & 8.28*). Abstract patterns continued, particularly cross-hatching. On both haft and blade,

Elder Dempster pocket fruit knives
A fleet of Elder Dempster Line's souvenir fruit knives, all by Walker & Hall from 1905 - 1912.
Plates 8.19 & 8.20

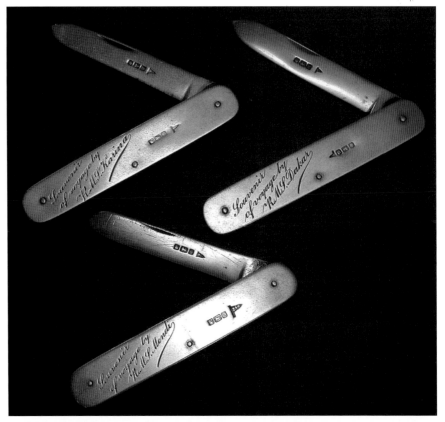

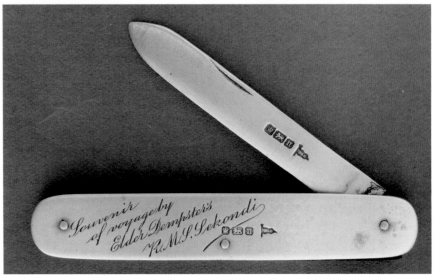

(right): Mark of Thomas Bradbury & Sons of Sheffield, using the London assay in 1883. The narrower blade is a pip-remover.
Plate 8.21

a sometimes crudely engraved fern frond was a popular motif at this time (*plate 8.29*). The reverse scales continued to be engraved with the usual pair of sunbursts that had been the standard 'reverse-scale-pattern' since about 1790.

With the end of the First World War and the ascendancy of the *Arts Décoratifs*, fruit knife bolsters and hafts themselves became more pointed, following the simpler geometric shapes of the movement but the steady waning of interest in pocket fruit knives did not encourage more adventurous designs. Plastics were also used as a scaling material from c.1900 onwards. By the 1920s they were decorated in a fancy and colourful deco chequer pattern, usually incorporating iridescent metal flakes (*plates 8.15-16*).

Elder Dempster knives

During the commercial era of the early 1900s, the renowned cutlery and silversmithing firm of Walker & Hall was commissioned to make quite large pocket fruit knives with silver scales. These were either given away or sold as attractive souvenirs to customers who cruised on Elder Dempster's African Steam Ship Company's fleet, which was founded in 1852. There are several different boat names but the most common is RMS Sekondi, which was acquired by the Company in 1896, re-named *Sekondi* in 1901 and scrapped in 1910. Each knife was engraved with *Souvenir of Voyage by Elder Dempster RMS Sekondi* ending with a flourish (*opposite page plates 8.19-20*). Fruit knife collectors often insist on possessing at least one Elder Dempster knife.

Decline of pocket fruit knives

At the turn of the 19th century, pocket fruit knives were still given as gifts or purchased as souvenirs, some as Valentines (*plates 8.31-2*). Even at the cheaper end of the market, a charming inscription would greatly enhance such a gift. From the collector's point of view such items are quite scarce and give a personal insight into peoples' lives. By the time of the Second World War, production of pocket fruit

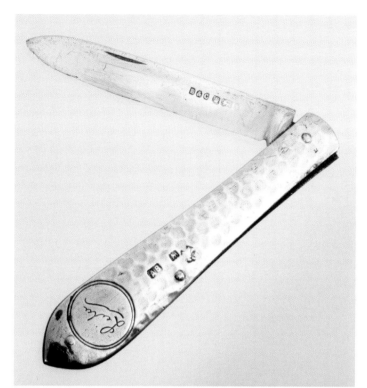

knives had dropped considerably. Although they would still have been a traditional and charming gift, they seem to have become rather outmoded at this time and examples from the 1950s and later are practically non-existent. Scales of nacre or plastic became dull and plain, as if the makers were only producing them under sufferance! People hardly used them at all judging by the unused condition of many pieces from this time. Even the more versatile stainless steel-

Gilt and hammer-finish silver-hafted knife by A B of London 1905, the blade by Brookes & Crookes of Sheffield 1905 - another example of inter-purchasing between companies.
Plates 8.22 & 8.23

Pages from Dixon's catalogue of 1920, showing price ranges for their pocket fruit knives; note how some are still being offered as current stock although having been made during the 1860/70 period; also the stainless steel blade and the aslant pipper blades - not to be confused with the nut peelers (top) which were thicker but were occasionally added to a pocket fruit knife (see *plate 8.7*).
Plate 8.24

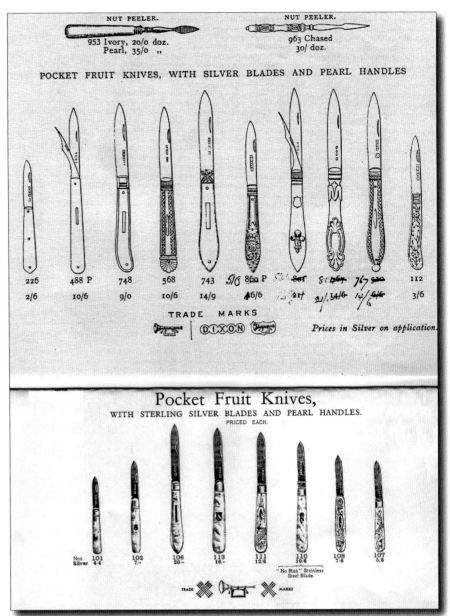

Makers
As the vogue for pocket fruit knives declined in the UK, the number of firms making them also declined to just a handful. Silver blades were occasionally added to a multi-bladed pocket knife bringing the craft of folding fruit knife-making full circle after 300 years. Today only a handful of 'mesters' or independent Sheffield cutlers have the skill to make specially handcrafted pocket knives, often scaled and occasionally bladed with precious metal. The bladed fruit knife was gradually phased out.

art of using these metals for making significant numbers of blades seems to have ceased during the 1950s.

Manufacturers' catalogues
By the early 1900s, cutlery and silversmithing firms in both Sheffield and Birmingham produced their own catalogues and these have turned up in the USA, priced in dollars. In many, a line, or half-page at least, was devoted to pocket fruit knives. A few list their products as being sold on a sheet of card and attached by cotton thread (*plate 8.50*). These catalogues showed the full range of items available with

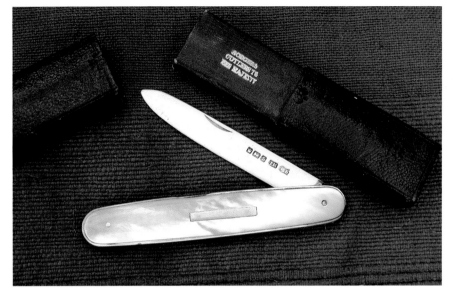

Although collectors may consider this a rather plain knife, it shows that the firm of Joseph Rodgers produced pocket fruit knives of good quality at this time: 1909. Note also their additional trademark of the star & cross and the stamp on the box to HER majesty referring to Queen Victoria's royal warrant.
Plates 8.25 & 8.26

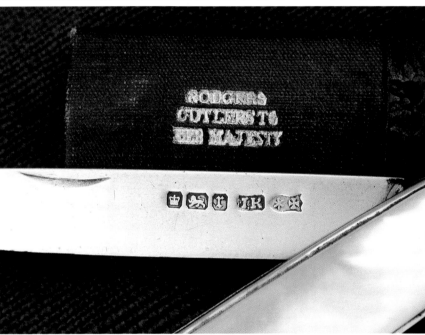

wholesaler's discounts, from small and plain knives at the lower end to finely-engraved blades or carved nacre-scaled hafts at the top. Some of the finer items shown often hark back to styles that evolved up to 100 years previously and many of these would have been made 30 or 40 years before. Many show the extra tools - pippers, saws and orange peelers - as the norm. However, hardly any show knife-and-fork sets from this time suggesting that only the knives were favoured, a sign of downsizing on these items as their luxury appeal started to wane.

Specials, Souvenirs, Prizes and Ghurka knives

Only a few special items exist from this period. Although no records have shown how the name came about, the steelmaker Sir Robert Hadfield might have been honoured by Thomas Marples, who made a more luxurious knife called 'The Hadfield' in about 1903. This knife was made from finest prismatic nacre, inlaid with decorative, rococo-style silver bands and *piqué* work in the French style, forming a decorative oval centre for the scales (*plate 8.41*).

An example of a multi-bladed *réchange* knife by Green of Windsor c.1840 but with a later silver blade by J Y Cowlishaw, 1910 and retailed by the Army & Navy stores, haft scales of grey buffalo horn.
Plate 8.27

The lowest quality knives were sometimes sold as seaside souvenirs and some may well have been attached to postcards. (*plate 8.36*). Organic knives, usually made from bone and inscribed *Remember Me* in inked lettering, also began to be made from c.1870 onwards. Extrapolating from the idea of inlaying dark horn hafts with colourful Abalone shell chips, European souvenir knives began appearing in about 1900 with hafts of dark horn, inlaid with colourful shell chips, shaped as flowers and leaves and silver traceries recording the name of the resort. Typical are Aix les Bains or Wiesbaden, though their blades of blonde horn are quite fragile and have often become chipped.

Pocket fruit knives were still recognised as traditional gifts and some can be found from this time, engraved with lavish inscriptions, as prizes at such events as dog shows (*plate 8.56*).

Pocket fruit knives were even modelled on Ghurka *kukri* fighting knives, stamped Ghurka Knife (c.1910) but like most of these imitative fads, this phase was short-lived (*plate 8.57*).

A series of knives commemorating the marriage of King George V & Queen Mary were made in 1911 in various styles, ranged according to price (*plate 8.58*).

Tube or 'pencil' fruit knives
These appear to have enjoyed a brief vogue from c.1890 to some time during the early 1900s. When closed they exactly resembled

(left): Chinoiserie decoration with bamboo, by Arthur Staniforth, 1895. As late as 1930 (below) some makers still favoured later Victorian acanthus scrolls and lambrequins but combined with a slightly deco Nordic boat, by Constantine & Floyd Ltd. Ferns were also a typical motif at this time, (also by Constantine & Floyd, 1910: below). Plates 8.28 & 8.29

silver-cased pocket pencils, which were designed to be elegant but practical and portable. Like their earlier sliding counterparts (*plate 8.42*) from the late 18th century, these Birmingham-made knives again suffered from the silver case becoming dented, although the blade was still easier to extract. However, should it become stuck then the shortness of the extraction

Knife blade with unusual overstriking Empire mark, and bird 1900.
Plate 8.30

A cheaper knife with slightly retro Victorian decoration of grasses and *piqué clouté* panels, somewhat cruder than the 1860-80 period. Despite the slight cheapness of the piece, the purchaser had the blade finely engraved for Helena Middleton, likely as a Valentine gift. The knife made by Thomas Marples, 1891 who was a prolific Sheffield manufacturer at this time.
Plates 8.31 & 8.32

knob would have made the blade difficult to open, as testified by several with parallel scratches suggesting the use of a vice or pliers! By the end of the First World War they were fairly rapidly phased out. All appear to have been stamped with a patent registration number: Rd. number 373659.

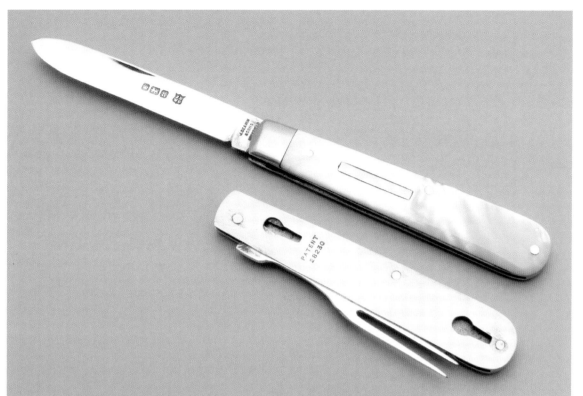

PAGE 211

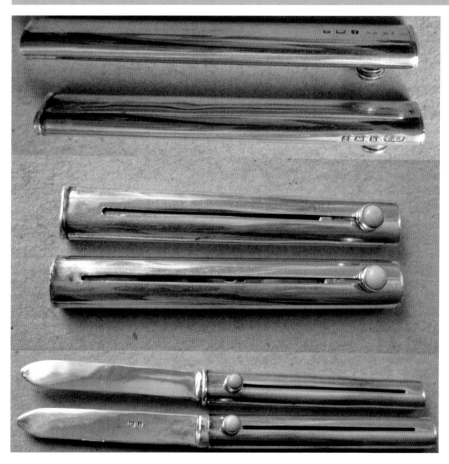

Later slotting knife and fork set by James & William Deakin, 1905. The Patent number refers to the fork blade's flared ricasso which, by closing the fork blade, creates a safety lock.
Plate 8.33

Two Birmingham-made sliding fruit knives reminiscent of those from the beginning of the 19th century, but with slightly more robust casings and with turquoise buttons to advance and retract the blade, both by Thomas H. Vale, 1908 and 1909.
Plate 8.34

Deco-style pocket
fruit knife by William
Needham, 1935,
complete with George
V & Queen Mary silver
jubilee mark.
Deco knives are fairly
scarce.
Plate 8.35

Two cheaper knives,
upper with plastic scales
imitating nacre by Francis
Howard 1931 and (lower)
a Brighton souvenir by
William Needham 1923.
Plate 8.36

(far right):
a gold-scaled knife by
Singleton & Priestman,
1897 but the haft
purchased from L & CH of
Birmingham, probably due
to no gold-marking facility
at Sheffield until 1904.
Plate 8.37

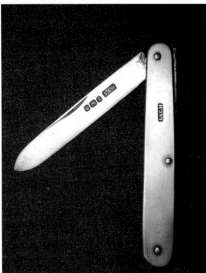

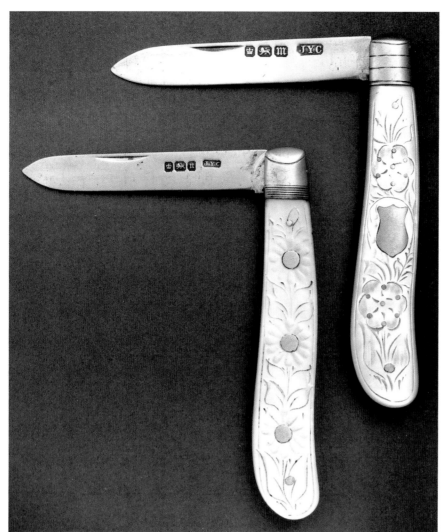

Typical cheaper quality knives of the early 20th century, also showing the change over of JYC to J.Y.C of Cowlishaw's firm c.1904-5. The JYC mark was still occasionally used on later knives. The decoration is still typically later Victorian in style.
Plate 8.38

Group of three souvenir knives: (top) of ivory c.1870 inscribed: *Remember me* with a sprig of oak leaves in ink, (mid & below) two horn knives of dark and blonde horn with heat-pressed silver overlay and inlaid with chips of abalone shell, c.1900.
Plate 8.39

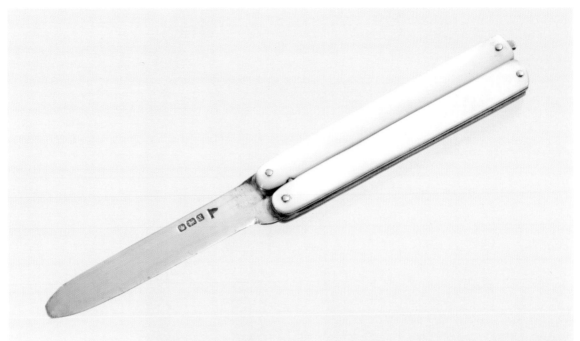

Unusual butterfly-
mechanism fruit knife by
Walker & Hall, 1925.
Plate 8.40

A 'Hadfield' knife by
Thomas Marples, 1903.
Scaled with top-quality
prismatic nacre and
ornamented with Rococo-
style *piqué posé* and *piqué
clouté* in silver.
Plate 8.41

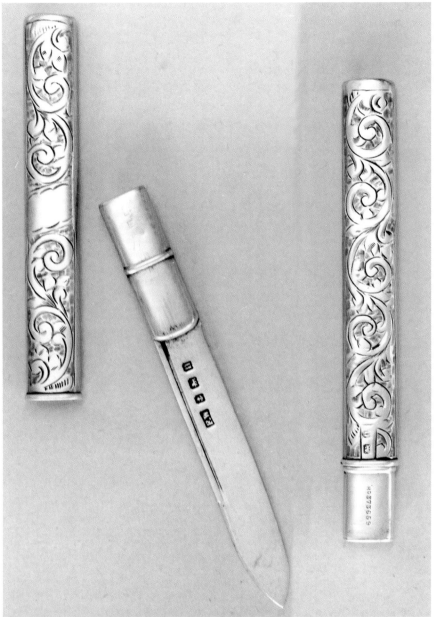

Silver 'tube-pencil' fruit knife by F. Webb who were pencil case makers in Birmingham, 1912 engraved with scrolling foliage. Note the Registration number for this design of knife.
Plate 8.42

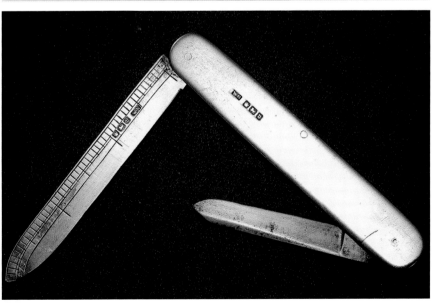

A less usual pocket-*cum*-fruit knife by William Needham 1913, an imperial scale rule engraved onto the fruit blade.
Plate 8.43

Slight variation of the
spoon-type orange peeler
c.1900, complete with its
patent number: 560047.
Plate 8.44

Retail cutler or silversmith?
This knife was constructed
and sold by the cutlery
firm of Thomas Turner
but the silver blade was
produced by Henry Atkin,
and assayed in 1890.
Plate 8.45

An ivory-scaled pocket
fruit knife by Thomas
Marples, 1923, note the
late use of the acanthus-
engraved bolster and the
raised knobs on the scales
- a retro design from the
1880s and echoed on a
printing block below it
for a generic fruit knife
catalogue c.1890-1910.
Plate 8.46

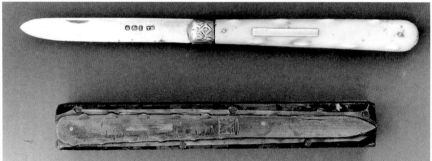

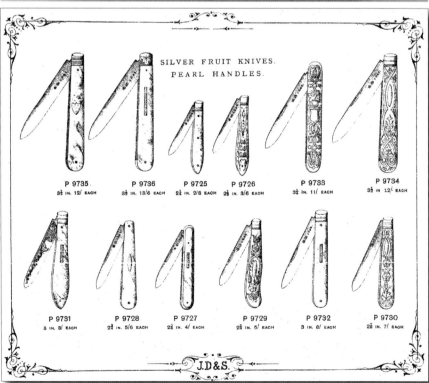

Page of fruit knives
from James Deakin &
Son's catalogue showing
how size, rather than
decoration, affected the
price, c.1900.
Plate 8.47

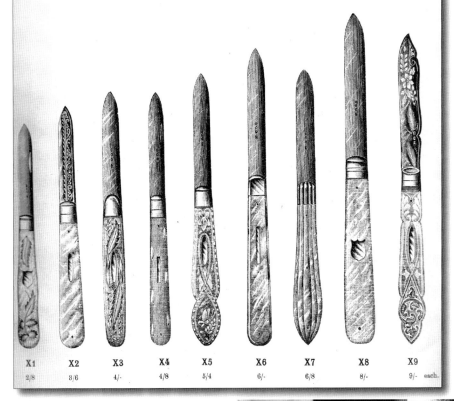

PEARL FRUIT KNIVES, STERLING SILVER BLADES.

MOUNTED ON CARDS.

CORPORATE MARK.   XL ALL   GRANTED 1789.

X1	X2	X3	X4	X5	X6	X7	X8	X9
2/8	3/6	4/-	4/8	5/4	6/-	6/8	8/-	9/- each.

Page of fruit knives from Parkin & Marshall's catalogue, c.1910 showing lower-range prices for that time and their XL-ALL mark in imitation of Wostenholm's renowned IXL punning trademark.
Plate 8.48

Using a shielding parser to carve out a shield for a knife haft (the breastplate is normally strapped around the chest).
Plate 8.49

Another page of fruit knives from Parkin & Marshall's catalogue, c.1910 and showing the upper range of their wares at this time. Many still show styles dating back to the 1860s & 70s. Note that these were mounted on cards to prevent their being scratched but keeping costs down by not having to supply a leather purse, (below).
Plates 8.50 & 51

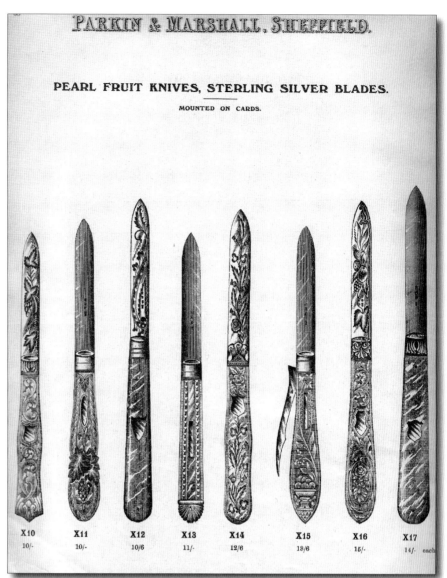

PARKIN & MARSHALL, SHEFFIELD.

PEARL FRUIT KNIVES, STERLING SILVER BLADES.

MOUNTED ON CARDS.

X10	X11	X12	X13	X14	X15	X16	X17
10/-	10/-	10/6	11/-	12/6	18/6	15/-	14/- each

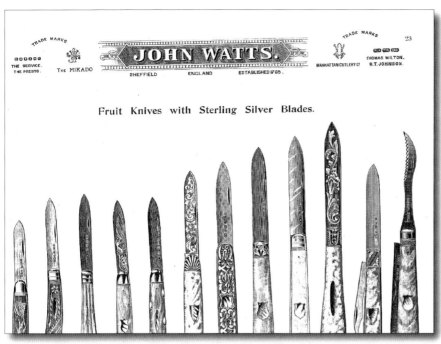

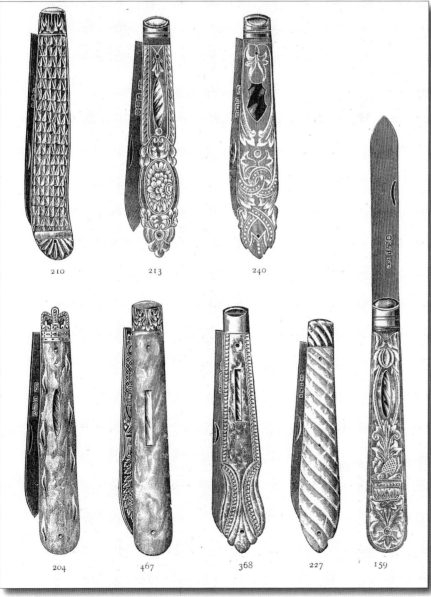

Pages from the catalogue
of John Watts, 1905 and,
as always, showing older-
styled stock. Note how
the blade for number 213
has been slightly extracted
to show its tip, not to be
confused with a worn tang
(ref. pages 262-3).
Plate 8.52

Page of fruit knives from
Wingfield & Rowbotham's
catalogue, c.1915
and showing Hygienic
(stainless) steel introduced
into fruit knives.
Plate 8.53

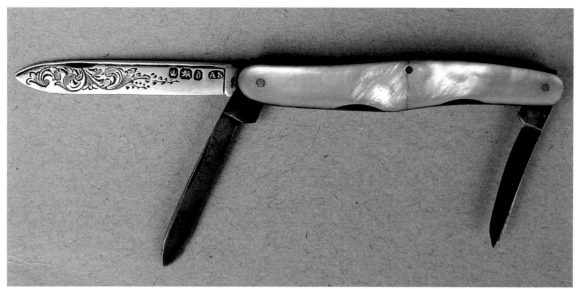

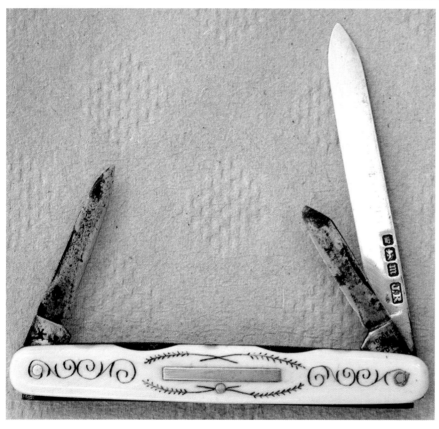

Two multi-bladed pocket fruit knives, (*upper*) by Arthur Staniforth, 1896 and (*lower*) by Joseph Rodgers & Co., 1904. The obverse side of this knife is shown at the end of the preface.
Plates 8.54 & 8.55

A plain pocket fruit knife by Thomas Marples, 1909 and presented by Spratts at the Portsmouth Canine Association dog show in 1911: an unusual prize, and amazing how the bold engraving has been fitted onto the already-hallmarked blade.
Plate 8.56

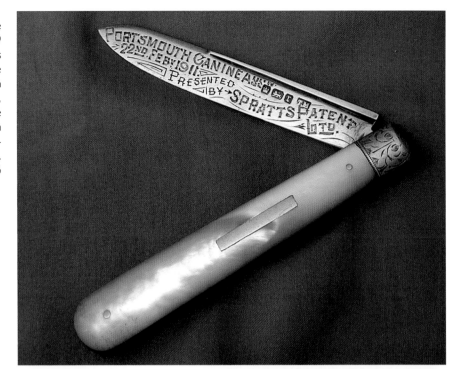

Despite its partly-obliterated hallmarks, this *kukri*-style pocket fruit knife by William Needham, c.1910, seems to have enjoyed a brief, possibly commemorative vogue at this time.
Plate 8.57

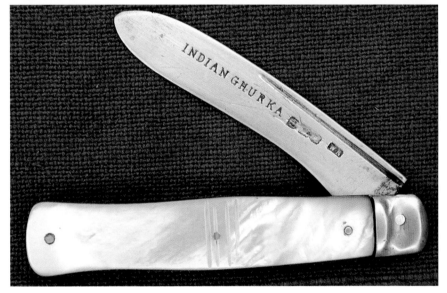

Fruit knives were still evidently popular enough to warrant a commemorative issue for the wedding of King George V and Queen Mary in 1911, by J. Wilmot (Birmingham maker).
Plate 8.58

A 1924 retro design by John Batt & Co. Ltd echoing the fruit and cornucopia style of the 1860s and 1870s.
Plate 8.59

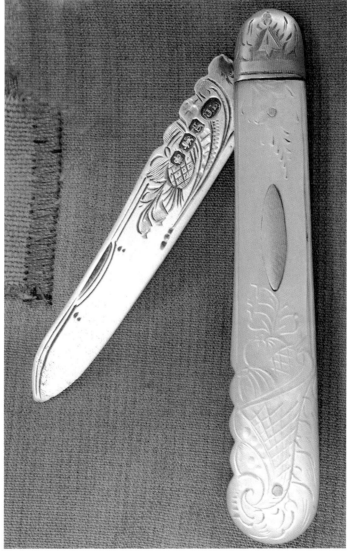

Superb shop display-style collection of pocket fruit knives showing a mix of 19th century English items (base, centre and corners) and American (outer surround), complete with a hallmark explanation, by Imogen Ranson, Chattanooga National Knife Museum.
Plate 8.60

Agate hafted knife with engraved silver band by Adie & Lovekin Ltd of Birmingham 1897. Hardstone hafts such as this, were likely produced to promote the Scottish hardstone industry.
Plate 8.61

Pocket fruit knives from other countries

Three typical later
19th century American
pocket fruit knives.
Plate 9.1

A fine Art Nouveau style knife, complete with a pipper blade (or seed pick). Many USA-made pocket fruit knives were made with this accessory, especially as it had become fashionable back in England at this time. Manufactured by the Meriden Britannia Company c.1890, the trailing clematis design is appealing and is found on many other electro-plated knives by the same company, in which case the company's name is stamped in gothic letters on the blade.
Plate 9.2

Another knife by Meriden Britannia Company slightly copying the Flying Bird motif, popular on English knife hafts in the 1890s. Note the wear to the plating, including the rather crude rivets, and the Deco-style frieze. Marked M.B.Co on the ricasso of the pipper blade only.
Plate 9.3

Smaller-sized knives, bladed with coin silver c.1850, with trailing plant motifs along their hafts.
Plate 9.4

Fruit knives from the USA

American pocket fruit knives seem to have first been made sometime during the 1830s, probably copying the popular fashion in England. They were also a small and very saleable adjunct to small silverware produced by American silversmithing firms. Although the fashion may have been copied, the style of American fruit knives was not. The blades tended to be made with the 'French nail nick' – a long groove that extends from the double-edged swage (USA *swedge*) along the top of the blade, only occasionally found on English knives. Some were also made with a French-style single action using a rounded tang which made for a

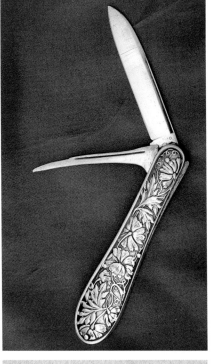

smoother opening and prevented tang wear.

Many knives came with an additional tool, usually a pipper blade or 'seed pick'. Orange peeler blades, saws and the confusingly-named nut pick are virtually unknown, as the makers would have had to pay extra to copy them since they had been patented in the UK, unlike the pip-removing blade.

Showing the use of the pipper (seed pick) blade, this Aesthetic period fruit knife's casing stamped with scrolling botanical motifs was given to Myra (*au verso*) MVPL. Marked STERLING only and with a rather scratched blade. *Plate 9.5*

PAGE 227

Styles

Hafts were almost invariably made from die-stamped silver sheet over base metal. Plainer examples were left plain but occasionally shaped in a period Gothic style with small indents. Decorative knives were engraved with organic motifs – curling fern fronds, scrolls and leaves being typical and tending towards the European Aesthetic Movement of the 1870s and 1880s. Nonetheless, some manufacturers extrapolated from this producing their own more individual designs. By the turn of the century there was a mix of American and European-influence styles, particularly during the British Arts & Crafts period. The Meriden Britannia Company produced a number of silver-plated knives embossed with a beautiful *Clematis* design trailing along the haft, more in the Art Nouveau-style (*plate 9.2*).

Throughout these art periods, many American knives were machine-stamped and embossed with motifs. One of the most common incorporated a classical head (known as 'The Empress', *plate 9.12*) in profile in the base and a rose in the bolster area, another brief revival of neo-classical combined with late 19th century taste.

Standards

There was no regulation for silver in the USA at the time apart from Baltimore where between 1814 and 1830 an Act regulated the silver content of items made and sold in that city (Karsten, 1986). American silversmiths used a 90% silver alloy 'as good as the coinage' and known as *coin* silver. The smith either stamped the COIN mark onto pieces of silver or it bore no quality regulating mark at all. If the smith

Two well-known exponents of pocket fruit knives were the renowned firm of Gorham (G-mark *above*) and Albert Coles (*below*: 1836 - 1880), both from New York. Note how the other blade marks reflect English hallmarking with (*above*) the right-facing sterling lion (post 1865), and anchor. Also that these marks were so worn out that they are barely legible in a deep stamp! (*Below*) the pseudo-duty mark of William IV but which more resembles the profile of Edward VII and the mark of Albert Coles in a French-style lozenge cartouche.
Plates 9.6 & 9.7

used Sterling silver (92.5%) then a lion, imitating the English assay, but facing to the right, was used (*plate 9.6*) or it was (less confusingly) stamped STERLING.

American smiths tended to copy English hallmarks and imitative Georgian heads can often be found

Another piece by Gorham but ricasso-marked, with neo-classical haft decoration, c.1870 and on a more Aesthetic piece (*below*), the Sterling mark denoting its superiority to coin silver.
Plate 9.8 & 9.9

on American blades, even though these items were at least mid 19th century or later. Most of these marks are unidentifiable as to who made the knives and when. The Birmingham anchor mark was frequently used by the renowned firm of Gorham and the flying Eagle

Two fine pocket fruit knives that typify the work of Albert Coles, c.1860-70 and interestingly copying the English cornucopia style of the same period, although the acanthus and anthemion decoration (on both) are more typical of the English neo-classical revival period (1815 - 1830).
Plate 9.10

by Coles (*see plate 9.7*). Date letters were even used so that American fruit knives can only be differentiated from English on stylistic grounds.

Notable makers.

Most notable were the firms of Albert Coles whose A over C in a French styled lozenge and Gorham, whose plain G or gothic 𝕲 like an English date letter, are often found on better quality fruit knives. Based in New York, Coles worked between 1836 and 1880. Gorham became renowned for inventive flatware designs during the Art Nouveau period and his decorative

knives are highly collectable. Other American firms included the Empire Knife Company (1856-1930), the aforementioned Meriden Britannia Company (1852-1898: M.B.Co.) and Wallace Brothers Silver Company (1875-1879). Messrs Tift & Whiting of Attleboro' near to Boston also produced finer-quality knives, as always tending to European styles but occasionally more 'home-grown' aesthetically-designed knives can be found. Their curious conjoined triple mark comprising a cockerel, T&W and a third mark of a hammer-bearing arm often confuse collectors who attribute the mark to Russia!

After 1850-1870, American taste tended to reflect the upcoming English Aesthetic movement style.
Plate 9.11

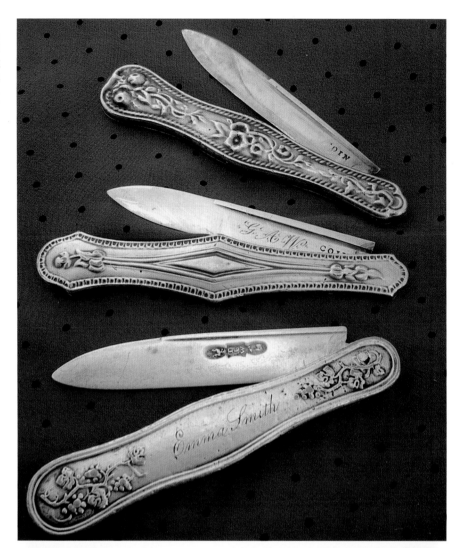

The 'Empress' cameo motif is found on many turn of the century knives.
Plate 9.12

In his 1986 booklet, *Silver Folding Fruit knives*, Bill Karsten identified other types of American fruit knives including those with proud advertising slogans – "Given away by Smith Stevenson & Co.", a clothiers in Meriden. He has also noted wrap-around brass handles marked M for Miller Brothers (1863-1926) some made with ivory scales and steel blades by an unidentified maker N.A.G.A.F, and even one made entirely from ivory (excepting the riveting pins) by J. Ward & Co., Bronxville, New York.

An exceptionally fine Aesthetic style pocket fruit knife, possibly by Gorham, lacking a maker's mark but given to *Jennie* as a Christmas gift in 1884.
Plate 9.13

Typical electro-plated haft in Aesthetic taste by Gorham c.1880-1890. The marks are again very worn out indicating Gorham's high output.
Plate 9.14

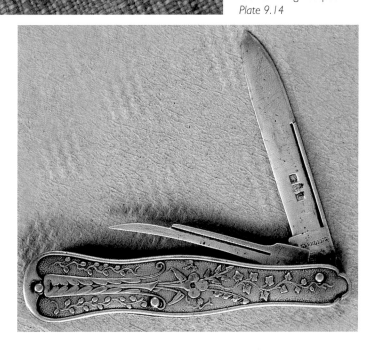

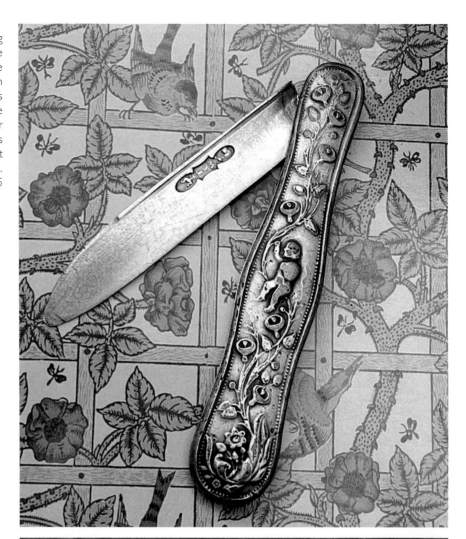

Knife by Tift & Whiting showing a distinctly more Aesthetic Movement style which was appearing on British knives at about this time (c.1850). Despite the wear to the silver plating on the haft, this enchanting design has not lost any of its appeal.
Plate 9.15

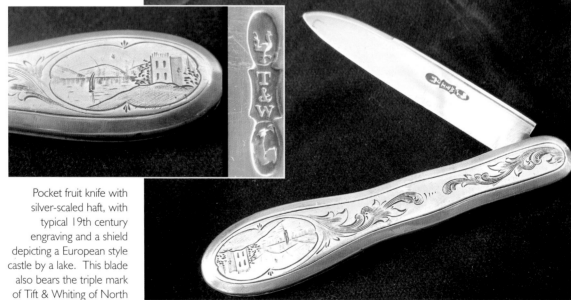

Pocket fruit knife with silver-scaled haft, with typical 19th century engraving and a shield depicting a European style castle by a lake. This blade also bears the triple mark of Tift & Whiting of North Attleboro, Massachusetts, 1840-1858.
Plate 9.16

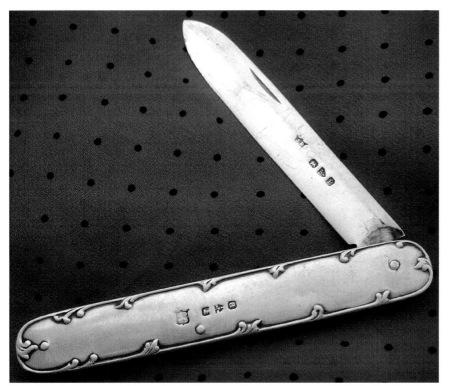

Knife by James Deakin and Sons of Sheffield, who used the Chester Assay Office on this occasion (1898); this is a typical turn-of-the-century knife with scrolled edges – a style often used by American knife makers, especially Albert Coles.
Plate 9.17

Ownership markings were usually added to order by the manufacturer (Christmas 1884 previous page) but more amateur donations (March 1876 right) were sometimes scratched on blades or shields.
Plate 9.18

Donation inscription to Emma Smith on a Tift & Whiting fruit knife, c. 1850.
Plate 9.19

Knife by Gorham & Co., c. 1870 when Chinoiserie was popular. The bamboo motif on a hammered background typifies this trend and where the thick silver plating has worn away, the underlying yellow base metal adds an extra dimension. Some adjustments have been made to the blade and the vice marks are visible near the STERLING-marked ricasso (ref. Chapter 10).
Plate 9.20

Another fine piece by the Gorham Company the haft depicting a sleigh being chased by wolves. The reverse side comprises a plain hammer-marked thin sheet of silver.
Plate 9.21

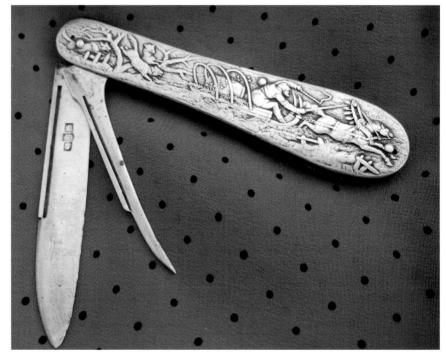

Inscriptions

Inscriptions on American fruit knives are quite diverse, except that *Mother* is quite commonly found suggesting a gift from a child. Unsurprisingly, female names abound as recipients, but a few bear donation markings from loving daughters to fathers. Other gifts have been made more specifically to teachers e.g. *'from her pupils'*.

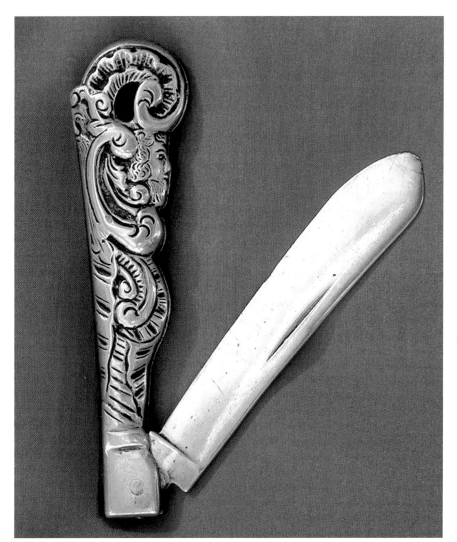

Pocket fruit knives from the Netherlands are occasionally found. mainly made during the 1750 - to early 1800s period. Earlier items such as the above are unmarked and decorated in a Baroque - Rococo manner. Many are steel-bladed.
Plate 9.22

Rest of the world

So far I have recorded fruit knives (and forks) from the UK, France, Switzerland and the USA. The Netherlands enjoyed a brief vogue for pocket fruit knives in the mid to later 18th century. Hafts of cast silver, quite heavy and cast with strange caryatid-like faces which peer out from the sides. The blades are either of unmarked silver or of carbon steel.

Germany also enjoyed a brief vogue during the early 18th century, but I have only ever seen two sets, unmarked and provenanced purely on stylistic grounds.

At least one of the renowned Carl Fabergé's workmasters, Gabriel Niukkanen (*plate 7.50*), made small purse-sized pocket-cum-fruit knives, c.1880, incorporating a steel blade, a fold-out spike for cigar piercing and scissors within a gold haft overlaid with gold wire traceries and centred with cut precious stones, typical of Russian pre-revolutionary extravagance.

I am sure that Italy, especially, Spain and other European countries must have produced pocket fruit knives but I have not yet discovered any!

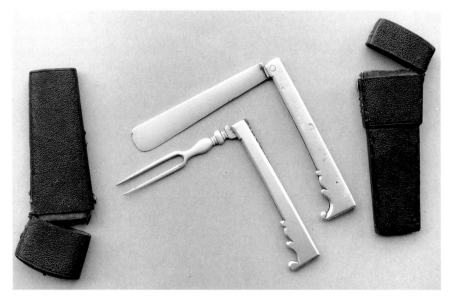

Travelling cutlery was particularly *à la mode* in Germany during the late 17th to late 18th centuries. Many steel sets were produced but few were bladed with silver, presumably for fruit. This set in separate shagreen containers c.1700.
Plate 9.23

The small ricasso-standard marks are German except for the small quatrefoil mark on the right which is a Belgian quality mark for 900 silver. This sliding-blade fruit knife combines deco style with Roman Lictors' *fascicules* (wood bundles depicting strength) c.1910.
Plate 9.24

Modern French, American and other pocket fruit knives - a change of direction

Despite diminished interest in the UK, which has reduced the Sheffield pocket knife industry to a dwindling handful of custom knife makers (or *mesters*), interest in the USA and the rest of Europe, particularly France, has been maintained throughout. Pocket and fruit knives tend to be custom-made as commemoratives or special editions, some with inlaid jewels and superbly patterned Damascus steel blades. Although the trend for impressing the ladies whilst eating fruit *al fresco* may be considered as somewhat

archaic, these modern knives have been crafted to combine age-old skills and excellence with modern technology. The resulting knives are more collectors' pieces and many are breathtaking to behold. The use of such knives might be considered as rather showy by today's standards and, bearing their cost in mind, unwise lest anything might happen to them.

Throughout the UK and rest of Europe and especially the Americas, these are now considered to be the acme of pocket 'knifery'. Although the 19th century factories that produced high-quality wares may no longer exist, except as local culture museums, the custom knife-making industry, in the form of smaller workshops, is flourishing and advancing all the time.

German pocket fruit knife
and fork set, unmarked
but c. 1700. Note the
fine scrolling fruit design on
the hafts interspersed with
gold wire.
Plate 9.25

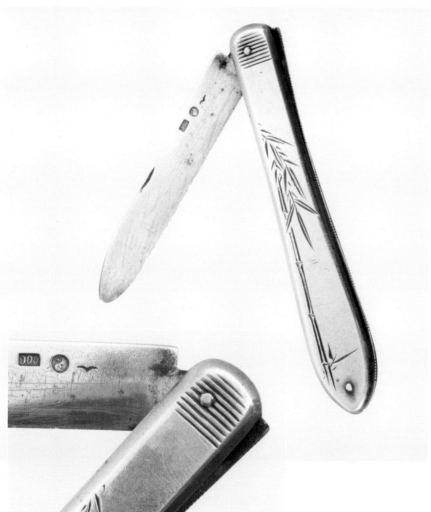

Far eastern pocket fruit
knife, probably made as a
European export c.1900.
Plate 9.26

Massive (thickly nacre-
scaled) fruit knife by
William Needham,
Sheffield 1928. The design
is quite plain and the
mechanism crisp showing
that as the fruit knife trade
was rapidly waning in
Britain, well-made knives
were still being produced.
Plate 9.27

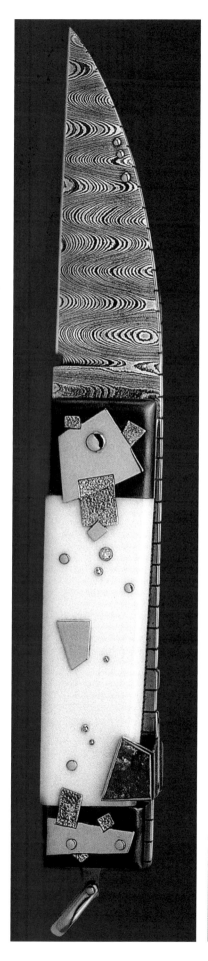
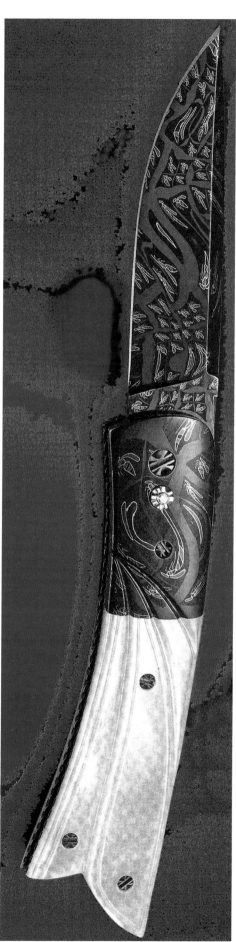

Contemporary custom
pocket knife-making has
a cult following these
days with craftspeople
in both Europe and the
USA producing the most
amazing and complex
items, typified by these
two pieces from Darom,
2003. Quite apart from
the stunning Damascus
steel blades, each has
been finely-adorned with
precious metals (and along
the spines) gemstones
in the manner of fruit
knife-making.
(left): by Dellana 1999,
titled *Collage*.
(right): by Barry Gallagher
2002 titled *Hornets*.
Plates 9.28 & 9.29

PAGE 240

A final knife from Darom's book, by Johan Gustaffson of Sweden, 2001 titled *Multi-coloured mosaic* and showing the intricate care taken to produce such a pattern of colours from the interference spectrum.
Plate 9.30

10 Collecting, Construction, Pitfalls, Fakery and Faults

Collecting

Construction

Pitfalls & fakery

Faults
Plate 10.1

Collecting

Collectors of fruit knives can be categorised into: those who collect anything as long as it is in MINT condition; those like me who collect different designs and types; those who prefer only the best quality items and will pay anything to secure them; and the few who collect in particular periods (18th century only, Georgian, Victorian or 20th century). The last category leads onto those who collect sequences or 'runs' of dates.

Sequence collectors will naturally become obsessive trying to locate knives with certain dates, and members of their families are often asked to look for certain date letters, especially from those years when production was lower than average. The main Georgian period between 1797 and 1817 is a natural stumbling block in this pursuit since the date letter is barely ever visible, as Sheffield fruit knives made within this 20 year period were invariably tang-hallmarked with the date and crown combination mark (*ref. chapter 4*). Sequences are extremely useful to the researcher and date runs of knives and forks stand as a record of the years in which pocket fruit knife making was most plentiful.

For example, Sheffield knives were copiously made in the years 1819, 1822 and 1825-6 but less so during the years in between suggesting that the large numbers assayed during those 3 years would have been plentiful enough to maintain adequate stock levels during the intervening periods.

Sequences also show how the designs for fruit knives came and went, when they were most popular, and also which workshops shared the same pearl cutters or patterns. They also keep track of subtle changes in hallmarking legislation or style, such as the change of the Victorian duty mark cartouche at Sheffield in 1862. Sequences also show that pre-1800 Birmingham fruit knives are scarce.

I have been fortunate in finding Ted Kleinman whose 'run of dates' for both Sheffield and Birmingham is one of the most complete that I have seen. His family kindly gave me permission to reproduce the sequences that he collected shortly before he died.

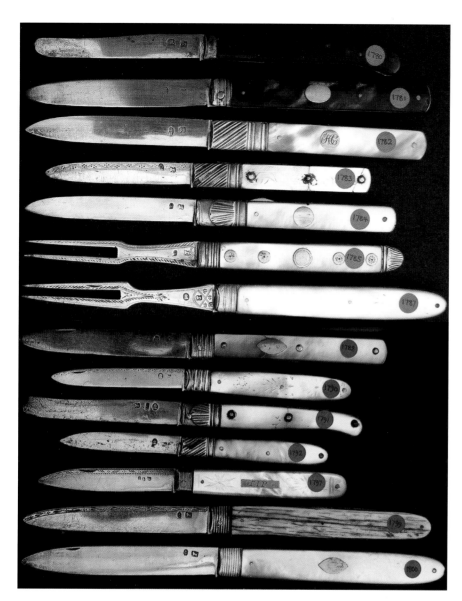

**Ted Kleinman
sequential collection of
Sheffield pocket fruit
knives & forks**

Sheffield 1780 - 1800.
Some of these blades
were removed from their
hafts for date checking.
Until c.1815 most do
not show date letters
but there are a few rare
exceptions.
Plate 10.2

Sheffield 1853 - 1862.
Plate 10.6

Sheffield 1894 - 1906.
Plate 10.9

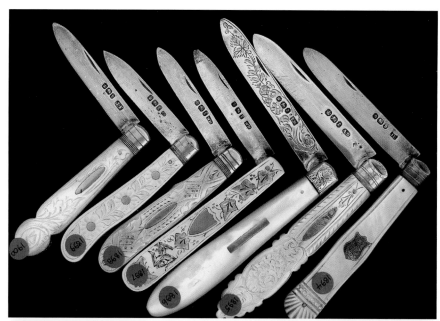

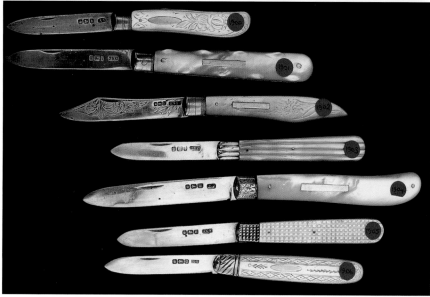

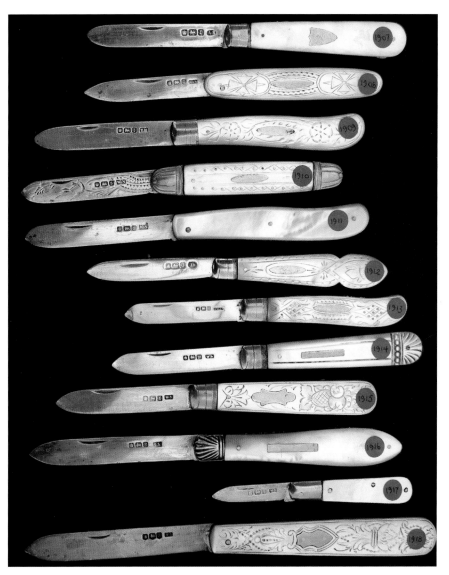

Sheffield 1907 - 1918.
Plate 10.10

Sheffield 1961 and one
Chester 1895.
Plate 10.13

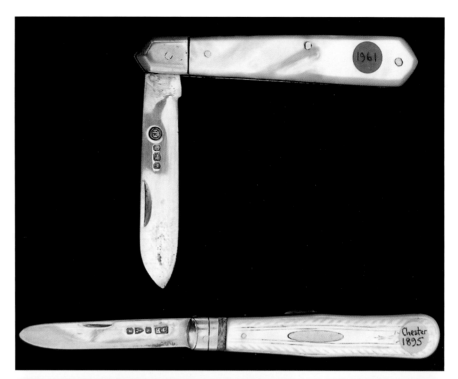

Birmingham 1843-1849
A typical George Unite
knife on the right.
Plate 10.14

Construction & Glossary (also page 269)

In this world of *Caveat Emptor*, some knowledge of the construction of pocket fruit knives and forks is essential.

Folding fruit knives follow the same constructional pattern as pocket knives. The scales are attached by rivets, usually of silver, to webs or linings made of copper or a copper alloy such as brass. The webs are the base part of the handle and need to be strong enough to take the strain from those rivets that are connected to the spring. At the same time they need to be discreet so as not to spoil the overall appearance of the knife. At the junction of the blade, a bolster of copper or alloy is attached to the webs with solder. The copper surface is then silver-plated.

The conjoined webs form a slot for the blade, which is normally spear-pointed or maybe scimitar-shaped for early or art period pieces. The blade is cut with a crescent-shaped nail nick or a French nail nick, which comprises a groove along the blade's upper edge and is combined with a swage (double-edged) point (*plate 10.18*). The blade is attached at the base end to a ricasso (extension or junction of the blade and tang) and a small filed lug, known as the kick. The kick determines how level the blade will lie in the haft when folded since it touches the underside of the spring.

The haft end of the blade comprises a square extension of itself, pierced centrally, and known as the tang. The edges of the tang are crisp when the knife is new but with use the soft silver square corners gradually become rounded. With

Fruit knife components from two knives but marked with scratched-on Roman numerals to distinguish the knife into which they will be fitted.
Plate 10.15

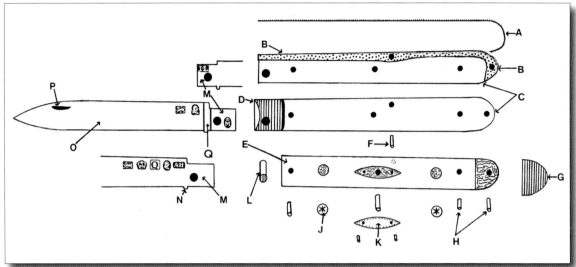

Nomenclature.

Some names survive from the industry days but many of the smaller components' names have become lost over time and have been re-invented (italicised here):

A — *decorative spine,*
B — spring
C — webs or liners
D — bolster
E — scales
F — *spring balance rivet*
G — cap
H — scale rivets
J — rosettes
K — shield
L — *hinge rivet (for blade attachment)*
M — tang
N — kick
O — blade
P — nail nick
Q — ricasso (*see also page 63, Chapter 3*).
Plate 10.16

Series of fruit knives comparing: rivet concealment (bottom to top/left to right): domed rivet (c.1770), flush rivet (c.1930), part blended rivet (c.1780), blended rivet (c.1930) and concealed (internal) rivet (c.1900).
Plate 10.17

much wear, the corners become even more rounded so that the (blade) end of the spring sinks down into the haft and pushes the blade up. The kick, which prevents the fragile blade edge from knocking against the underside of the spring, can be filed to extend the blade's working life: the blade level can be adjusted so that it folds down into the haft once again. Once the kick has been filed away and the tang is so rounded that the blade still springs out of the haft, then the knife mechanism is worn out (*Plate 10.28*). Removing the blade and soldering silver flat wire to the tang edges will restore the tang's original shape and dimensions but this is a difficult job and the knife should only be restored if considered to be worth the effort.

The spring is made from carbon spring steel and lies along the back of the haft, curling around the knife base into a solid bed of

metal which secures it in place. A thin strip of decorated precious metal (spine) is soldered along the spring-back to give it a fine finish and sometimes the underside of the spring is engraved or filed with tiny transverse or zigzag lines. About halfway along, another rivet holds the spring in place so that the end bears forcibly onto the blade tang holding the blade open or closed. This balance rivet is usually concealed within shallow depressions drilled into the scales so that it remains hidden from view. The hinge rivet attaches the blade to the knife bolster and comprises hardened silver wire or is capped with silver to blend it into the bolster surface, or is recessed into the bolster (usually found on later 19th & 20th century items). Rivets are often concealed beneath tiny discs of precious metal, sometimes engraved, and known as rosettes. Victorian and later springs tend to be vertically rectangular in cross-section, exerting twice the pressure onto the tang than in knives from earlier periods, which explains why these later knives tend to suffer much more from worn tang problems.

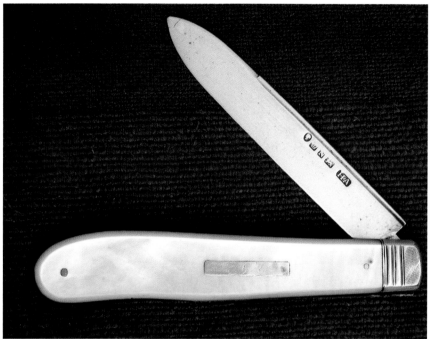

A swaged blade by
Henry Atkin, 1856,
therefore made with
a 'French' nail nick
along the blade.
Plate 10.18

Condition and Pitfalls

Condition is the most important
factor to some collectors and no
matter how unusual or interesting a
knife may be, if the scale is cracked
(the most usual fault) then the item,
in their view, is not worth having.
Nacre, especially, is most prone to
this fault and from a personal point
of view, if cracked, it will devalue the
item by about half. Cracks can be
hairline if the pearl becomes at all
stressed, or more severe if dropped
and can result in chips. Tiny chips or
'nibbling' are not too severe a fault
although perfectionists will reject
such items. The nacre on some
knives is usually of prime quality for
the obverse scale and may have the
fine prismatic pink and green colour,
whereas the reverse scale is of
second quality, perhaps a dull cream
colour, or greyish, occasionally
with a natural layer mark or muscle
'scar' from the living mollusc– often
mistaken for damage (*Plate 10.46*).

Blades are often creased or have
bent tips resulting from a strain
injury (opening a cocoa-type tin with
a silver blade is the most usual!)

A very pretty knife c.1860,
but the bone blade is
much too short and has
been re-shaped following
a mid-blade break.
Plate 10.19

Ends of two *couteaux-sans-clous*. The left example is complete with finely decorated ends but the right-hand piece has had its steel blade broken at some time and the remainder sawn off. This is quite a common fault and although the knife may be interesting enough, it is still incomplete.
Plate 10.20

To restore the blade's normal appearance following this type of damage is surprisingly difficult. Many knives are stiff to open and close. The blade should glide in and out of the haft and requires a little oil on the blade tang to ease the mechanism. Beware of letting the blade fly back too hard or it may become damaged. The kick will normally prevent the edge from striking against the spring but a very few knives have a slotted shock absorber of grooved horn or bone, to receive the edge of the point, and situated at the far end of the blade slot.

If the cap is missing from a knife or fork, the end naturally appears unfinished.

Like all serious collectors, people with the 'magpie urge' are quickly attracted to these charming objects of a bygone age and can become fanatics. There are also (inevitably) those who are less scrupulous and

will feed this collection mania by supplying altered pieces.

At the end of each section I have inserted a guide to devaluation in square brackets. Bear in mind that this is my personal guide and that other collectors may have their own rules concerning devaluation. Always check the hinge or bolster rivet - can you see it? It should be blended in. The knife action: if good the blade will 'walk and talk' - glide out and in closing with a slight snap. These common faults, combined with tang wear and more obvious flaws (cracks), are the main problems.

There are many other more subtle and serious flaws - - - -

1 Fakes - these are invariably contemporary with the items, usually with counterfeit hallmarks that are recognisable as such due to their often distorted appearance: a string-

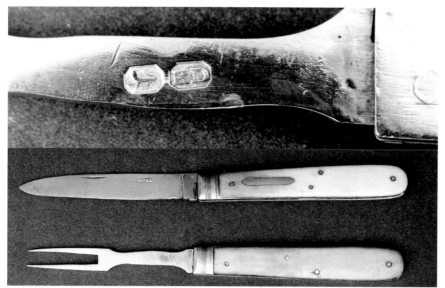

I. Fakes
These are invariably contemporary with the items, usually with counterfeit hallmarks that are recognisable as such due to their often distorted appearance:. The string-bodied sterling lion is typical c.1820-1880.
Plate 10.21

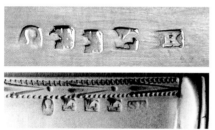

bodied sterling lion is typical. [If contemporary this will often double the value due to scarcity!]

2   Transposed blades – a worn-out or broken blade has been replaced with a perfect one from another knife. Checks - Does the knife back match perfectly with the level of the spring or is it slightly higher or lower? Does the bolster rivet blend in properly? The blade rivet of Victorian knives with decorated bolsters will normally have been blended into the bolster with filed, engraved/chased decoration and should be almost invisible. In the example illustrated the blade is from a Georgian knife c. 1790, the haft c. 1890 [Serious devaluation of 90%, *plate 10.24*].

3   Short and re-shaped blades. Check - when folded does the blade reach to the end (or very near to the end) of the blade

slot? Sometimes a creased or broken tip has been re-shaped and thereby shortened by filing. This is one of the commonest faults. [Medium to severe devaluation depending on how much is missing: 30-80%].

4   Broken and repaired blades – check the ricasso area. Also - are there bubble craters (tiny black depressions) or a lump of solder, or a grey-black discolouration of fire stain on the metal? If so this means that the blade has been repaired and this can be confirmed by checking the blending in of the bolster rivet (see 2). [Severe devaluation 50-80%, dependent on skill of repair (visibility, texture, craters &c)].

5   Hidden cracks can be concealed beneath nacreous paints and nail varnish. Look for strips of pearl that don't quite match in or rub off with nail varnish remover! I have even known some dealers to stick their price labels strategically over cracks! [Medium to severe devaluation: small nibbles less 10%, hairline cracks less 50%, larger cracks

Two sets of 'Bat-wing' hallmarks c.1825. These are found on some fruit knife blades by Samuel and William Kirkby of Sheffield (mark registered in 1821. These marks are contemporary forgeries and even the duty mark is odd - the king's head face-on rather than in profile. The assay master at this time, Lewis Sayles must be assumed not to have noticed this breach of the law as no record of litigation is known.
Plate 10.22

2. Transposed blades
A worn-out or broken blade replaced with a perfect one from another knife. Note the oddly curved knife blade back and that the blade is not marked. The blade does not sit open in a straight line and the blade rivet is visible versus that of the fork.
The blade (*below*) from a Georgian knife c.1790, the haft c.1890.
Plates 10.23 & 10.24

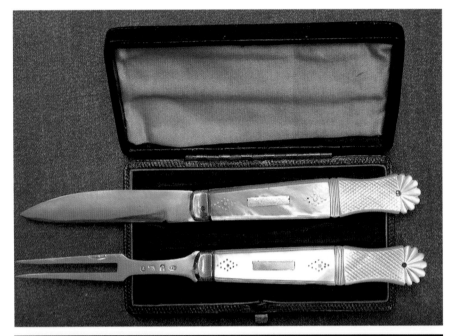

and missing chips less 70-90%].

6 Worn out mechanism. Checks – does the blade sit up out of the haft? Does it spring out again if pressed back in? It shouldn't. If not severe, the blade can be adjusted to fit back by filing away a small amount of the blade kick. In this instance a knife cannot be judged as perfect so check the condition of the tang even if the knife looks good. If the tang corners have been worn away and the end of the spring drops down into the bolster area, then the tang is seriously worn.

[Severe devaluation: less 80%].

7 Squeezed bolsters. If the tang has worn and/or the blade is so loose that it 'flops in and out', this can be unscrupulously improved by squeezing the sides of the bolster in a vice – look for matching flattened areas or parallel scratches or vice imprint marks on either side of the bolster (*plate 10.32*) and a stiff action; always examine the tang. [Severe devaluation: less 80%].

3 Short and re-shaped blades
Note how this blade does not extend the full length of the blade slot. It is missing nearly a centimetre of blade!
Plate 10.25

to open the knife too often or open carefully while squeezing the knife's back. Some people unscrupulously use super-glue to prevent recurrence. [Medium to high devaluation dependent on ability to correct the fault: less 20-50%].

9 Rust from the spring and verdigris from the webs will often discolour nacre, bone and ivory brown and green respectively if damp has affected the knife. Occasionally the nacre has been burnt (dark brown and flaky), through leaving the knife on a hot surface or a repairer may have attempted soldering without removing the blade from the haft. [Medium to high devaluation: less 20-80% dependent on disfigurement].

4 Broken blades
The ricasso of a knife blade, subsequently gilt to hide the repair, is betrayed by the presence of bubble craters when the repair was cooling.
Plate 10.26

8 Popped rivets. The spring balance rivet can pop out from its recess, leaving the sides bulging (nacre scales can often be cracked by this). This problem can be very carefully corrected by pushing down on the spring and manipulating the spring rivets back into their recesses, but the problem can easily recur. This will mean that the top edge of the spring balance rivet has become slightly burred. Try not

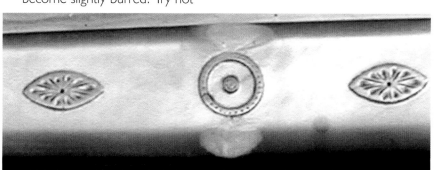

5 Hidden cracks
Can be concealed beneath nacreous nail varnish and paints – look for strips of pearl that don't quite match in or rub off with nail varnish remover! A typical, if rather crude, attempt at crack concealment.
Plate 10.27

6 Worn out mechanism
A classic instance of blade 'sit-up'. If the tang corners have been worn away and the end of the spring drops down into the bolster area, then the tang is seriously worn.
Plate 10.28

More problems with worn tangs: (*above*) a normal blade kick and (below it the JYC blade) a typically filed kick. This blade also looks transposed - it does not coordinate with the haft back and the rivet is too short and unblended.
Plates 10.29 & 10.30

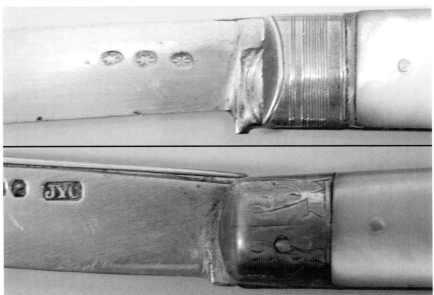

(left): uneven tang wear showing gradually increasing wear (l-r) and tang grooving where the spring pressure is to one side *(right)*. Note the vice marks on this blade (right).
Plates 10.31 & 10.32

10 Broken webs bringing about the collapse of a knife through the tension of the spring. Sometimes a single broken web will cause some hinge weakness and will bulge outwards each time the blade is opened and closed. [Severe devaluation: less 80%].

Knives with broken webs are hard to repair without taking them apart. Any job that involves reconstruction must be carried out very carefully. Nacre is extremely brittle and must have frustrated many an apprentice who used the pinning hammer just one blow too close. Cracks in nacre and other materials, are irreversible and can only be dishonestly concealed.

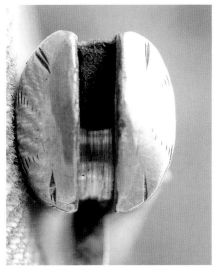

A typically worn tang (*left*) and its correspondingly rising blade (*below*).
Plate 10.33

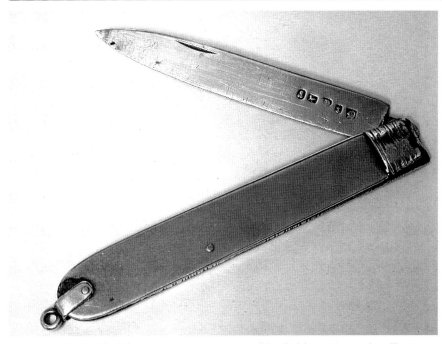

This Birmingham George IV knife is missing its scales which were probably damaged when someone added the shackle later in the 19th or early 20th century. To compensate for the damage, the webs have been silver-plated and the rivets filed down.
Plate 10.34

11 Inscriptions. Opinions are divided over these and some prefer an object to have no previous ownership markings (unless it belonged to a celebrity). However, inscriptions are fascinating and a part of the object's history - maybe, like the inscription shown, they are somewhat amateurishly engraved. Erasures (plate 10.40) can almost completely devalue a piece. [Minor to severe (erasure) devaluation: less 30-80%].

7 Squeezed bolsters
(Left): this knife's bolster
(face-on) has been
squeezed in a vice in an
attempt to conceal the
worn tang - the action is
consequently very stiff!
Plate 10.35

8 Popped rivets
(right) – Both the right
hand web and scale have
detached due to the spring
balance rivet popping out!
Plate 10.36

9 Rust
This shows rust staining
from the spring where the
knife has been affected by
damp.
Plate 10.37

10 Broken webs

- can bring about the collapse of a knife through the spring's tension. Sometimes a single broken web will cause some hinge weakness and will bulge outwards each time the blade is opened and closed.
Plate 10.38

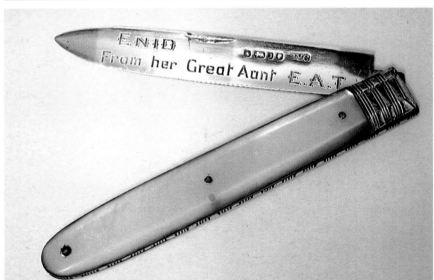

11 Inscriptions.

Opinions are divided over these. Inscriptions are fascinating: a part of the object's history even if they are somewhat heavily or amateurishly engraved. The blade assayed in 1876 but the haft looks more like c.1815 - another likely 'marriage'!
Plate 10.39

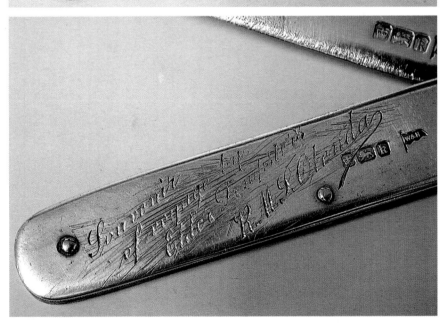

Erasures can completely devalue a piece. Note the badly-sharpened blade as well!
Plate 10.40

Restorative measures and how to spot them

1 Cracks in other materials (especially tortoiseshell) are more easily concealed since they can be filled with coloured resin and blended in by filing and polishing. [Medium devaluation: less 50%].

2 Inscriptions on blades and haft shields are sometimes removed or even scratched out! In either case this removes the item's history and is tantamount to

1 Cracks.
Plate 10.41

2 Inscriptions.
Plates 10.42 & 10.43

vandalism! Blades will have a rather thin and flexible patch if this has occurred and may be strangely or unevenly shiny. [Severe devaluation: less 80%]. Shields were often decorated around the edge and if erasure has occurred then part of the border engraving will also have been affected. [Medium devaluation: less 40%, not so serious if removed near to time of manufacture – difficult to evaluate].

3 Decorative spines on springs become damaged or partly detached and a vendor will often 'improve' an item by abrading away all traces of the silver and any adherent and underlying

solder. If the item were made for the cheap end of the market (ref. page 110) it may not have been made with a silver spine but normal-sized and decorated pieces would always have had a precious metal spine. [Medium devaluation: less 30-60%].

4 Lower quality nacre taken from near the edge of the shell is sometimes layered or pitted. Although this is not serious, it is unusual to find second quality nacre used as scaling material

for finer-quality items. [If contemporary, quirks such as this should not affect value].

5 Later decoration is unusual but sometimes a plain early knife has been 'prettified' with later (usually Victorian) engraving. Not too serious provided that the owner is aware of this. [Minor to medium devaluation: less 20-50% dependent on whether decoration drastically alters the style of the knife or not].

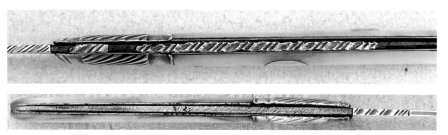

3 These two knife backs show typical spine damage and (below) how unscrupulous people try to rectify this by removing all the decorative silver and solder. You can still see the cable effect of the original gadrooning on the spring. *Plates 10.44 & 10.45*

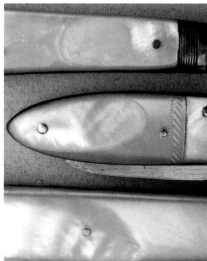

4 Unusual to find second quality nacre used as scaling material for the end of the gold fork (right). To the left three nacre hafts showing natural pearl layers. Some have found this worse than cracks and have even resorted to disguising this with fillers and paints. *Plates 10.46 & 10.47.*

6   Finally, boxed items should always fit exactly and not rattle about inside, nor should the box bulge unduly or the lid not quite join up with the lower half of the box. This is not a serious fault but the buyer should not have to pay above the odds for a so-called original box. Boxes have also been substituted from other items such as corn razors, quill knives, and even from small scent bottles!

5 Later decoration is unusual but this knife has been 'prettified' with later (usually Victorian) engraving. *Plate 10.48*

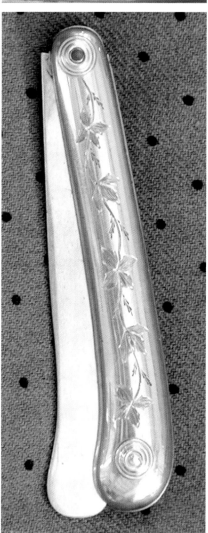

Typical nacre crack concealment using pearl nail varnish, since cleaned away from 5 (p.261).
Plate 10.49

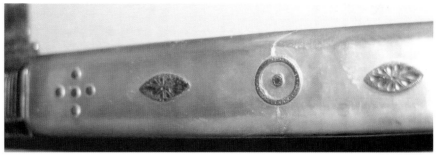

Damage or wear to silverplated blades is obvious but this abraded area shows how thick the silver plating can sometimes be.
Plate 10.50

Pocket fruit knife by William Needham, Sheffield, 1927 - no fault with this; the action is smooth, the scales undamaged and the blade undamaged.
Plate 10.51

For such small items, there are many faults and pitfalls: some are obvious but many are not, so be careful.

Glossary

Anthemion Radiating pattern from a central base, like a palm leaf, found in classical Greek art and design.

Arcadian Design relating to rural simplicity in Ancient Greece. An example might show shepherds and shepherdesses dancing.

Berge Type of twin-bladed springless pocket-cum--fruit knife with inter-supporting blades, supposedly invented by a Parisian cutler of the same name.

Bolster The fulcrum of a knife – where most pressure is applied during cutting, therefore thickened with base metal and silver-coated, it also hides the tang from view.

Cameo Profile portrait in relief.

Cap Protective and ornamental metal end of a knife's haft.

Double action Pocket knife with squared tang so that the blade is opened or closed in a two-part action: the blade can be half-closed.

Estaing French 18th century Admiral who gave his name to a knife with both an extendable blade and a removable silver sleeve for this blade.

French nail nick Groove running along obverse and upper side of the blade. Associated with a swaged blade.

German Silver An alloy comprising copper, nickel and zinc which was frequently used as a knife mount or occasionally as a 19th century fruit knife blade.

Gigogne A three-part straight knife in a sheath: the outer blade of steel, the inner knife blade of precious metal and a toothpick inside the fruit knife: nesting knives.

Hard spring Associated with double action (above), refers to a stronger-than-usual spring that can close a blade forcibly.

Incuse (or inaglio) hollowed-out pattern or design (reverse of cameo).

Kick Small metal extension of tang or ricasso so that the height of a closed blade can be adjusted and prevent the edge from knocking against the spring.

Nacre Shorter name for Mother of Pearl.

Nail Nick A crescent-shaped grrove cut near the blade tip to facilitate blade opening.

Piqué work Wire inlay work, sometimes comprising a pattern of rosettes.

Piqué clouté Wire inlay work in section (as dots).

Piqué posé Wire inlay work in length.

Ricasso The extension of a knife blade bridging the tang and the blade proper. On steel pocket knives it also acts as a trade-marking area. Only some pocket fruit knives have a noticeable ricasso.

Rivet Metal wire piece used to hold the knife together and act as a hinge for the blade.

Rosette small circle or shaped flat cover for a rivet or part of a decoration.

Scale Strip of (usually) organic material attached by rivets to a haft and acting as a grip for the haft.

Shield Plate of shaped precious metal let into the scale for the engraving of ownership markings.

Shielding parser Twin-bladed tool with cutting edges, operated by a bow drill and bobbin action, within a shield-shaped template.

Three Georgian forks with blades half opened, showing the spring positions for (*front to back*): single action (spring slightly raised), concealed single action (spring barely raised), and double action (spring not raised) mechanisms.
Plate 10.51

Single action Pocket knife with rounded tang so that the blade is opened or closed in a single smooth action.

Soft spring Metal stop to prevent over-opening of folding blade, or a spring that exerts minimal pressure on a single action knife

Spine Thin, decorative and precious metal coating to the spring.

Swage (Swedge – USA) Chamfered portion of blade back nearest the point, often forming a double edge.

Tang Squared or rounded extension of the blade, centrally drilled to form the blade hinge. Often hallmarked during the Georgian period.

Web (liner) Inner metal lining of a pocket knife, comprising twinned strips of metal to which the bolster and scales are attached.

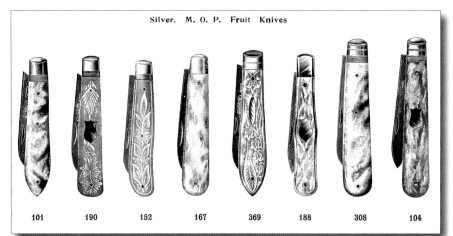

Silver, M. O. P. Fruit Knives

101   190   152   167   369   188   308   104

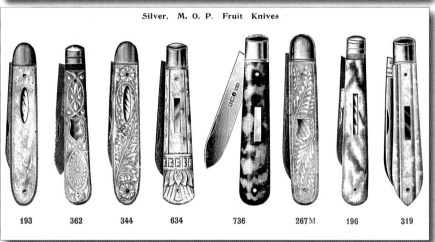

Silver, M. O. P. Fruit Knives

193   362   344   634   736   267M   196   319

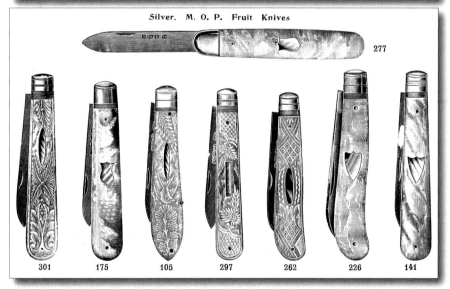

Silver, M. O. P. Fruit Knives

277

301   175   105   297   262   226   141

Pages of pocket fruit knives
from William Needham's
catalogue, c.1920 showing
contemporary and late
19th century styles. A few
blades have been drawn
slightly open to show their
tips and this should not be
confused with wear to the
tang (pages 262 & 263).
Plates 10.52 to 10.53

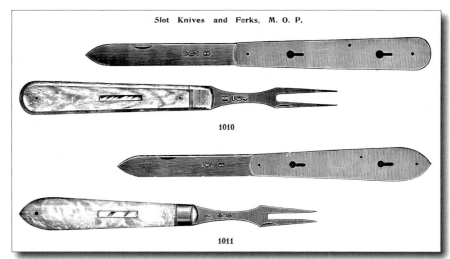

Slot Knives and Forks, M. O. P.

1010

1011

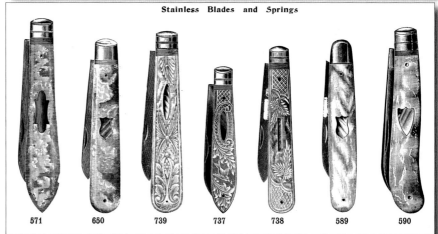

Stainless Blades and Springs

571   650   739   737   738   589   590

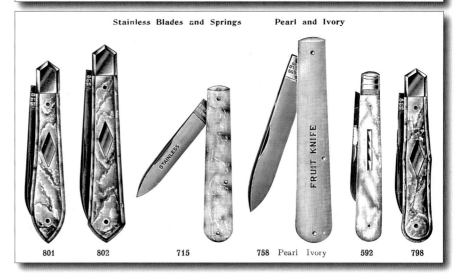

Stainless Blades and Springs   Pearl and Ivory

FRUIT KNIFE

801   802   715   758 Pearl Ivory   592   798

11 Pocket fruit knives: list of makers, references and further reading

Pocket fruit knives: references and further reading

Adams, W (Bill) et al. 1999 *Sheffield exhibition knives*. Old World Publishing Ltd., Oregon.

Ashford, R 1977 Folding fruit knives. *The Antique Collector*, August: 60-63.

Beuque, E & Frapsauce, M (reprinted) 1982 *Dictionnaire des poinçons des maîtres orfèvres français du XIVe siècle á 1838.* F de Nobele, Paris.

Bradbury, F 1968 (12th edition) *Guide to Marks of origin on British and Irish Silver plate, 1544-1968.* J W Northend Ltd., Sheffield.

Carré, L 1928 *Les poinçons de l'orfèvrerie française du XIVe jusqu'au début XIX siècle.* Paris.

Chapuis, A & Loup, G 1919 *La Montre Chinoise. Relations de l'Horologie suisse avec la Chine.* Neuchatel, Attinger Frères.

D'Allemagne, H R 1928 *Les accessoires du costume et du mobilier.* Vols. I-III, Paris J Schemit, reprinted 1970, Hacker Art Books, New York.

Darom, D 2003 *(Art & Design in modern) Custom folding knives.* Edizioni Saviolo, Vercelli.

Dove, A B L 1986 Some observations on gold and its hallmarks. *Antique Collecting*, September issue.

Fougeroux de Bondaroy 1771-2 *L'Art du Coutelier en ouvrages communs.* LF Delatour, Paris

Hall, D 2005 *Silver-bladed folding fruit knives.* Private Press.

Howe, C 1986 Back the Knife. *Homes & Gardens*, September: 68-7.

Jackson, Sir C J Ed. Pickford, I 1989. *Jackson's silver & gold marks of England, Scotland & Ireland.* Antique Collectors' Club, Woodbridge, Suffolk.

Jones, K C 1981 *The silversmiths of Birmingham and their marks: 1750-1980.* NAG Press Ltd., London.

Karsten, W C (Bill) 1986 *Silver folding fruit knives.* Knife World Publications, Knoxville, Tennessee, USA.

Klinka-Ballesteros, I et al. 2003 *Les orfèvres d'Orléans.* Musée des Beaux Arts d'Orléans. Somogy éditions d'art.

Levine, B 1985 *(et seque) Levine's guide to knives and their values.* DBI Books Inc., Northbrook Illinois, USA.

Moore, S J 1975 Folding fruit knives and forks. *Antique Dealer & Collectors' Guide*, September: 77-83.

Moore, S J 1983-4a The history of the folding knife. *The National Knife Magazine*, December: 5-7; February: 8-13; March: 8-10.

Moore, S J 1984b Pocket knives at table? Whatever next! *Petit propos culinaires*, 16: 35-41.

Moore, S J 1984c Some fruit knife and fork oddities. *The National Knife Magazine*, November: 22-24.

Moore, S J 1988a The development of de luxe folding knives within the history of alfresco eating. *The National Knife Magazine*, July: 20-24.

Moore, S J 1988b *Penknives & other folding knives.* Shire Publications, Aylesbury.

Moore, S J 1989a Silver-plated folding fruit knives and forks. *Silver,* 22 (2): 8-12.

Moore, S J 1989b Desirable pocket knives 1. Folding fruit knives. *Antique Dealer & Collectors' Guide,* **42** (9): 54-57.

Moore, S J 1989c Desirable pocket knives 2. Sheffield hallmarking on folding fruit knives. *Antique Dealer & Collectors' Guide,* **43** (1): 36-39.

Moore, S J 1989d Desirable pocket knives 3. Silverplating techniques applied to folding fruit knives. *Antique Dealer & Collectors' Guide,* **43** (5): 49-51.

Moore, S J 1989e French folding fruit knives. *Antique Collector,* **60** (9): 58-63.

Moore, S J 1991a Gold-bladed knives. *The National Knife Magazine,* September **15** (3): 32-33.

Moore, S J 1991b Bladed with gold. *Antique Dealer & Collectors' Guide,* **45** (5): 20-22.

Moore, S J 1991c The evolution of English folding fruit knives. *The National Knife Magazine,* **15** (6): 26-28.

Moore, S J 1992a Metal-hafted folding fruit knives. *The National Knife Magazine,* **15** (7): 24-26.

Moore, S J 1992b Georgian Duty marks (on Sheffield folding fruit knives). *Antique Dealer & Collectors' Guide,* **45** (8): 40-42.

Moore, S J 1994 A taste for music? (Musical fruit knives). *Antique Dealer & Collectors' Guide,* **48** (1): 22-23.

Moore, S J 1996 Fruit spoons, as sometimes included with folding fruit knives/fork sets. *The Finial,* **7** (1): 14-15.

Moore, S J 1997a Collecting French and mechanised fruit knives. 1 *Silver Magazine,* May/June: 18-23.

Moore, S J 1997b Collecting French and mechanised fruit knives. 2 *Silver Magazine,* July/August: 20-26.

Moore, S J 1997c Collecting French and mechanised fruit knives. 3 *Silver Magazine,* September/October: 38-41.

Moore, S J 1999a *Cutlery for the table (a history of table and pocket cutlery).* Hallamshire Press, Sheffield.

Moore, S J & Thomas B 1999b Historical motifs on silver folding fruit knives. *Silver Magazine,* Jan/Feb.: 46-49.

Pagé, C 1896 *La coutellerie depuis l'origine jusqu'à nos jours.* Volumes I-VI, H Rivière, Châtellerault.

Pascal, D 2001 *Collectible* (sic) *pocket knives.* Flammarion, Paris.

Pascal, D 2004 *(L'aventure des) Couteaux de poche.* Hachette Collections, Paris

Perferttini, J 1997 & 2005 *Le galuchat.* Editions, H Vial.

Perret, JJ 1771 *L'Art du Coutelier,* 3 vols., LF Delatour, Paris

Scott, D 1987 For elegant eating. *The Antique Collector,* May: 120-1.

Secker, C E 1976 Folding fruit knives. *Antique Collecting,* **11** (3): 24-28.

Sheffield Assay Office 1911 *The assay office register.*

Smith, J 1816 *Explanation or Key to the various manufactories of Sheffield.* Reprinted by the Early American Industries Association, 1975.

Sketchley *Sheffield Directory* (Bristol) 1774.

Tardy 1942 (et seque) *Les poinçons de garantie internationaux pour l'argent.* Tardy, Paris.

Tardy 1942 (et seque) *Les poinçons de garantie internationaux pour l'or, le platine et le palladium.* Tardy, Paris.

Appendix: Sheffield, Birmingham and other cutlers and goldsmiths known to have made pocket fruit knives.

Note 1: With rare exception have any other makers been found listed at other Assay Offices such as Chester, London and Dublin. Many of the Birmingham and Sheffield makers were listed at other offices.

Note 2: The dates shown alongside the makers have been recorded from actual fruit knives and must not be confused with when the actual mark was registered.

SHEFFIELD

AA	George Butler & Co.: 1880, 1920
A&	probably Henry Atkin (Plater's mark): 1840
A&D	Allen & Darwin: 1900
A.H	Aaron Hadfield or less commonly, Hatfield: 1820
AH	Alexander Hunt: 1820
AH	A. Hadfield or Martin Brothers: 1850
A&N	Army & Navy Stores (additional mark as retailer): 1890
A&O	Henry Atkin & John Oxley: 1830
A&O	Atkin & Oxley (Plater's mark): 1830
AS	Arthur (Worrall) Staniforth: 1890
AWS	Arthur Worrall Staniforth (Plater's mark): 1890
B&C	(in single punch) Brown & Clark: 1860
B&C	(incuse) Brookes & Crookes: 1860
B&C	Brookes & Crookes: 1895 (in 3 separate

punches after 1893 but noted as such since 1871)

B&C	(in single punch) Bradley & Cohn: 1900
CE&FDLD	Constantine & Floyd Ltd. (at Birmingham): 1920
CL **TL**	Levesley Brothers: 1860
CS FS	Saunders & Shepherd: 1890
C.W.F	Charles William Fletcher: 1900
E.B	Edward Butler: 1890
EH	Edward Hutton (of William Hutton & Son): 1880
EM JM	Mappin Brothers: 1870
ES	Ebenezer Smith: 1800
E.T	unknown but could be Edward Thomason (Birmingham): 1830
FH	Francis Howard: 1930
G:A **&CO**	George Ashforth & Company: 1775
GH	George Hardesty: 1820
G.H	Harrison Bros. & Howson: 1900
GU	George Unite: 1860 (at Birmingham)
GW	George Warriss: 1890
GW&CO	Gregory Wostenholme & Company: 1850
H.A	Henry Atkin: 1860
HA	Henry Archer: 1860
H&A	Horton & Allday: 1907 (at Birmingham)
H&B	Hardy, Bell & Company: 1835

H.C	Henry Cook: 1875	JEB	Walker & Hall (J.E. Bingham): 1870
H&F	Hukin & Fenton: 1860	JF	James Fenton: 1860 (at
HG	Henry Greaves: 1890		Birmingham)
H.H	Harrison Brothers & Howson: 1850	J.G & Co	John Gilbert (at Birmingham, Plater's mark): 1830
HH&	Walker and Hall: 1870	JH	John Hunter: 1870, 1900
JEB	(J E Bingham was principal of Walker & Hall: 1875)	J.I	John Ibberson: 1775
		J.L	Joseph Law: 1820
HJC	H J Cooper & Co: 1900 (also reg'd at Birmingham)	J.M	Joseph Mappin & Son: 1850
		J.N	John Nowill: 1830
H.M	Henry Morton: 1890	JN	John Nowill & Sons: 1880
H&S	Harwood & Sansom: 1850	JN	John Needham: 1850
H&S	Hirsch & Stern: 1880	JN	(incuse) John Needham: 1880
HW & Co	Henry Wilkinson & Company: 1860	J.N&S	John Nowill & Sons: 1910
I&JB	John & Jonathan Bell: 1840	J.R*+	Joseph Rodgers & Sons Ltd.: 1880
IC	James Crawshaw: 1825	JR	(in double oval cartouche) John Round & Son Ltd.: 1880
I.L	John Law: 1795		
IN	Joseph Nowill: 1815		
I.O	John Oxley: 1850	J R W	(in separate and different cartouches) John Watts: 1900
I.P	Jonathan Parkin & Abraham Wigan: 1790		
IR	John Roberts: 1780	J.S	Stevenson & Law (Plater's mark): 1890
I.S Co	Joseph Shemell & Company: 1780	JS &S	John Sherwood & Sons: 1870
I.S.G	Israel Sigmond Greenberg (at Birmingham): 1895		
I.T or J.T	Joseph Tibbitts: 1775	JT	James Thompson: 1860
I.W	John Watkinson: 1775	JYC	James Yeomans Cowlishaw: 1840, 1880
I.W	John Winter: 1780 (sometimes struck sideways, ref. pages 97-8)	J.Y.C	James Yeomans Cowlishaw: 1910
		𝔍𝔜𝔠	James Yeomans Cowlishaw (Plater's mark): 1840
JB	James Burbury: 1830		
JB	Jonathan Bell: 1860	JW	in conjoined circles - J Wilmot (Birmingham): 1900
JB	John Batt: 1925		
JD &S	James Deakin & Sons: 1895		
JD WD	James Deakin & Sons: 1905	JW	in conjoined circles – Joseph Westby: 1920

LAMPREY	Joseph Stephenson: 1770	**T.C** **J.W.C**	Cooper Brothers: 1895
L.H	L Heinzelmann: 1900	**TF**	Thomas Freeman: 1845
LL	Joseph Law, Atkin & Oxley: 1820	**TM**	Thomas Marples: 1870
MB	Maurice Baum: 1895	**𝕿𝕸𝕾**	Thomas Mappin & Sons: 1850 (as Plater's mark)
M&C	Mackay & Chisholm: 1870		
MH&Co	Martin, Hall & Company: 1870	**TPL**	Thomas Pagan Lowe: 1860
NC	Thomas, James & Nathaniel Creswick: 1830	**TP&S**	Thomas Prime & Son: 1870 (registered at Birmingham)
O&E	Osborn & Elliott: 1870	**TR**	Thomas Royle: 1880
		TS	Thomas Sansom: 1820
R&S	Roberts & Slater: 1840	**V&J**	Villers & Jackson: 1900
READ	John Read: 1770		
R.K **&Co**	or **R.K** Robert Kippax & Company: 1775, 1800	**W&Co**	Waterhouse & Company: 1800
RM **EH**	Robert Martin & Edward Hall: 1860	**WB M**	William Briggs (Plater): 1830
R.P	Robert Pringle & Sons: 1900	**W.F**	William Fox: 1780 (sometimes struck sideways, ref. page 76)
S.C I.H	Samuel Colmore (with) John Harrison (Close Plater at Birmingham): 1770	**W&K**	Wardell & Kempson: 1815
		W.C	William Carter: 1850
SF	Samuel & Ann Fox: 1800	**W.C**	(incuse) William Coldwell: 1800
SH	Samuel Harwood: 1835	**WH**	William Hutton: 1845, 1860
S.K	(sometimes incuse) Samuel Kirkby: 1810	**W&H**	(in a pennant) Walker & Hall (also at London): 1900
SK	Samuel & William Kirkby: 1830	**WM&S**	William Morton & Sons: 1900
S&P	Singleton & Priestman: 1900	**W.N**	William & Jonathan Nowill: 1820
		WN	William Nowill: 1840
TB or **T.BEST**	Thomas Best: 1820	**W.N**	William Needham: 1890, 1920
TB **JH**	Thomas Bradbury & Sons: 1900 (also reg'd at London)	**W.S**	William Smith: 1785
		WW **&** **JH**	White, Henderson & Company: 1870

WW.H	W.W. Harrison & Co.: 1900	ML	Matthew Linwood: 1800
W.W	William Webster & Son: 1870, 1900	T.F	Thomas Freeman: 1830
W W & S	*idem* plater's mark	TH	Thomas Hastelow: 1830
Y&W	Yapp & Woodward (at Birmingham): 1850	T.H	T.Hayes: 1890
		T.H.V	Thomas H. Vale: 1910
		TL	T. Latham & E.
		&	Morton: 1870. (also
BIRMINGHAM		EM	reg'd at Chester)
A&LLᴅ	Adie & Lovekin Ltd: 1900	T.M	Thomas Millington: 1890
A.T	Alfred Taylor: 1860	TP & S	Thomas Prime & Son: 1864 (also reg'd at Sheffield)
C.C	C.H Cheshire (also reg'd at Chester): 1900		
D&F	Deakin & Francis: 1890	W&C	Mary Wheeler & James Bartholomew Cronin
EB	Edward Brailsford: 1890	WS	William Steen (junior): 1840
E.T	Edward Thomason: 1800		
		BRISTOL	
F&Co	Foxall & Company: 1860	W.C	William Chandler (cutler): 1790
FC	Francis Clarke: 1840		
F.W	Francis Wallis: 1910	**DUBLIN**	
GU	George Unite: 1840	C.L	Charles Lamb: 1907
GW	Gervaise Wheeler: 1840		
		LONDON	
H.G	Henry Griffith: 1880 (also reg'd at Chester)	AB	A B: 1900
		AJS	A.J. Strachan: 1820
H&T	Hilliard & Thomason: 1850 (also reg'd at Chester)	GA	George Adams: 1860
		GIBBS	Joseph Gibbs: 1770
HW	Horace Woodward: 1880	GRAY	John Gray: 1770
		TB	Thomas Bradbury & Sons:
I.C	(incuse) John Clemments: 1870	JH	1907
IT	Joseph Taylor: 1780	WS	William Stroud: 1804
JC	James Collins: 1820		
J.F	John Fenton: 1860		
J.W	Joseph Willmore: 1800		

19 Index

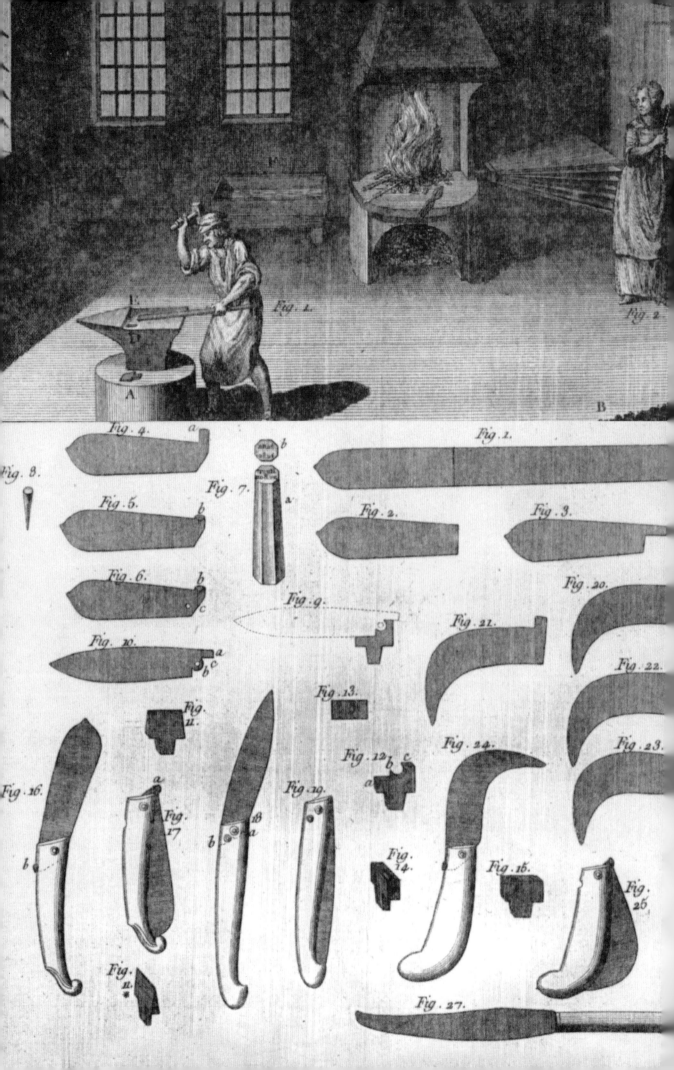